ARGENTINE INTERNATIONAL TRADE UNDER INCONVER- TIBLE PAPER MONEY 1880–1900

BY

JOHN H. WILLIAMS, Ph.D.

ASSOCIATE PROFESSOR OF BANKING IN
NORTHWESTERN UNIVERSITY

SOMETIME ASSISTANT PROFESSOR OF ECONOMICS
IN PRINCETON UNIVERSITY

AMS PRESS
NEW YORK

Reprinted from the edition of 1920: Cambridge

First AMS edition published in 1971

Manufactured in the United States of America

International Standard Book Number: 0-404-06979-7

Library of Congress Catalog Card Number: 75-178302

AMS PRESS INC.
NEW YORK, N.Y. 10003

PREFACE

As is stated in the opening chapter, the present inquiry was begun at the suggestion of Professor F. W. Taussig, to whom I am especially indebted for kindly and unfailing advice and inspiration. Though some preliminary work was accomplished at Harvard University during the academic year 1916–17, most of the data were assembled and the book written in Buenos Aires (from July, 1917, to May, 1918), whither the writer went for that purpose as Sheldon Travelling Fellow.

For valuable assistance in collecting materials acknowledgment is due to Dr. Alejandro E. Bunge, Director General de Estadistica de la Nación, and to Sr. Ricardo Pillado, who prior to 1916 was for many years Director General de Comercio é Industria. Sr. Pillado has an intimate personal acquaintance with the period of Argentine economic history here studied, and has for many years been a keen student of his country's economic problems. For information and insight gained from conversations with Sr. Pillado, as well as from his books, I am most grateful.

Most of all, I am glad of this opportunity to express my gratitude to Sr. Carlos Alfredo Tornquist, the distinguished head of the banking firm of Ernesto Tornquist y Ca., Lda., which since its inception in 1830 has played so prominent a part in the economic and financial upbuilding of the republic. It was Sr. Tornquist's father, the late Sr. Ernesto Tornquist, who as intimate friend of Presidents Pellegrini and Roca, and as supporter of Finance Minister Rosa at the time of the Conversion Law controversy of 1899, played so large a part in restoring the finances of the government after the collapse of the Baring Panic, and in solving the problem of depreciated paper money.

Sr. Tornquist has the best commercial and financial library in Argentina. Until recent years, except by a small number of eminent students, not much attention has been given in Argentina to systematic research or to the preservation of documentary or other materials. Sr. Tornquist and his staff, by indefatigable canvassing of booksellers and searching into odd corners, have made an invaluable collection of Argentine books, documents, and periodical literature. The major part of the materials upon which the present investigation is based was obtained in Sr. Tornquist's library, where I was made thoroughly at home and given every aid and encouragement throughout the period of my stay in Buenos Aires. The inquiry will always be intimately associated in my mind with pleasant recollections of Sr. Tornquist and the members of his staff.

JOHN H. WILLIAMS

PRINCETON UNIVERSITY
MAY, 1920.

CONTENTS

CHAPTER VI

CHAPTER VII

CHAPTER VIII

CHAPTER XIV

CHAPTER XV

Examination of imports simpler matter than that of exports, and
the results more decisive, 236.—The overturn of the trade balance
took place not by increase of exports but by decrease of imports,
237.—Index numbers of value of imports and the gold premium,
1889–96, show a precisely inverse relation in every year, 238.—
But not in the years prior to 1889, 240.—This partly due to spirit
of extravagance fostered by the "boom," 240.—Comparison of
total imports, and imports of food, drinks, tobacco, and textiles
1886–96, 241.—But it was chiefly due to the *direct* connection
between imports of construction materials and railroad loans, 242.
—Comparison of railroad borrowings and imports of construction
goods, 246.—But this direct relation between borrowings and
imports applied to only part of the imports and the borrowings,
and is for our purpose of minor consequence, 248.—Comparison
of index numbers of import prices, wages, and the price of gold,
1886–96, 250.—Import prices rose more rapidly than wages, 251.—
The Argentine import trade appears to offer complete verification
of theory, 253.

CHAPTER XVI

On the whole, the data are adequate for the purpose for which
they are used, 254.—They indicate a pretty general correspondence
with theoretical reasoning, 255.—Two points brought out by the
inquiry deserve special emphasis, 256.—The import trade provides
the clearest verification, and probably would be found to do so in
any agricultural country on an inconvertible paper basis, 256.—
There need be no "dislocation" of exchange, 258—This inquiry has
been concerned with the train of sequences characteristic of a
"transition period" between "states of equilibrium," and not with
the broader implications of the theory of international trade.

ARGENTINE INTERNATIONAL TRADE UNDER INCONVERTIBLE PAPER MONEY 1880–1900

CHAPTER I

THE PROBLEM

FOR the student of international trade the period from 1880 to 1900 of Argentine economic history is of peculiar interest. During the greater part of it, Argentina was on a depreciated paper money basis, gold having been driven completely out of circulation, and standing at a premium which ranged from 35 per cent in 1885 to 354 per cent in the third week of October, 1891. As is always the case under a régime of depreciated paper, the price of gold fluctuated violently, often moving over a range of twenty to thirty points in a single day.

Contemporary with the depreciated paper régime, and indeed, as I hope to show later, an intimate part of it, there was a program of heavy borrowing of foreign capital, particularly of British capital. The borrowing was maintained throughout the eighties, culminating in loans of such extent as have probably never been equalled, in time of peace, by a country of so small a population as was that of Argentina.

Add to the depreciated paper money situation and to the borrowing program the fact that in these twenty years Argentine foreign trade underwent a revolution, that the "unfavorable" balance of trade which had existed from early times was suddenly converted into a "favorable" balance in 1891, and that this overturn was punctuated by the Baring Panic, the most severe crisis in Argentine history, and one has the broad outlines of the period I am to study.

The purpose of this study is to work out the interrelations among these factors — depreciated paper money, foreign borrowings, and foreign trade — and by so doing to make an inductive examination of the theory of international trade and foreign exchange under a régime of depreciated paper money. Several studies have been made of the balance of international payments in its relation to foreign trade. These, however, have usually been concerned with gold-using countries. The factor of depreciated paper has been absent. That the latter essentially alters the nature of the problem, and makes necessary the formulation of an independent explanation, is apparent from a casual examination of the case.

The presence of depreciated inconvertible paper money removes some essential parts of the mechanism which is presupposed in the usual explanation. Summed up baldly, the bases of the usual statement of the theory of international trade and foreign exchange are as follows:

1. The trading countries are on a gold basis.
2. Through the mechanism of the specie points, gold flows freely between the trading countries.
3. When gold flows out of a country the level of prices within that country falls, and in consequence exports increase and imports diminish: and conversely, when gold flows in, the price level rises, so that imports are encouraged, and exports discouraged.

Given this mechanism, a comparatively slight disturbance of the balance of international payments, as for example an increase in borrowings, will set the machinery in motion and effect a change in the merchandise imports and exports. A disturbance sufficiently marked would result in an overturn of the trade balance.

But how explain such an overturn without the mechanism? How explain the fact that such an overturn did occur in Argentine foreign trade in 1891, notwithstanding the fact that the currency of the country was depreciated inconvertible paper money, and that there was consequently no gold in circulation? Since gold could not circulate within the country, the changes of prices presupposed in the usual statement of the theory could not take place, or at least they could not occur from the same cause, or operate upon foreign trade in the same manner.

This problem of international trade and foreign exchange under a régime of depreciated paper money has been considered by Professor F. W. Taussig in an article which appeared in the *Quarterly Journal of Economics*, in May, 1917.[1] At the conclusion of the article Professor Taussig expresses the conviction that, despite its difficulty, verification of theory must be attempted in this field of economic inquiry as in any other. He mentions the possibility of attempting verification with some prospect of success in the case of Argentina, in view of the fact that the particular change in the balance of international payments that took place there, the heavy foreign borrowings, was of sufficient duration and of sufficiently pronounced character to give rise to the hope that its effects upon exchange and trade might be traced with some distinctness.

This study, begun at Professor Taussig's suggestion some months before his article was published, is an attempt to find the verification there mentioned. What I propose to do is to trace historically each of the three large factors in the situation, the paper money, the balance of international payments (and this means particularly the borrowings of foreign capital in the period here studied), and the foreign trade: and to try to work out the interrelations that existed among these factors.

[1] *International Trade Under Depreciated Paper: A Contribution to Theory.*

CHAPTER II

PRELIMINARY DISCUSSION OF PRINCIPLES

As has been said, it was the presence of depreciated inconvertible paper money which differentiated the problem of international trade in Argentina from that which the theorist ordinarily has in mind. We may best indicate the general purpose of this study, therefore, and the broad lines which it is to pursue, by some general discussion of inconvertible paper money and the forces which determine its value.

There is no theoretical reason why inconvertible paper money should not be worth its full face value. Instances are not lacking of emissions of inconvertible paper that have not depreciated, the most notable, perhaps, being that of France during the Franco-Prussian War. There is at least one remarkable instance in which paper money rose above par. In March and April of 1889 and again in October Brazilian credit stood so high that the paper milreis actually sold in foreign exchange transactions for more than the intrinsic value of the coin which it represents.

There is proof, then, that an inconvertible paper money need not depreciate. So long as it will circulate freely, that is, so long as people do not distrust their government, or have no strong feeling against using paper, such as existed in California during and after the Civil War; and so long as the quantity of inconvertible paper is not greater than the quantity of specie and convertible paper that could be maintained in circulation, it will retain its value and perform all the functions of money.

Nevertheless, the experience of all countries is proof that inconvertible paper rarely does retain its full face value.) The cause of its depreciation has usually been "over-issue," the great curse of inconvertible paper. Argentine writers are virtually unanimous in ascribing the vicissitudes of their monetary history

6

to excessive issues of paper: and although, as will appear later, I shall take some exception to this view, it is undeniable that over-issue was *one* of the main determinants of the value of Argentine paper money.

Argentine writers have ample reason for their reiterated assertions that over-issue has been due to extravagance, to maladministration, and, at times, to motives that have the color of downright dishonesty. Inconvertible paper money is apt to be looked upon by an unscrupulous governor, or even by one who is merely near-sighted, as a means of getting something for nothing.[1] Inconvertible paper is in the nature of a forced internal loan. Whenever the government finds itself in a tight pinch what is more simple than to issue a few millions of paper pesos? A new issue will buy guns for the army, new battleships, a new House of Congress, larger salaries for government officials. And these things may be had merely by starting a printing press.

Paper money was not infrequently issued in Argentina for no better motives than these. More often it was issued to meet some special emergency, such as a budget deficit due to extravagant expenditure, or to meet the expenses of civil rebellions or foreign wars. In the great boom of the eighties, a chief cause of the liberal issues appears to have been the desire to keep the boom going, a dread of the consequences when the inevitable contraction should come.

Not only did the government have an interest in increasing the quantity of paper in circulation, but the banks as well. Until 1887, virtually all of the paper was issued by banks that were semi-governmental in character. Their directorates were composed in part of private persons, and in part of members appointed by the government. Their operations were subject to government regulation. They acted as fiscal agents of the government and made loans to it from time to time. When the government needed paper it applied to the banks. Theoreti-

---

[1] The present fondness for lotteries and horse-racing is witness to the fact that the spirit of something for nothing is still very much alive in Argentina. There are lotteries at frequent intervals whose first prizes range from 50,000 to 300,000 pesos each; and the chief prize of the annual Christmas lottery is 1,000,000 pesos.

cally, the banks were required to maintain 'a reserve of specie behind their notes. Precise figures of the amount of this reserve are lacking, but it appears to have been about one-third of the notes.

On their own behalf the banks welcomed opportunities to make new issues, for if in place of one gold peso they could use three paper ones, they could do three times as much lending: and they need not be so careful as to what the money was lent for, or on what security. Since the provision for a specie reserve was, except in rare instances, not lived up to, the cost of the paper money was little more than a printer's bill. Such a situation offers a powerful inducement to speculation. In the late eighties the banks made loans lavishly for all sorts of madcap enterprises. Personal credit was expanded to such limits as have rarely been witnessed in any country.

There is ample cause, therefore, for the virtually unanimous opinion among Argentine writers that maladministration, extravagance, a wild desire to get something for nothing, have produced excessive issues of paper money, and consequently depreciation. Many of them have gone farther than this, however, and have said that excessive issues, due to maladministration, have been the *sole* cause of depreciation. It is this point of view to which exception must be taken: and it is because, as a student of international trade, my chief interest in Argentine paper money consists in pointing out other factors that helped to regulate its value, that I have thought it necessary to begin with this general discussion of paper money.

One of the factors that regulated the value of the paper was the possibility of redemption in gold. At no time during the whole of the period of this study did the government publicly accept the fact of inconvertible paper money as a permanent condition of things. In the early eighties there was a series of monetary reform measures. In 1883 specie payments were actually begun; and although they came to an end in 1885, announcement was made that merely a two years' suspension, and not the permanent abolition of specie payments, was intended. The famous Guaranteed Banks Act of 1887 was also, in theory, an attempt to guarantee the full face value of the bank notes.

At no time, therefore, was the prospect of redemption wholly absent: and the value of the paper fluctuated as this prospect seemed nearer or farther away. Civil war would send the gold premium up on the run. Lack of confidence in the government, a cabinet crisis, a rumor of scandal in a state bank, an attack on government policy in Congress, any of these things and many more would cause a disturbance of the gold premium. When the Revolution of July, 1890, broke out, turning President Celman out of office, the premium rose to 186,[1] as compared with 139, the maximum for June. But when some degree of confidence was restored by the succession of Señor Pellegrini, the premium dropped to 155.[2]

Fluctuations of this sort may take place without any change in the quantity of paper money. These modifications, however, are of minor importance. They are merely some causes of the short-time fluctuations of the value of the paper, and serve to indicate how unstable a situation is created by a régime of depreciated paper, and how sensitive is the premium on gold to every new event. It must be admitted, moreover, that fluctuations from these causes were fundamentally due to the fact that public confidence had already been shaken by the reckless issues of paper, founded on no legitimate need. They were the inevitable concomitant of depreciated paper money, and not a fundamental cause of its depreciation. Their presence serves rather to confirm than to weaken the affirmation that the real cause of depreciation was excessive issues of paper.

There is, however, a factor that affects the premium on gold, or the value of paper money, more fundamentally: and which, as I hope to show, deserves to be classed as a main determinant, coördinately with the quantity of paper issued, of the underlying, long-time movement of the premium on gold. And the operation of this factor forms a significant part of the explanation of Argentine foreign trade in the period from 1880 to 1900.

---

[1] Monthly average for July, 1890. [2] *Ibid.*, August, 1890.

This factor is the balance of international payments. Inconvertible paper money circulated freely within Argentina: but for foreign transactions it was worthless. The foreigner must be paid in some money that he could make use of, some money of whose value he could be certain. He must be paid in gold, or in bills of exchange representing gold. That the balance of international payments has some relation to the value of inconvertible paper money would appear to be indicated by the fact that the extent of the depreciation of paper is habitually, and with approximate accuracy, stated by means of a comparison of the paper with gold. We express the value of the paper in terms of a premium on gold. In other words, we express the value of the domestic currency by comparing it with the standard money of international transactions.

Outside of the large cities there was no such thing in Argentina as a "premium on gold." The farmer paid his rent and his wages in paper and sold his produce for paper. The laborer received his wage in paper and expended it in the same form. Indeed, it would have been difficult to make the ordinary country person understand what was meant by a "premium on gold." W. R. Lawson tells of his inability to make use of gold coins in some of the interior towns even as late as 1890.[1] He was looked upon with suspicion for offering them in payment of his purchases.

It was only in the cities, then, where foreign trade was conducted, in Buenos Aires and Rosario, that there was a "premium on gold." And this premium owed its existence to the fact that international transactions made necessary an exchange of gold for paper and vice versa, a continual comparison of the one with the other. It is obvious that in such a situation the movements of the gold premium would be determined not merely by the conditions of supply of and demand for paper, but also by the conditions of supply of and demand for gold. If it is true that an increase in the quantity of paper would tend to lessen its value and cause the premium on gold to rise, it is no less true

[1] "The Argentine Crisis: Its Financial Aspects," *Fortnightly Review*, liv, p. 454.

that a decrease in the quantity of gold would have precisely the same effect, without any change in the quantity of paper.

If the balance of international payments were such that Argentina owed to the outside world a deficit not covered by her exports, or by capital coming to her as the result of government loans, investments in railroads, and the like, that deficit would have to be made good in gold: and the export of gold would have precisely the same effect upon the gold premium as would a new issue of inconvertible notes. It would cause the premium to rise. And conversely, a "favorable" balance of payments, by starting a flow of gold to Argentina, would bring down the premium, and cause paper to appreciate in terms of gold, without any change having taken place in the quantity of paper.

If gold were being imported as the result of a favorable balance, and at the same time paper were being issued, the tendency would be for the two factors to neutralize each other. Paper might be issued without the premium's rising at all: or, if the issue were very large, the premium would not rise so far as it would have done but for the imports of gold. This combination of opposing forces did occur in the middle years of the eighties, 1885–88: the premium rose, but only very slowly, and to a comparatively small degree. From 1891 to 1894 there were large issues of paper, poured into a circulation already redundant to the point of suffocation: yet because of certain external arrangements of the foreign debt impeding the outward flow of specie, the premium showed a marked decline in those years. The years 1884 and 1885 afford an instance of still another sort. In 1884 paper was converted into gold at par; there were no issues whatever of paper money: yet an unfavorable balance of payments, by causing a demand for gold for export raised the price of gold, exhausted the resources of the banks, threatened a commercial crisis, and forced the suspension of specie payments. In other words, paper depreciated without any change in its quantity.

These instances are sufficient to indicate that there are grounds of fact for believing that the balance of international payments did play an important part in regulating the value of

Argentine paper money. This interrelation between the value of inconvertible paper money and the balance of international payments becomes still more significant in the case of Argentina when it is considered how large a part the balance of payments plays in the economic life of that country. There are few countries whose economic life depends so entirely on contact with the outside world. Without foreign trade and foreign capital Argentina would be a frontier community. Its resources are purely agricultural and grazing. Its eight millions of inhabitants occupy a country one-third the size of the United States, a country capable of producing grains, wool, hides, and meats in quantities immeasurably greater than those needed by the home population. On the other hand, it lacks combustibles [1] and minerals. It is virtually without manufactures, and has not the materials or the facilities for their development. Its business of making a living, therefore, consists of an exchange of its raw materials for the finished products of the outside world; with the result that in proportion to population and to domestic trade its foreign trade is enormously large. Prior to the late war the foreign trade of the United States was but a small portion of its total trade: in Argentina foreign trade is the breath of life. If there is a bad harvest there is immediately a "slump" in exports; as a direct consequence, the spending power of the country is cut down; there is a decline of imports. The national budget of the following year shows traces of these effects of the bad harvest. For example, in 1901 there was a bad grain harvest. Exports declined 9,000,000 pesos; imports for 1902 showed a decline of 4,000,000 pesos in imports of iron and construction materials; the depression was visible too in imports of textiles and beverages and still more in articles of luxury. The revenue for 1902 showed a decline of about 10,000,000 pesos gold. The bad harvest made itself manifest in every branch of the country's economic life: and it did so, not by limiting supplies of home-grown food for home consumption, but by obstructing the currents of foreign trade. In the case of Argentina it is strictly true

[1] Oil deposits at Comodoro Rivadavia are now being worked by the government with some success.

that the prosperity of the country depends on its foreign trade. Foreign trade gives the measure of all improvement, all progress of a financial or economic order.

To build up a large foreign trade, Argentina, like all young countries, has needed capital to develop her agricultural resources. Almost all of the large industries, the banks, the railroads, the meat refrigerating plants, the importing and exporting houses, have been developed by foreign capital and are still in the hands of foreigners. How entirely dependent Argentina still is upon foreign capital may be seen from the fact that ninety per cent of the internal loans of the national government is held abroad. The whole economic structure, in a word, is erected on a single basis and with a single aim, that of buying and selling, borrowing and repaying, with the outside world. If the farmer finds his foreign market cut off, he does not sell at home; the home population is too small to afford him an adequate market. He must simply stop cultivation, or grow just enough to feed himself. If he should already have raised his crop, and the international price should fall ruinously, he must sell abroad nevertheless and pocket his loss. If a new railroad is to be built, there are but two alternatives: either the government must borrow the capital abroad and build and manage the road, or it must give a building concession to foreigners, who will bring their capital from the outside world.

Enough has been said, perhaps, to indicate the importance of the balance of international payments in the economic life of Argentina, and to point out in general terms the significance of the interrelation between the balance of payments and the depreciated currency during the period of my study. Before proceeding to the actual investigation, however, it is necessary to consider the relation of these factors to the mechanism of foreign exchange, the machinery whereby the contact between paper money and the balance of payments was effected.

It is a familiar fact that inconvertible paper money tends to drive out specie, and that if enough paper is emitted gold will disappear completely from circulation. Once this stage is reached gold becomes a mere commodity like any other. Those needing gold for any purpose, whether for use in the arts or to make payments stipulated in gold, must procure the gold in the market.

In some discussions of the mechanism of foreign exchange in countries on a depreciated paper money basis, the process of expulsion of coin has been supposed to go much further. It has been said that virtually all gold, save that used in the arts, or that proceeding continually from gold mines within the country, is expelled from the country through the mechanism of foreign exchange: and that when that stage is reached gold exchange ceases to exist, and the international transactions of the country are conducted by means of a "paper exchange." The gold exchange may continue to be quoted, indeed, but it has not any real significance, it is said, since, there being no gold in the country, bills of exchange must be bought with and sold for depreciated paper money. The "real" exchange is therefore said to be a "paper exchange," and the so-called gold exchange is only a "nominal" exchange.

To cite an instance, I find the following in Mr. George Clare's *The A B C of the Foreign Exchanges:* [1]

When once the depreciation of an inconvertible paper currency becomes an accomplished fact, some of the fundamental propositions on which the theory of the exchanges is built up will appear to call for reconsideration. How, for instance, are we now to reconcile our conception of a par of exchange, or of a standard of value, with the new state of affairs: and if we are at fault in our elementary definitions, what becomes of the superstructure which we have based upon them? True, there is still the nominal metallic par to refer to: but, except that it serves as a sort of standard by which to measure the extent of debasement, it might for all practical purposes just as well be non-existent. And to tell the student that the specie par with the Argentine is about 48*d*. but that the rate fluctuates at present (1892) between 12*d*. and 13*d*. is merely to add to his perplexity.

In order to understand the actual situation as regards the exchanges in Argentina during the twenty-year period covered by this study, and to understand how essentially different it was from Mr. Clare's conception of it, it is necessary to explain more fully the reasoning that underlies this conception.

[1] First edition, 1892, London: reference is to fifth edition, reprint of 1914, pp. 150–151.

Let us assume, for a beginning, a time when Argentina was on a specie basis. The Argentine gold peso, as created by the Law of November 5, 1881, is equal to 47.58 British pence. Sterling exchange being quoted in Buenos Aires in British pence, the mint par is thus 47.58.[1] Let us assume now that with exchange at par lavish issues of inconvertible paper money were made in Argentina. The paper being of no use outside the country, foreign transactions would continue to take place on a gold basis. Suppose now that the balance of international payments became unfavorable to Argentina, so that Argentina was called upon to remit the deficit to Europe. That deficit would be remitted in gold, for the following reason:

International payments are effected by bills of exchange. Those having remittances to make to foreign creditors seek exchange for that purpose. They represent the demand for exchange. Those who have remittances to receive from their foreign debtors receive payment by means of bills of exchange, which they turn into cash by selling them. They represent the supply of exchange. On the side of demand are the importers, those having to make remittance of interest on foreign capital, immigrants who are sending their savings to the home country, and the like. On the side of supply are the exporters, those who have succeeded in borrowing foreign capital, foreign tourists in Argentina receiving funds from their home country, and so on.

In the situation originally assumed, exchange was at par, because the demand for and supply of bills of exchange were equal. Suppose now that the balance of payments becomes unfavorable to Argentina. Suppose that Argentine imports increase, or that interest charges on the national foreign debt, or on capital invested in railroads, grow heavier, with no corresponding increase in the other side of the equation representing the exports and new annual borrowings. Then the demand for exchange to make these remittances will become greater than the supply, and exchange will go "against" Argentina. That is, the price of exchange to the Argentine buyer will

[1] The Argentine gold peso equals $0.965 U.S.

become greater. He will have to pay more of Argentine money for a bill of exchange worth a given number of pounds sterling. Since in Buenos Aires exchange is expressed in British pence, this would mean that exchange would fall. Instead of being able to buy 47.58 pence with an Argentine gold peso, one would receive something less. If the excess of demand over supply were considerable, exchange would continue to fall, to say 46. Much lower it would not go, for with exchange at that point, the Argentine debtor would find it more to his profit to ship gold to his English creditor, and pay the cost of transportation thereon. This rate of 46 is thus the "gold export point." [1]

It is clear, therefore, that in the case I have assumed, of an unfavorable balance of payments, exchange would fall to the gold export point, and the deficit in the balance would be paid by a flow of specie from Argentina to England. Continuing, then, with the train of reasoning underlying the concept of a paper exchange:

Through the workings of the foreign exchange mechanism, as just described, it is supposed that virtually all gold disappears from the country, except for some minor quantities which find a market in supplying the demand for gold in the arts, or for the payment of contracts expressly stipulated in gold.[2] Once the gold is expelled, the mechanism of the gold exchanges must of necessity cease to function. For, to go back to the assumed case:

Suppose that on account of a continued unfavorable balance, exchange were to continue "against" Argentina. The country having now been drained of gold, there is no longer a "gold export point." A person having a foreign remittance to make must buy exchange willy-nilly: and since he has only the depre-

---

[1] This figure is given only as a rough approximation. The cost of shipping gold varied with freight rates, interest rates, and other factors. During most of the period of this study the gold export point appears to have been somewhat higher than 46. In fact, 47 was often thought a low rate; and gold was shipped frequently at 46 to 47.

Gold might also proceed from mines in the country; but in Argentina there are no gold mines. There is no source of gold save the ordinary one of foreign transactions.

ciated paper money, he must buy his exchange with this: and since a bill of exchange represents command over gold, he must give for it whatever gold is worth in terms of paper. Instead, therefore, of the exchanges being confined within the narrow limits of the gold points, now that there has been removed the regulating factor of gold shipments which kept exchange within those points, the fluctuations will become incomparably wider: and will keep pace approximately with the fluctuations of the premium on gold.

Thus, as paper depreciates, exchange will fall lower and lower. Instead of stopping at 46, it will fall to 40, to 35, and finally, if the depreciation of paper be very great, to the 11 or 12d. that Mr. Clare mentions. A favorable balance of payments, on the other hand, by increasing the supply of exchange, will cause the rate to rise. It might cause exchange to rise from 12d. to 20d., for example, but always, so long as paper was depreciated, exchange would remain below par.

Theoretically, this train of reasoning appears sound enough. Had Argentina not been receiving large sums from Europe on account of borrowings during the period when the paper issues began to be multiplied, and the paper to depreciate, it is possible that some such situation as this might have come about: although in view of the fact that gold exchange was maintained even during the disastrous Baring Panic of 1890 and 1891, it seems unlikely. In any case, it is not so much my purpose to criticise the theory as to point out that, so far as Argentina was concerned, it was not borne out by the facts. Gold exchange, as I have said, was maintained throughout the period. Nor was it merely a "nominal" exchange, that might as well for all practical purposes be ignored.

So far as the relation between the balance of payments and the value of paper money is concerned, it is indeed true that the relation would exist under a paper exchange quite as much as under the gold exchange that was actually in operation. One could prove that the value of the paper depended not merely on its quantity in relation to home needs, but also on its quantity in relation to the demand for and supply of bills of exchange, representing gold. That comes to much the same thing as my own statement, that the value of paper money depended not solely on the conditions of demand for and supply of paper, but also on the conditions of demand for and supply of gold. And as regards the overturn in the trade balance, and the means whereby it was brought about, the conclusions, as we shall see when we come to that subject, would be much the same, whether we had in mind a paper exchange or a gold exchange in a country on a depreciated paper money basis. For, as I hope to show in later portions of this study, the essential factor in the situation is not the particular mechanism of foreign exchange which was in operation: but the presence of depreciated paper money, and the relation of the paper to the international balance of payments.

There are, however, some points of difference between a paper exchange and a gold exchange operating in a paper money country which have significance; and which therefore warrant a description of how exchange was actually dealt in in Buenos Aires during the period covered by the present study. Exchange was not bought with and sold for paper, but for gold. Exchange was sold by the banker, and the purchase price drawn against the customer's gold account with the bank. In other words, instead of one money there were two: the depreciated paper which circulated throughout the country, and was legal tender for all domestic transactions; and gold, which was bought and sold only in the foreign trade centers, by the money changers and on the Buenos Aires stock exchange, where balances in gold dealings were settled at the end of each month. To buy a bill of exchange you first bought gold, and with the gold bought exchange. Importing and exporting houses bought gold at frequent intervals, through their brokers, in order to purchase exchange for their over-seas settlements. When the government had to remit interest on the foreign debt, it bought exchange with gold, and if it had not on hand a stock received by means of foreign loans, or from such revenues as were required to be paid in gold, it had to go into the market for the coin. There was thus a continual buying and selling of gold for paper and paper for gold.

Of the opportunities which this situation created for speculators, and the violent fluctuations of the gold premium occasioned thereby, I need not speak at present. The essential point at this stage is to make it clear that foreign exchange was not bought with and sold for paper; that there was no "paper exchange," but instead a gold exchange, and a continual buying and selling of paper for gold: that, in other words, there were two distinct monetary systems, the domestic paper money system, and the foreign trade monetary system of gold exchange and gold wherewith to purchase it.

Fundamentally, of course, the situation was a good deal the same as it would have been under a paper exchange. The *underlying* transaction was an exchange of depreciated paper for foreign exchange; and every person who purchased exchange made a calculation as to how much paper it had cost him to buy gold for that purpose.

There was, however, one significant difference between the exchange mechanism that operated in Buenos Aires and a paper exchange. The cardinal point of the theory of paper exchange is that, once gold has been driven out and a paper exchange has taken the place of the metallic exchange, gold cannot move freely between the trading countries. There is no specie, and it is for that very reason, says the theory, that exchange fluctuates so violently, destroying the notion of a par of exchange and destroying the mechanism of the gold points. The mechanism of gold exchange having been destroyed, the whole train of consequences so familiar to the student of international trade falls to the ground. Since specie cannot move between the trading countries, one cannot explain changes in the price levels of the two countries by reference to gold movements: and consequently one cannot so explain changes in the balance of trade, which, in the theory for gold countries, are brought about by the influence of gold movements upon the level of prices. There would be no gold movements, for example, to explain the overturn of the Argentine trade balance in 1891.

Such is the conclusion to be drawn from the theory of the paper exchanges. In point of fact, however, there were gold movements between Argentina and the outside world. The operation of the exchanges permitted the flow of specie in much the same manner as would have been the case had there been no depreciated paper money. There was still a par of exchange: not a "nominal" par, but a par between the Argentine gold peso that was being bought and sold in large quantities on the stock exchange, and foreign gold monies. There were still specie points, which operated in precisely the same manner as they do in gold-standard countries. For, as I have said, the first step in the operation of dealing in exchange was to buy gold. As to this, there was no choice. Once in possession of the gold, the buyer of exchange faced exactly the same question as he would have done in a gold-standard country: should he buy exchange with his gold, or ship the gold itself? If exchange was above gold export point he bought exchange. If it had fallen to the gold point, it was to his advantage to ship the gold and pay transportation cost thereon. So, too, with the seller of exchange. Should gold exchange rise high enough above par to more than cover the cost of importing gold, he would send for gold rather than sell exchange at so great a loss.

Thus we find in 1888 an import of about $45,000,000 of specie; and in 1889 an export of about $12,000,000. For the seventeen years 1884 to 1900, imports of specie amounted to more than $158,000,000, and exports to about $90,000,000. It is impossible to explain away such heavy shipments of specie, as due entirely to shipments for purposes of speculation, or to the fact that in 1890 the government enacted that part of the customs dues must be paid in gold.[1] The size of the specie movements, and more particularly their dates, indicate clearly that the mechanism of exchange was operating as in a gold country, and that specie flowed in and out in obedience to the machinery of the gold points. The year 1888 was the year when borrowings reached their height. Argentina, then a country of less than four million people, borrowed about $250,000,000 (gold) in that year. In 1889, on the other hand, borrowings declined, and the interest

---

[1] As a matter of fact, virtually all customs dues continued to be paid wholly in paper.

charge began to assume alarming proportions. As in a gold country, the movements of gold were in entire accord with these changes in the balance of international payments.

Gold exchange and gold movements between the trading countries there were, then; and in these respects the Argentine case differs from that of a paper exchange. The difference, however, is merely one of mechanism, and does not materially alter the conclusions of theory regarding international trade in a country on a basis of depreciated currency. For, after all, it is not the question of mechanism, but the fact of the presence of depreciated paper which is of real significance. It is the presence of depreciated paper that makes the case of Argentina different from that of a gold-standard country. Gold did flow into and out of the country in obedience to the mechanism of gold points, to be sure: but gold could not flow into and out of the monetary circulation of the country. Gold stood constantly at a premium. Consequently an influx of gold into the country would not raise the price level, nor an outflow of gold lower it, as would be the tendency in a gold-standard country. Gold movements would not, therefore, affect exports and imports in the same way, or by the same means, as they would in a gold-using country. For the theorist of international trade this is the significant difference between the Argentine case and that of gold standard countries.

From this, however, one is not to jump to the opposite conclusion: that gold movements are of no importance, or that they do not affect prices at all. I have already discussed the effect that international movements of gold have on the value of inconvertible paper money. Gold cannot, to be sure, enter into circulation, but gold coming to the country would have quite as much effect upon the value of money as if it had done so. Only, it would be the opposite effect: it would not cheapen money and raise the price level, but would cause money to appreciate and the price level to fall. It would do so by increasing the supply of gold, and thus cheapening gold in terms of paper.

This is not the place to set forth in any detail the conclusions of my study, or to state to what extent the investigation of the

Argentine case appears to provide verification of the theory of international trade and foreign exchange under conditions of depreciated paper money. This preliminary discussion will have served its purpose if it has indicated the nature of the principles which this study is intended to test. It was important, too, to make known at the outset the fact that in so far as the machinery of exchange is concerned, the Argentine case does not accord with theory, that there was no "paper exchange," no "dislocation" of exchange: and to point out that so far as the main conclusions of theory as to the effect of depreciated paper on foreign trade are concerned, the question of exchange mechanism is of secondary importance, the significant factor in the situation being the presence of depreciated paper money, and the interrelation between this money and the balance of international payments.

Before concluding this introductory chapter it may be conducive to clearness to explain briefly the general scheme of the narrative account that follows. I am to study the interrelations of three factors — depreciated paper money, foreign borrowings, and foreign trade — with a view, finally, to explaining the overturn in the trade balance in 1891, when an excess of imports over exports, until then the normal state of things, was changed into an excess of exports over imports, "a favorable" balance which has existed ever since. I shall divide the work into two main sections: the first will consider the facts of paper money and of borrowings, and show the relation between them. It will be shown that the value of the paper depended in large part on the conditions of borrowing; and that, on the other hand, the borrowings themselves emanated to a considerable extent from the paper money situation. This interrelation, as I have said, was the significant factor in the Argentine case. The second section will consider the effects of this interrelation of paper money and borrowings upon the foreign merchandise trade: and will consist mainly of a study of prices and costs, of the manner in which these were affected by depreciated paper money, and of the influence of the fluctuations of paper money, prices, and costs upon the operations of importers and exporters. The purpose of this latter section will be to explain how, in a country using depreciated inconvertible paper money, changes in exports and imports are brought about.

The twenty-year period of this study divides itself naturally into two parts: (1) 1880 to 1885, and (2) 1885 to 1900. The first period is of minor importance for our purpose, its chief interest consisting of the fact that it provides the most striking single instance of the effect of borrowings on the value of the currency. This is the period of monetary reforms, of the adoption of specie payments, in 1883, and of their suspension, in January, 1885.

The second period is the important one. Through it all, paper was inconvertible and depreciated. It consists of a period of inflation and speculation culminating in the Baring Panic of 1890 and 1891, and of a subsequent nine or ten years of depression and very slow recovery. It ends with the Conversion Law of 1899, the act famous in Argentine history for having furnished at last a stable basis for the currency. From that time on the problem of a fluctuating premium on gold disappears.

PART I

INCONVERTIBLE PAPER MONEY

AND

THE BALANCE OF INTERNATIONAL PAYMENTS

CHAPTER III

ARGENTINE MONETARY HISTORY TO 1885

THE decade from 1880 to 1890 is the great "boom" period of Argentine economic history. It is not too much to say that in those ten years Argentina underwent a greater economic development than in all the preceding decades of the century. In 1880 a strong central government was established under the presidency of General Julio A. Roca. In 1881 Buenos Aires was declared the federal capital. In 1881, also, the great reform of the currency took place, the Law of November 5th still serving as the basis of the Argentine system of currency. And it was in Roca's administration that the program of borrowing, intended for the opening up of the land for settlement and the building of railroads on a scale hitherto undreamed of, was conceived, and put in process of operation.

Prior to 1880 the modern Argentina can scarcely be said to have existed. Until then, Argentine history is one long tale of internal strife and foreign wars. It was in 1861 that the fourteen provinces which, together with ten "national territories," comprise the present Argentina, united to form a federation. In 1864 together with Brazil and Uruguay the new republic waged war on Paraguay, a war which terminated in 1870 with the death of Lopez, the dictator of Paraguay, and the destruction of nine-tenths of the population of that country. At this period Argentina was nothing more than a backward frontier community. Her chief industry was grazing; but Argentine wool was of poor quality, and the sheep, poorly cared for, were much afflicted with epidemic diseases.[1] Agricultural methods were primitive. Wheat, which has since become one of the great staples, was not grown in sufficient quantities to supply home consumption; no wheat was exported before 1875. The foreign

[1] H. Gibson, *The History and Present State of the Sheep-breeding Industry in the Argentine Republic,* 1893, Chapter VI.

trade (imports and exports combined) amounted in 1870 to 79,000,000 pesos, as compared with 256,000,000 pesos in 1889. The population, according to the census of 1869, was 1,830,000, and was confined largely to the eastern and northern provinces. This scanty population inhabited a country equal in aggregate extent to the United Kingdom, Austria, Italy, and Spain.[1] The South and West of Argentina was a vast uncultivated territory stretching away to the Andes on the West and to Patagonia on the South, and inhabited almost exclusively by Indian tribes.

Most interesting for our purpose is the condition of the currency prior to the monetary law of 1881. Jorge Pillado begins his study of Argentine paper money [2] with the following sentence, which serves as a key to Argentine monetary history in the nineteenth century: "Argentine paper money, besides its regular functions as an element of exchange, has served the official finances of all periods, as a tax forced upon the country in difficult moments of its political life." Whenever the party chiefs for the moment in power needed resources to suppress an internal rebellion, wage foreign war, defray extravagant expenditure of one sort or another, they usually turned to the simple expedient of the printing press. To name only one instance, when civil war broke out in 1859 between the province of Buenos Aires and the other Argentine provinces, the Buenos Aires legislature authorized, between July and December, three emissions of paper money for a total of 85,000,000 pesos. These were followed by a further emission of 50,000,000 in 1861.

An idea of the lavish scale on which resort to these forced loans was had may be obtained from the figures of emission on various dates. The first issue, in 1822, was for 290,000 pesos. By 1826 the total amount in circulation was 2,694,856; in 1835 it was 15,000,000; in 1854, 204,000,000; and in 1865, 298,000,-000.[3] The population at this latter date was about one million

[1] H. B. Callender, *Fortnightly Review*, liv, p. 445; "The Argentine Crisis."

[2] *Anuario Pillado*, 1900, p. 1.

[3] *Anuario Pillado*, p. 10 *et seq.;* Martinez and Lewandowski, *La República Argentina en El Siglo XX*, Part IV, Chapter III, pp. 474–475 (Madrid, 1912).

and a half, and it had not doubled in fifty years. It is not surprising, therefore, that by 1865 the value of the paper peso had fallen to three to four cents gold.

In 1866 an attempt was made to stabilize the currency, by means of a system of conversion, a system of interest to us because of its similarity to the famous scheme of 1899, by which the problem of debased currency was finally settled. A "Bureau of Exchange" was established in connection with the Bank of the Province of Buenos Aires. The bank was to deliver, through this bureau, 25 pesos in legal tender notes for one peso in gold, and vice versa. This office functioned from February, 1867, to May, 1876. At first, the plan appeared to work successfully. In the first year the bureau accumulated 3,481,000 gold pesos. By 1873, the gold reserve had risen to 16,862,000 pesos. But after that date the stock of gold dwindled rapidly, chiefly by reason of the fact that the province could not keep its hands off the accumulated gold. A law of June 30, 1873, authorized the retirement of three millions from the conversion office. This act, together with the large loans made by the provincial bank to the federal government, the expenses of the Civil War of 1874, and finally the financial crisis of 1874-75, when the federal government was on the verge of bankruptcy, forced the bureau to terminate its operations: and paper money again became inconvertible.[1]

One clause of the law creating the Bureau of Exchange in 1866 had declared that "the provincial bank might issue the paper money necessary for the execution of the law." It is this clause that appears to have been most assiduously attended to. When the conversion bureau was opened in 1867, the amount of paper in circulation was 298,458,000 pesos. By 1873 the provincial bank had emitted through the conversion bureau 420,000,000 pesos of new legal tender notes.

In 1872 the Banco Nacional was founded, by private capitalists but with the aid and encouragement of the national govern-

[1] On the conversion system of 1866, see J. M. Rosa, *La Reforma Monetaria en la República Argentina*, p. 33 *et seq.* (Buenos Aires, 1909). (Señor Rosa, as finance minister, introduced the Conversion Law of 1899.)

ment. Of the total stock of 20,000,000 pesos, the government was to subscribe two millions in government bonds. The bank, in addition to the ordinary operations of discount and deposit, was to act as the financial agent of the government, and was to make loans to government. As an offset for these services, the bank was to be permitted to issue its notes to an amount of double the paid-in capital, the notes to be full legal tender, and redeemable on demand. The bank began operations November 1, 1873, when the first signs of the approaching crisis were already apparent. To strengthen its position, the provincial bank restricted its emissions, but the national bank, taking advantage of the more prudent policy of its provincial rival, issued notes and made loans liberally. By June, 1874, when civil war broke out precipitating the crisis, the Banco Nacional had issued 4,500,000 of paper pesos, and was burdened with 6,000,000 pesos of bad debts. The result was that when conversion of the provincial issues was suspended in 1876, the notes of the Banco Nacional had likewise to be declared inconvertible.[1]

The net result of the conversion scheme, therefore, was an enormous increase in the paper money. From 298,458,000 pesos, the amount that was already suffocating the country in 1866, the fiduciary circulation increased more than threefold by 1876. The national department of statistics gives the total amount of paper in circulation throughout the country at the end of 1881 as 882,000,000 pesos,[2] and assigns to the paper peso a value of about four cents gold.

After the crisis of 1874-76 there was a healthy reaction. New arrangements were made for the payment of the national debt to the provincial bank. The condition of the banks improved. The foreign trade increased 60 per cent between 1878 and 1880. Wheat made its appearance for the first time among the exports.

By far the most important event of the late seventies was the reduction of the Patagonians and the opening up of great stretches of southern lands for settlement. In 1878, General

---

[1] *Anuario Pillado*, pp. 35-44.

[2] *Extracto Estadistico de la República Argentina, Correspondiente al Año 1915*, p. 297. Published by the Dirección General de Estadistica de la Nación. Buenos Aires, 1916.

Roca, then minister of war, led a series of expeditions, known as the "Salidas de Roca" (Roca's Sallies), into Southern Argentina to conquer the Indian tribes, which were accustomed to make raids for long distances into the inhabited parts of the country, killing the settlers and driving off their herds. Roca's troops quickly overcame the Indians, sent some of the survivors as slaves to the plantations of the northern provinces, and drove the remainder beyond the Rio Negro into Patagonia. To protect the southern frontier a great ditch was dug along the Rio Negro. This together with a line of forts effectually put an end to any further danger of invasion.

From these events may be dated the beginning of the land boom that swept over Argentina during the eighties. As soon as life and property were secure from Indian raiders, land values began to rise, and the land was gradually taken up by settlers.

There appeared to be no impediment in the way of a period of unexampled economic development except the disordered state of the currency. The enormous depreciation of the paper peso I have mentioned. An equally disturbing element was the lack of uniformity in the currency. National money did not exist. Each province had its own money, and the same money had a different value between one province and another, and even between cities in the same province.[1] In Buenos Aires there were four varieties of paper, as well as foreign coins. In the other provinces, Chilean, Bolivian, Peruvian, and other gold, silver, and copper coins circulated side by side with provincial paper, with the notes of the Banco Nacional, the notes of private bankers, and even of ordinary business houses. There was convertible paper and inconvertible paper. Of the silver coins, many were from Chile, Bolivia, and Peru; and of these many

[1] In Mendoza (West Argentina) 13½ to 15 silver pesos were needed to buy a Chilean condor (gold), though the condor was officially valued in 1876 at 9.15 pesos: in Rio Cuarto, 150 miles from Mendoza, the condor could be had for 1½ pesos less than in Mendoza. (See W. I. Buchanan, ex-United States minister to Argentina, "La Moneda y la Vida en la República Argentina," in *La Revista de Derechi, Historia y Letras, 1898*, ii, p. 203. The same article appears in English in United . . ates Special Consular Reports, xiii.)

were under-weight. [1] The most famous was the "melgarejo,"
a light-weight silver peso, which got its name from that of the
president of Bolivia who first ordered their coinage, and forced
the Bolivians to accept them as full-weight coins, incidentally
shooting some of the more respectable business men, who
objected. It is not surprising that in many parts of the country
merchants settled accounts according to the weight of gold.
Scales were an indispensable instrument in all offices and stores.

As an illustration of the prevailing confusion, the Commission
of Mendoza [2] appointed by the national government to report
on the condition of that province, cited the case of a merchant
who, wishing to fetch merchandise from the Atlantic coast, had
his capital in the form of Mendoza paper money. He would have
to go through the following operations:

1. Exchange in the market his Mendoza money for Chilean
   coin, in fractional money, since no other existed in
   abundance:
2. Exchange the fractional coins into pesos:
3. Arrived at the seaport of Rosario, Santa Fé, he would
   exchange the pesos for Bolivian cuatros; and with these
   would pay for his goods:

[1] The following are some of the coins that circulated in Argentina prior to the
Law of 1881:

1. Spanish-American gold "onza" (ounce), 27.875 grains: valued officially
   in Argentina in 1876 at 15.75 pesos.
2. Chilean condor (gold coin), 15.253 grains: valued in 1876 at 9.15 pesos.
3. Chilean, Bolivian, and Peruvian silver pesos, 25.9 grains: valued in
   1876 at 92 centavos.
4. The "melgarejos," emitted by Bolivia, Chile, and Peru under their
   national seals: weighed 20.9 grains, *i. e.*, 5 grains under weight.
5. Twenty centavo silver pieces of Chile, Bolivia, and Peru.
6. European and North American coins, as American eagle, napoleon,
   Spanish doubloon, the pound sterling, Brazilian 20-milreis piece: and
   Mexican, Central American, Brazilian, Spanish, French, Belgian, and
   United States silver coins.
7. Some copper pieces.

And, in addition, there was the paper money, convertible and inconvertible,
issued by the Banco Nacional, by the provincial banks, by private bankers, and
by ordinary commercial houses. (See W. I. Buchanan, *ibid.*, p. 201 *et seq.*)

[2] The province of Mendoza is in the west of Argentina, in the foothills of the
Andes. It is famous for its grapes and wines.

4. Lastly, he would sell his goods in Mendoza for paper money of the bank of Mendoza.[1]

Some improvement of the currency was imperative. The Banco Nacional complained to the minister of finance in 1878: "The lack of a national money is so injurious to the legitimate interests of the country that it is not possible to continue a day longer in these conditions."[2] The federal executive presented to Congress a project for currency reform in 1878; but no action was taken until after the Revolution of 1880, when the finance minister of Roca's administration, J. J. Romero, presented a measure which was enacted into law on November 5, 1881, and has ever since been the basis of the monetary system of the republic. The law established a bi-metallic standard, the units to be the gold peso, of 24.89 grains, 9/10 fine, and the silver peso, of 385.8 grains, 9/10 fine, the legal ratio being thus 15.55. The law was intended principally to provide national coins which should circulate throughout the country. A mint was established, and it was provided that eight million gold pesos and four million silver pesos be issued, whereupon the circulation of foreign coins was to be prohibited. Thus, it was hoped, the Bolivian, Chilean, and Peruvian coins which circulated all through the country, but particularly in the northern and western provinces, would be got rid of. Foreign coins were to be accepted at the mint at their bullion value, under the ratio established by law. Banks of issue existing in the republic were, within two years from the passage of the law, to renew their issues in accordance with the new monetary unit. New issues of denominations under one peso were prohibited, and outstanding notes of this kind were to be withdrawn from circulation within a period of two years.[3]

It is interesting to observe the subsequent history of this somewhat pretentious enactment. The bi-metallistic provision

[1] *Anuario Pillado*, p. 49.

[2] Romero got rid of the "melgarejos" by fixing for them a mint price which was four centavos above their bullion value.

[3] *Anuario Pillado*, p. 50 *et seq.*

was a failure from the outset. Silver ceased to be coined in 1884, when 2,805,839 pesos had been issued. Gold was coined until 1896, the total amount being 31,722,625 pesos, about four times the number that the act called for.[1] Yet in 1896 there were no gold coins in circulation, any more than there had been in 1881. At the end of 1886, when 11,225,000 gold pesos had been minted, the director of the mint advised against further issue, and called attention to the fact that "the gold coined has been shipped or melted down, for which reason it is useless to continue coining under present circumstances."[2]

The Law of 1881, though it brought about a measure of uniformity, did not get to the root of the currency difficulty. Whatever might be enacted with regard to new metallic units, the money that circulated from hand to hand was the old depreciated paper. The real problem was to replace the great mass of 882,000,000 pesos of practically worthless notes with a currency having a dependable value. Between 1881 and 1883 a number of measures were directed to this end. By law of September 25, 1881, the Bank of the Province of Buenos Aires was ordered to retire from circulation its notes, amounting to over 600,000,000 pesos, within two years; and, to this end, an executive decree of August 26, 1882, required the provincial bank to begin the conversion of its paper before July 1, 1883, the old legal tender notes to be replaced by so-called "metallic notes" (i. e., gold notes) at the ratio of twenty-five of the old for one of the new. By law of October 19, 1883, this measure was extended to all banks of issue, the law providing that the executive should indicate a period within which all of the old emissions must be retired from circulation, after which there should circulate only the new metallic notes, redeemable in gold at par. An executive decree of December 22, 1883, fixed a period of six months for the fulfillment of the terms of the law. The same decree restricted the privilege of emission of the new metallic

---

[1] *Extracto Estadistico de la República Argentina*, 1915, p. 299.

[2] P. Agote, *Finances of the Argentine Government*. Edition IV, 1887, p. 595 *et seq.* (An official investigation and report to the national government by the chairman of the Department of Public Credit: contains texts of laws relating to banks, currency, taxation, debt, etc.)

notes to five banks: the Banco Nacional, the Bank of the Province of Buenos Aires, the Provincial Bank of Santa Fé, the Provincial Bank of Córdoba, and the private banking firm of Otero
& Co.[1] To insure compliance with the terms of the Act, a
Bureau of Inspection of Banks was created, under the ministry
of finance.

At the end of 1883, therefore, Argentina for the first time had
a practicable monetary system. The old notes were withdrawn
from circulation, and in their place the country enjoyed the
benefits of a national paper currency, convertible into gold on
demand and at par. The effect on the quantity of paper in
circulation was, of course, extraordinary. The 882,000,000 pesos
in circulation in 1882 were replaced by 61,739,000 pesos in new
national metallic notes by the end of 1884.[2]

The conversion decreed in 1883, however, lasted only a short
time. Even if we date the period of conversion from July 1, 1883,
the time when the Bank of the Province of Buenos Aires began
the replacement of its old notes with metallic notes, the period
during which paper was convertible and on a par with gold was
of only eighteen months duration. By the end of 1884, Argentina
was in the throes of another financial crisis, which, though it
was of short duration and had practically no industrial effect,
was sufficient to cause the suspension of conversion, and to bring
about a return to forced paper currency, a condition from which
no escape was effected until 1899.

In January, 1885, President Roca, upon the petition of the
Banco Nacional and the Bank of the Province of Buenos Aires
found himself forced to decree the suspension of conversion for a
period of two years. In March, 1885, by another executive decree, the Banco Nacional, and shortly afterwards those of the
Provinces of Buenos Aires, Santa Fé, and Córdoba, and the
bank of Muñoz, Rodriguez & Co. of Tucuman, were given
permission to issue their notes as legal currency without being
obliged to convert them.[3] In December, 1886, the government
authorized the Bank of the Province of Buenos Aires to increase
its issue of now inconvertible notes by seven million pesos. And

---

[1] *Anuario Pillado*, p. 52.   [2] *Ibid.*, p. 54.   [3] P. Agote, *ibid.*, p. 340.

in the same month, the suspension of conversion decreed in 1885 for two years was continued for another two years, until 1889. By that time the gold premium had risen to over 100 per cent, the country was on the eve of a new crisis, and all pretence of a return to conversion had been abandoned.

The reasons for the failure of the only attempt that has been made to maintain convertible paper on a par with gold, in 1883–84, are worthy of careful attention, as indicating in some measure the nature of our problem, and affording on a relatively small scale an illustration of the forces that were at work in the subsequent five-year period which terminated with the Baring Panic in 1890.

CHAPTER IV

BORROWINGS AND THE BALANCE OF PAYMENTS
1881–1885

To make possible the establishment and maintenance of specie payments in 1883 and 1884, as contemplated by the currency laws already reviewed, it was necessary to supply the banks of issue with reserves of gold. To find the gold, the national and provincial governments resorted to foreign borrowing operations. The national government had borrowed four million pesos from the Bank of the Province of Buenos Aires in 1866 to meet expenses of the Paraguayan War, and ten millions of paper in 1876, to avert the bankruptcy that threatened the government after the Civil War and the panic of 1874.[1] These debts the government paid off in part by a 6 per cent loan of 6,855,000 pesos.[2] To provide the Banco Nacional with a specie reserve the national government bought 60,000 shares of its stock, which it paid for by a 5 per cent loan of 8,415,500 pesos.[3] Meantime, on May 14, 1883, the province of Santa Fé authorized a 6 per cent foreign gold loan of 7,000,000 pesos, intended to pay off a

---

[1] Characteristically, the provincial bank was on each occasion granted permission to issue for its own account a corresponding amount of new paper pesos. (See *Anuario Pillado*, pp. 38, 46.)

[2] Issued in 1883, at 90. The law of September 25, 1881, authorizing the debt had intended it to be internal; but in fact the bonds were subscribed abroad, in recognition whereof the loan was declared external by law of October 17, 1883. Similar in purpose to the above loan was that of 1882, for 4,118,000 pesos; also a 6 per cent loan, and issued abroad at 90. (See *Memoria de Hacienda*, 1883, i, p. 72 *et seq.*: this is the annual report of the ministry of finance. See too, P. Agote: *Finances of the Argentine Government*, Ed. IV, 1887, p. 89.)

[3] After an unsuccessful attempt to float the loan at home in 1882, it was declared a foreign debt, June 28, 1883, and issued in England in 1884, at 84½, yielding the government 7,300,000 pesos gold (Ernesto Tornquist & Co., Ltd.: *Manual of Argentine National, Provincial and Municipal Loans*, p. 8: Buenos Aires, 1913).

prior loan of 1874, and to increase the capital of the provincial bank.[1]

All in all, therefore, the national and provincial governments, to provide the gold necessary for the establishment of conversion of the paper currency at par, issued between 1881 and 1885, 26,561,000 pesos (gold) of their bonds, which yielded 22,670,000 pesos (gold), and required an annual service for interest and amortization of 1,486,829 pesos (gold).

Had these been the only loans, the burden upon the national and provincial governments would have been tolerable, and specie payments would doubtless have been maintained. In fact, however, they were but part of a general program of borrowing, arising out of the plans of the new administration of General Roca for the development of the economic resources of the republic. Argentina, though a country of about 3,000,000 square kilometers, having in 1883 about 65,000,000 sheep and 14,000,000 cattle,[2] had as yet a population of only two and one-half millions;[3] and the bulk of it was in the eastern and northeastern provinces of Buenos Aires, Santa Fé, and Córdoba. The southern and southwestern parts of the country, though freed from Indian invasion, were as yet very sparsely settled, for the reason that they lacked adequate means of communication with the seaboard and with the more populous provinces of the east and north. The first Argentine railroad, a ten-kilometer road, had been built in 1854. By 1875, the total railroad mileage was 1170, and by 1880, 1512.[4] In the next five years the railroad mileage nearly doubled, the total miles open for traffic in 1885 being 2700. This increase, though small compared with that effected in the subsequent five-year period, when the railroad fever reached its height, is nevertheless indicative of the

[1] The loan was issued in two parts: 5,122,950 pesos being issued by Morton Bliss & Co. of New York, in May, 1883, at 85, and 2,049,180 in October, 1884, by the same firm, at 83. (See *Anuario Pillado*, pp. 148–149.)

[2] *Exposición Sobre el Estado Económico y Financiero de la República Argentina*, p. 85: Buenos Aires, 1893; official publication.

[3] Present population (figure for 1914) is 7,885,237: about 7 per square mile. Cf. United States, 31 per square mile (*Extracto Estadístico*, 1915, p. xiii).

[4] *Extracto Estadístico*, 1915, p. 535.

efforts that were being made, both by the national and the provincial governments and by private enterprise, to open up the land to cultivation and settlement. The activities of the governments were twofold: they encouraged the construction of private lines by guarantees of interest on the capital invested, and they intensified the policy of building state lines, already begun by the province of Buenos Aires, as early as 1857, with the Western Railway, and followed later by the national government.

By law of October 2, 1880, the national government authorized a 6 per cent loan of 12,000,000 pesos for the prolongation of the two national lines, the Central Norte and the Andino.[1] A series of laws from October, 1881, to June, 1884, authorized two 5 per cent loans for a total of 42,133,345 pesos (gold). The original purpose of these loans was the construction of harbor and sanitary works. An attempt made to float them in 1884, however, proved almost a complete failure. European lenders, disturbed by the unprecedented frequency with which Argentina was appearing in the loan market, were becoming wary. Only 14,000,000 pesos of the bonds were subscribed; and the sum realized, 11,440,800 pesos, was applied to the further construction of state railroads.[2]

Meanwhile, the provincial governments of Buenos Aires, Santa Fé, and Entre Rios issued in England their bonds for a total of 25,664,000 pesos (gold). In addition, the province of Buenos Aires issued a loan of 1,550,000 pesos (gold) to construct port works.[3]

The total government borrowings for railroad purposes in the five-year period 1881–85 thus reached a nominal amount of 53,112,000 pesos (gold): on which the actual sum realized, computed on the basis of the rates at which the loans were floated, was 46,989,800 pesos (gold). The service and amortization of these loans required an annual sum of 3,239,538 pesos (gold).

[1] The loan was issued in London in June, 1881, at 91, by C. de Murietta & Co. (*Memoria de Hacienda*, 1881, p. xx).

[2] *Memoria de Hacienda*, 1884, i, p. 6.

[3] The Riachuelo Port.

To the borrowings for currency and railroad [1] purposes, must be added those growing out of the political rearrangements of 1880, and those destined for various public works. After the Revolution of 1880, the federal government assumed two loans of the province of Buenos Aires, amounting to 14,018,000 pesos. Buenos Aires, till then the capital of the province of the same name, became the federal capital; and the federal government agreed to pay 5,000,000 pesos for the cession to it of the buildings of the provincial government.[2] In addition, the federal government agreed to pay its debt to the provincial bank.[3] As a part of the same program of federalization, the national government took over the Riachuelo Port Works and the Sanitary Works of Buenos Aires (city), both of which were already under construction by the province.[4] The capital for the completion of these works was finally secured in 1886 and 1887 by a 5 per cent loan of 42,000,000 pesos (gold), the famous "Customs Loan" which became the subject of bitter controversy in the early nineties.

Meanwhile, the province of Buenos Aires had undertaken the building of a new capital, La Plata, some twenty miles south of Buenos Aires, on the La Plata River. A provincial loan of

[1] List of provincial railroad loans, 1881–85 (gold pesos):

		Emitted	Rate	Realized
1. Buenos Aires,	1882, 6%	$10,330,000	90	$9,297,000
2. Buenos Aires,	1885, 5%	2,380,000	(?)	2,380,000
3. Entre Rios,	1883, 6%	7,715,000	85	6,557,750
4. Santa Fé,	1883, 5%	1,940,000	(?)	1,940,000
5. Santa Fé,	1885, 5%	3,299,000	81	2,672,190
	Total			$25,664,000

(Information concerning these early provincial loans is scanty; so that for one or two of the smaller loans I have been unable to learn the market rate at which they were issued. The best sources concerning these loans are:

Memorias de Hacienda (Annual Reports of the Finance Ministry).

Anuario Pillado, pp. 125–168.

P. Agote: *Finances of the Argentine Government*, Ed. V, 1889 (p. 93 *et seq.*).

[2] *Memoria de Hacienda*, 1884, i, p. 6.

[3] The full amount of the debt was 17,608,000 pesos: but, as has been said (see above, p. 37 and footnote 2), the government paid only eleven millions at this time. The financial obligations of the nation to the province were not paid in full until 1888, when accounts were finally squared by means of a national foreign loan of 19,868,000 pesos (gold). (See *Anuario Pillado*, p. 90.)

[4] As mentioned above, page 39, attempts to float loans for the completion of these works in 1884 were failures.

March, 1882, for 10,246,000 pesos, though intended partly for the payment of the debt of the province to the provincial bank, was destined chiefly for the construction of the new capital. In October, 1883, the province issued a new foreign loan of 11,271,000 pesos, at 94, the purpose of which was to defray the expense of the construction of port works in the new capital, known as the Ensenada Port. At the time, it was generally believed that La Plata was destined to become a great seaport. Its natural advantages were superior to those of Buenos Aires, the river at that point being deep enough to accommodate ships of the deepest draught, whereas, in Buenos Aires, before the building of the new Madero Port Works,[1] ships had to stand out in the roads, where they were loaded and unloaded by lighters.[2] Convinced of the bright future of La Plata, the provincial government showered money upon it. Costly state buildings were erected; an entire city was laid out on the most magnificent scale. The extravagance displayed in the construction of La Plata is one of the reasons why the province of Buenos Aires could never shake itself free from the financial difficulties which terminated in bankruptcy in 1891.[3]

Summing up the public borrowings during the five-year period of currency reform, 1881–85, we have:

PUBLIC LOANS, 1881–85

(Thousand gold pesos)

Purpose	Nominal Value	Amount Realized	Annual Service
Banks and currency	$26,561	$22,258	$1,487
Railroads	53,112	46,990	3,240
La Plata	21,517	19,892	1,506
Totals	$101,190	$89,140	$6,233

The result of the borrowing operations, therefore, was to increase the foreign debt of the national and provincial governments 101,190,000 pesos (gold) in five years, and to increase the

[1] Begun in 1887 and not completed until 1900.

[2] Even today the river at Buenos Aires requires constant dredging: and still the largest ships, of say 12,000 tons, have difficulty.

[3] An Argentine banker has described La Plata to me as "Argentina's white elephant." Today, however, La Plata enjoys a new lease of life as the seat of the Armour, Swift, and Wilson refrigerating plants.

service of interest and amortization of the debt by 6,232,617 pesos (gold). To this must be added at least 90 per cent of the small internal national loans [1] of the period, amounting in all to 1,543,000 pesos (gold), and 90 per cent of the internal municipal loan (city of Buenos Aires) of October 30, 1882 (3,863,000 pesos gold) [2]: so that, all in all, the increase of the public foreign debt becomes 105,046,000 pesos (gold), and the interest charge 6,611,037 pesos (gold).

Thus far, I have spoken only of the public borrowings. To arrive at the full extent of Argentine borrowings during the period, one must include the new foreign capital invested in private enterprise. Private borrowings did not in this period attain to anything like the proportions that characterized the subsequent five-year period which terminated with the Baring Panic. For the most part, they were confined to investment in railroads. Investments in land and land-mortgages, which played so large a part in the borrowings of the later years of the eighties, were as yet of minor importance. The total of new capital in private enterprise, computed from the official reports of the bureau of railroads,[3] the London *Economist*, Mulhall's *Handbook*,[4] etc., shows for the five years, 1881–85, an increase of 44,313,000

[1] Authorized by laws of September 2, 1881, and June 30, 1884, for the purpose of paying civil and military debts incurred in the wars of independence and the war against Brazil (*Anuario Pillado*, p. 101).

[2] For taking 90 per cent of the internal loans as foreign I have the authority of the noted Argentine banker, Carlos A. Tornquist, who, in the annual balance of payments drawn up by him for several years past, has followed this practice. More direct evidence on the period here considered is afforded by the following statement of the minister of finance in 1883: "The greater facility for the placement of the titles of our debt which the European markets offer, not only has provoked the exportation almost *in toto* of our internal debt, but has also brought about a change in the character of various of the emissions authorized as such (internal), and which by special laws have been declared external debt. This is the case with both emissions created for the two state banks (Banco Nacional and Bank of the Province of Buenos Aires)." *Memoria de Hacienda*, 1883, i, p. 83.

[3] Dirección General de Ferrocarriles; annual reports since 1892: contain statistics of capital invested in railroads in every year since 1857, the figures being based on the reports of the railroads to the bureau.

[4] There are several of these handbooks, published at intervals between 1878 and 1900, by the former editor of the *Buenos Aires Standard*. They contain excellent information gathered from official sources and by personal investigation.

pesos (gold), of which 31,313,000 represents investments in railroads, and 13,000,000 investments in other forms of private enterprise. Computing the interest charge at 5 per cent, we find an increase in the outgoings on private borrowing account of 2,215,650 pesos.

The total borrowings of Argentina, therefore, in the period of monetary reform and specie payments, may be summed up as follows:

TOTAL FOREIGN BORROWINGS AND INTEREST CHARGE, 1881–85
(Thousand gold pesos)

	Borrowings	Interest Charge
Public Loans.....................	$105,046	$6,611
Private Investments..............	44,313	2,216
Totals.....................	$149,359	$8,827

It has been a fairly common remark among Argentine writers on economic problems that the vicissitudes of Argentine paper money history have had nothing to do with borrowing operations, or with the balance of international payments. When, in 1890, the gold premium was shooting up by leaps and bounds, the Paris correspondent of *La Nación* reported to his paper an interview with various European bankers, in which the bankers took the view that the crisis, and the high premium on gold, was fundamentally due to the inability of Argentina to meet its enormous liabilities of interest owed abroad; the correspondent added the characteristic sentence: "In Argentina, on the contrary, every one knows that the crisis is due to bad government, to bad political and financial administration, and to excessive issues of paper money." [1]

And in Martinez and Lewandowski's *Argentina in the Twentieth Century*, one of the books on Argentina best known outside of that country, the same view is taken:

"What were, for example, the reasons that determined forced currency in 1885, during the first presidency of General Roca?" they ask. "Was it, by misfortune, that some economic calamity had taken place? Had the harvest been lost, or had there arisen some foreign war, or one of those revolutionary movements so frequent in South American countries? Was there in the inter-

[1] *La Nación*, March 28, 1890.

national markets some violent fall in prices, ruinous for Argentine products?

"Nothing of this sort had occurred. The harvests were abundant, and prices in foreign markets satisfactory.

"It has been said, too, that the commercial balance was unfavorable to Argentina, which was at the same time a debtor country and one dependent on immigration. And it is even added that the republic was suffering a crisis of development, without having behind it reserves of accumulated capital.

"The affirmation which makes the depreciation of the paper money, and consequently the establishment of forced currency, consist in an adverse commercial balance lacks scientific basis, and is not supported by definite proofs." [1]

The authors go on to say that "the true cause of the depreciation of Argentine paper has always been excessive issues of paper, the vitiating of the credit instrument of the country by the superabundance of paper money."

It is no part of my thesis, of course, to deny that Argentine governments have been extravagantly fond of the printing press as a way out of their financial difficulties. Argentine monetary history is full of such incidents. Nor is it necessary to prove, what is of course apparent, that excessive issues of paper money did not at various times play a large part in the depreciation of the paper. The brief history that I have given of the early years is itself a sufficient proof that they did. And in the period of the late eighties preceding the Baring Panic, there is ample evidence that excessive issues of paper contributed largely to the rising premium on gold. What I am interested in demonstrating, however, is that the *mere* increase of paper is not a sufficient explanation of the ups and downs of the gold premium, but that an important, and to my mind the controlling, element in the situation was the adverse balance of payments, in which the dominant factor was that of borrowings. The period of the Baring Panic I leave for later treatment: what I am interested in explaining at this point is the part played by the borrowings in the period of specie payments, the period terminating in the suspension of conversion and the return to inconvertible paper in 1885.

[1] 1912 Spanish edition, pp. 481–482.

It may be noted at the outset that in this period there were no issues of paper money. In 1883, as I have said, the great mass of old worthless notes was exchanged for new metallic notes, convertible at par. I find no mention of any further emissions until December, 1886, when, as I have described, the provincial bank of Buenos Aires was permitted to increase its paper money by 7,000,000 pesos.[1] In this instance, at least, therefore, it cannot be said, as Martinez and Lewandowski assert, that the depreciation of the currency was due to excessive issues of paper money.

The following table indicates the balance of Argentine borrowings for the five years 1881–85. The first column gives the amount of new capital that entered the country in each year; the second shows the annual amount paid for interest and amortization on the total foreign capital invested in the country; and the third shows the "balance," or excess of new borrowings over the interest charge.

BALANCE OF BORROWINGS, 1881–85

(Thousand gold pesos)

Year	New Borrowings 1	Interest Charge 2	Balance 1−2
1881	$14,075	$11,967	+$2,108
1882	25,293	15,724	+ 9,568
1883	47,399	19,496	+27,903
1884	39,732	27,574	+12,158
1885	38,732	22,637	+15,522

The table indicates that the borrowings reached their height in 1883, the year when specie payments were begun, and that in that year the excess of new borrowings over interest charge was greatest. The balance of borrowings for that year was nearly 28,000,000 pesos (gold), from which figure it dropped markedly to about twelve millions in 1884.[2]

[1] But see p. 55, where is described the manner in which the Banco Nacional was permitted to increase its issue. This occurred, however, in October, 1885: *i. e.; after* the suspension of specie payments.

[2] The private investments of 1884, 13,510,000 pesos, were about equal to those of 1883, 13,764,000 pesos. The government, however, as I have said, was experiencing difficulty in placing its loans in 1884, the Riachuelo Port loan and that for sanitary works in Buenos Aires being failures.

So far as borrowings alone are concerned, it thus appears the balance was "favorable" to Argentina throughout the period. When we turn to the trade balance, however, we find a different state of affairs. The following table gives the imports and exports from 1881 to 1885:

BALANCE OF TRADE, 1881–85 [1]

(Thousand gold pesos)

Year	Exports 1	Imports 2	Balance 1−2
1881	$57,938	$55,706	+$2,232
1882	60,389	61,246	— 857
1883	60,208	80,436	—20,228
1884	68,030	94,056	—26,026
1885	83,879	92,222	— 8,343

The favorable balance of 1881 is converted into an unfavorable balance in 1882, which grows markedly in 1883 and 1884, diminishing in 1885. And it is worth noticing that the unfavorable balance is brought about not by a diminution of exports, which show a slow increase until 1885 and in that year a marked advance, but by a remarkable development of imports. The value of the imports in 1884 is about 59 per cent greater than in 1881. This expansion of imports, coincident with large borrowings, is a common enough phenomenon, which appears even more markedly in the latter half of the eighties, when the borrowings were much greater than in the first half.[2]

[1] *Extracto Estadistico*, 1915, p. 4.

[2] In part, it was the direct result of the borrowings. The Argentine governments and the private enterprises which borrowed capital in England for purposes of construction in Argentina, and especially for railroad construction, desired not so much actual money as materials for the building of the railroads. These materials could be secured as cheaply in England as anywhere else. A considerable part of the loans for railroad purposes, therefore, as well as those for the construction of port works, reached Argentina in the form of construction materials. The classification of Argentine imports prior to 1885 is so crude that it is impossible to say precisely what part of the imports was for construction purposes. I have, however, been able to extract the following imports of iron, machinery, and construction materials:

1884	18,249,000 pesos (gold)
1885	23,309,000 " "

It is fair to say, therefore, that from 15 to 20 per cent of the imports during these years were the direct result of the loans negotiated in England. Since the part of

We are now ready to sum up the balance of international payments, and to compare with it the movements of foreign exchange. The following table gives the balance of payments year by year for the period 1881–85. On page 48 the balance is shown by chart.

BALANCE OF INTERNATIONAL PAYMENTS, 1881–85 [1]

(Thousand gold pesos)

Year	Credits [2] 1	Debits [2] 2	Balance 1–2
1881	$72,013	$67,673	+$4,340
1882	85,682	76,970	+ 8,712
1883	107,607	99,932	+ 7,830
1884	107,762	121,630	—13,868
1885	122,611	114,859	+ 7,752

the loans thus directly expended in England would not give rise to exchange operations, they do not, strictly, belong to our problem at all.

Granting, however, that a part of the loans was thus expended, and should be omitted from the calculation, the fact remains that a considerable part of the railroad loans (as well as the whole of the loans for other purposes) must have been needed in the form of money in Argentina. A part must have been expended on domestic materials and for labor. The London *Economist* states that 11,000 men were employed in building railroads in Argentina in 1883 (*Economist*, 1883, ii, p. 1311). Part of the railroad loans would be used in paying the wages of these men. These funds would be secured by means of bills of exchange, and would form a part of the total supply of exchange.

[1] The balance as here given includes only imports and exports, and borrowings and payments of interest and amortization, year by year. Other items which should properly be included in the balance, as immigrants' remittances, tourists' expenditures, and the like, are omitted, for the reason that these items are not capable of computation in the period of my study. In this early period, the country being undeveloped, and the population small, these items were of minor importance as compared with borrowings or foreign merchandise trade. Mulhall's *Handbook*, 1878, places immigrants' remittances at about 2,000,000 pesos, the figure being based on an actual count of small drafts remitted to Europe by the banks in that year. Other items would probably be smaller still. One item, which in the balance for some countries is of considerable importance, maritime freights, should not be included in the Argentine balance, owing to the fact that, by the method of evaluating imports and exports, maritime freights are included in the official trade figures. See below, Chapter VII, p. 107, for discussion of this point. Regarding immigrants' remittances, it may be pointed out that, since they belong in the "debits" column, they would increase rather than lessen the unfavorable balance of 1884, and thus contribute still further to the fall of exchange in that year.

[2] By "credits" is meant borrowings plus exports, or the supply side of the exchange equation. By "debits" is meant interest payments plus imports, or the demand side of the exchange equation.

The chart indicates that, whereas up to 1884 the balance of payments had been favorable to Argentina, in that year there was a reversal of conditions, the interest charges and imports combined showing an excess of about fourteen millions over the combined exports and borrowings.

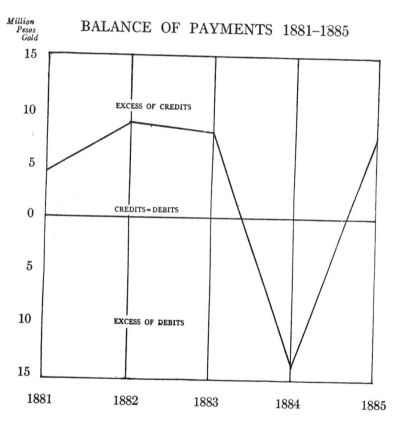

We may now proceed to note the effect of this reversal of the balance upon foreign exchange, and thus upon the currency. Recalling the fact that the demand for exchange comes from the importers and the payers of interest and that the supply is represented by the exporters and the borrowers, and applying these facts to the chart, the zero line would represent the equation of demand for and supply of exchange. Up to 1883, since exports plus new annual borrowings exceeded imports plus annual interest payments, the supply of exchange was in excess of the demand. But in 1884 conditions were reversed; so that the demand for exchange exceeded the supply. This increase had its logical effect, that of driving down the rate, or to put the same thing in other words, of causing a decline in the value of Argentine currency, a decline so great as to force the suspension of specie payments.[1]

The chart on page 50 shows the movement of the rate of exchange on ninety-day sterling bills in 1884 and 1885. We have here, in a space of two years, three distinct situations as regards exchange and currency conditions. In the first period, January to December, 1884, the exchange is in terms of gold; gold is also the basis of the currency; paper is convertible into gold at par. From January to April, 1885, gold exchange has broken down; the rate, instead of stopping at 46, the gold export point, as would normally have been the case under a system of gold exchange, continues to descend rapidly, to $34\frac{1}{2}$.[2] By April, 1885, however, we have still a third situation: the quotations

[1] The fall of exchange, however, did not, as one would expect, result in a heavy shipment of gold. In 1884 imports and exports of gold were about equal; in 1885 exports exceeded imports by only two millions, viz.:

EXPORTS AND IMPORTS OF GOLD

(Thousand gold pesos)

	Exports	Imports
1884............................	$4,510	$4,910
1885............................	8,443	6,306

.(*Extracto Estadistico*, 1915, p. 203.)

The absence of large gold exports is to be explained in part by the export of securities, which were shipped to Europe in large quantities (see P. Agote: *Finances of the Argentine Government*, Ed. IV, 1887, p. 348), and in part by the brief duration of the crisis. In 1885 Argentine cereals experienced a sudden rise of price in Europe, with a resulting increase of 20,000,000 pesos (gold) in the exports of 1885, as compared with 1884. Borrowing soon began again, moreover, on a large scale, and the balance of payments in 1885 was once again favorable to Argentina.

The principal cause of the absence of large gold exports, however, appears to have been the action of the official banks in supplying cheap exchange during 1884. (See p. 51.)

[2] Between March 28 and April 11 exchange went as low as 29. (See *Anuario de la Dirección General de Estadistica*, 1885, pp. 333–336.)

RATE OF FOREIGN EXCHANGE

(ON 90 DAY STERLING BILLS)

1884–1885

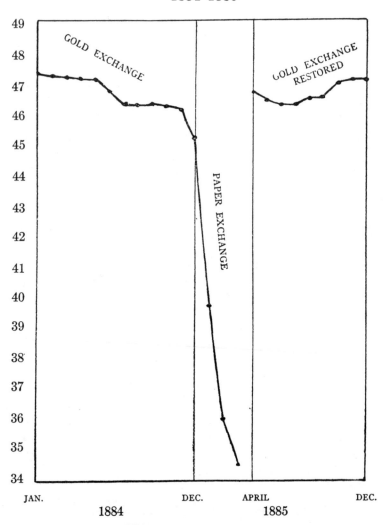

of exchange are again in gold, the same as those prior to the collapse of January, 1885. But there is this difference between the two situations. In the former period paper money stood on a par with gold: gold was not only the basis of the exchanges but also of the domestic monetary system. In the latter period, paper money is inconvertible and depreciated, its value relatively to gold being represented by the fluctuations of the gold premium. We have after 1885, therefore, two distinct currency systems, that of depreciated paper for domestic purposes, and that of gold and gold exchange for foreign transactions. This is the state of affairs which obtained throughout the remaining period of our study, 1885–99, and to which attention has been called in Chapter II.

There would appear to be no question, then, as to the cause of the suspension of specie payments. Suspension was due to the unfavorable balance of payments of 1884, and the consequent fall of exchange. One further point, however, requires explanation. The deficit in the balance of payments occurs in 1884; the breakdown of exchange and the suspension of specie payments do not occur until January, 1885. The interval represents the period of struggle on the part of the official banks to weather the storm, and maintain the conversion of the paper peso into gold at par.

The Bank of the Province of Buenos Aires gave up the struggle in June, 1884,[1] suspending specie payments. This brought an enormous burden upon the other state bank, the Banco Nacional, which, however, continued for another seven months to convert paper into gold on demand, at par. For these seven months the bank refused to recognize the depreciation of the Argentine paper peso in exchange operations. Not only did it convert paper into gold at par, but it furnished foreign exchange at a rate considerably higher than the merchant would have been able to buy it for in the open market. And in its exchange transactions it accepted paper equally with gold.[2]

[1] W. I. Buchanan: "La Moneda y La Vida en la Republica Argentina," p. 206 *et seq.*

[2] That is, it accepted paper as though it were of the same value as gold.

This measure of the Banco Nacional, "without precedent," says Agote, "in the history of commerce, served to stave off the disastrous commercial crisis which would inevitably have occurred had the commercial community, instead of having been supplied with cheap exchange, been left to make its external remittances through the ordinary channels." [1]

By the end of the year the Banco Nacional and the provincial bank had disbursed a total of 77,000,000 pesos [2] in converting paper into gold on demand and in exchange operations. The Banco Nacional, in particular, had suffered heavy losses owing to difference of exchange, to say nothing of the interest on the uncovered credits that the bank had been forced to have recourse to in Europe. In December, 1884, the bank applied to the government for relief, and in January, 1885, by a series of executive decrees, specie payments were suspended. It is then that we see the actual market rate of exchange, representing the true value of the Argentine paper peso in exchange transactions. Up to January, as we have seen, the bank accepted the paper peso at a rate based on the assumption that the paper peso was still worth a gold peso; a rate which was in consequence several points above what the peso would have brought in the open market. In January, this artificial rate disappeared by virtue of the suspension of specie payments, and exchange straightway fell to $34\frac{1}{2}$, and even to 29.

By a decree of March, 1885, the banks were permitted to dispose of their specie reserves in exchange transactions; with the proviso that the sums so disbursed be replaced within two years. [3] Thenceforward, exchange operations took place exclusively in gold, the buyer of exchange having first to buy gold for that purpose, or to keep with his banker a gold account for foreign transactions, as well as his paper account for domestic purposes. Thus we find established, in April, 1885, a gold foreign

[1] P. Agote: *Finances of the Argentine Government*, p. 348.

[2] *Los Mensajes*, iv, 133; Message of President Roca to Congress in May, 1885. (The Messages of the Presidents are collected and edited by H. Mabragaña, in six volumes.)

[3] P. Agote, *ibid.*, p. 340 *et seq.*

exchange, and by the suspension of specie payments in January of that year, a depreciated domestic paper currency. It is this combination that provides the monetary mechanism for our study during the succeeding fourteen-year period, 1885–99, the period of the Baring Panic, of the overturn of the trade balance, and of the final fixation of the value of the paper peso by the Conversion Law of 1899.

To sum up the analysis of the period from 1881–85, there seems no ground for doubting that the reason for the suspension of specie payments in January, 1885, and the return to inconvertible paper, was the disturbance of the balance of payments caused by the heavy borrowings of foreign capital, which, by giving rise to heavy interest charges and to inflated imports, created a foreign indebtedness, the discharge of which brought about a pronounced fall of foreign exchange, which in turn exhausted the resources of the banks in unprofitable exchange operations, and thus broke down a system of currency founded upon a slender basis.

CHAPTER V

THE NATIONAL BANKING SYSTEM AND THE PREMIUM ON GOLD

FROM January, 1885, throughout the rest of the period of this study, Argentina was on an inconvertible paper basis, and gold stood constantly at a premium. Since the cause of the crisis of 1884–85 had been the attempt to hasten prosperity by a too liberal policy of borrowing, it might have been expected that the succeeding years would witness a more sober course. That President Roca himself had grasped the situation, and saw the remedy, is attested by his Message to Congress in May, 1885, in which he said, "If individuals, the nation and the provinces will practice economy, and desist from borrowing and large public works for a year or two, things will get back to normal." [1]

There is little evidence, however, that he took his own advice very seriously, for almost immediately the borrowing began anew. And when, in October, 1886, Roca was succeeded by President Juarez Celman, a shallow optimist and an incompetent administrator of doubtful honesty, Argentina entered upon a veritable rake's progress. Not all, by any means, of the events which occurred in Celman's administration are ascribable to the acts of government. The spirit of speculation was general, and in part was inherent in the circumstances of the situation. It characterized the European lenders no less than the Argentine borrowers. But this much is true, that throughout the period the national and provincial governments played the leading rôle: and that but for their extravagant leadership, the speculative, spendthrift spirit could never have attained the scope or the intensity that it did.

The fact which differentiated most sharply the five years from 1885 to 1890 from the preceding five years, was the changed

[1] H. Mabragaña, *Los Mensajes*, iv, p. 133.

attitude of government toward the currency problem. In the first period, as we have seen, there was a genuine effort to put the currency on a sound basis; a notable improvement was in fact effected, but specie payments broke down because of too liberal borrowing. In the next period, extravagant borrowing, on a scale which makes former borrowing appear negligible in comparison, went hand in hand with a most reckless expansion of the currency. This combination of foreign borrowing and issues of paper money (which are but another form of borrowing, a forced internal loan) had, as we shall see, its usual effects, a successive elevation of the premium on gold, becoming more and more rapid as 1891 neared, an unprecedented expansion of business, an extension of personal credit rarely paralleled in any country, and finally, in 1891, the inevitable crisis, followed by a long period of liquidation and depression from which there was no real recovery before 1900.

When specie payments were suspended in January, 1885, it was clearly the intention of the president to guard against any increase in the amount of paper in circulation. The five banks of issue then in existence were required, in December, 1884, to report the quantity of their notes in circulation under the Act of October 19, 1883. The reports showed a total circulation of 61,739,000 pesos.[1] This sum was therefore distributed among the banks, the amount of inconvertible issue of each bank being carefully defined in the series of decrees suspending conversion in January, 1885. To guard against over-issue, an inspection board, to be named by the executive, was provided for.

These decrees were approved by Congress on October 5, 1885, but with a significant modification. The Banco Nacional, which according to the executive decree was to have a circulation of 28,000,000 pesos, was now permitted to double its emission. In other words, within nine months of the suspension of specie payments the expansion of the currency had begun, and this in the face of the avowed intention to return to specie payments on January 1, 1887.[2] In December, 1886, the Bank of the Prov-

---

[1] *Anuario Pillado*, p. 54.

[2] P. Agote: *Finances of the Argentine Government*, p. 344.

ince of Buenos Aires was permitted by executive decree to increase its inconvertible notes by seven million pesos. And in the same month, Congress, at the suggestion of the new president, Celman, extended the suspension of specie payments for another two years, till January 1, 1889. "The return to specie payments," said President Celman in his message, "ought to repose on a solid basis; it ought to be decreed by the development of industrial and commercial wealth, by the accumulated fortune of the country, and not by law." [1]

Yet, if conversion were to be resumed at all, the year 1887 was clearly the time for it. The premium on gold was still low. The yearly average had been 37 in 1885 and 39 in 1886, and was 35 in 1887. It showed a slight decrease in spite of the unwarranted increase in the paper circulation. The reason for the decrease of the premium appears to have been the balance of international payments, which, because of the resumption of borrowing, was, for the time, increasingly favorable to the country.

Instead, however, of the return to specie payments which might well have been attempted in 1887, Argentina in that year resorted to a measure which, as it turned out, put conversion of any sort completely out of the question for the next twelve years. This measure was the Law of National Guaranteed Banks, or, as it is more often termed, the "Free Banking Law." Once again the initiative came from President Celman, who proposed the measure to Congress in September, 1887, his proposal being enacted into law on November 3d.

The Law of National Guaranteed Banks was, with some modifications, an attempt to imitate the National Bank system of the United States. The principal provisions of the law were:

1. *Any* banking organization was to be authorized to issue notes, provided:

   (*a*) that it have a capital of at least 250,000 pesos:
   (*b*) that it purchase national gold bonds to the full amount of the notes to be emitted by it.

[1] Message of President Celman to Congress, November 9, 1886, proposing the postponement of conversion until January 1, 1889.

2. These bonds were to be especially issued for the purpose as an internal gold loan, to be known as the Guaranteed Banks Loan, bearing $4\frac{1}{2}$ per cent interest, and amortizable by means of a fund accumulating at 1 per cent a year.

3. The note issue was to be limited to 90 per cent of the capital of the issuing bank.

4. The bonds were to be paid for with gold at not less than 85.

5. The gold was to be deposited in the Bureau of Inspection of Banks for two years, whereafter it was to be applied to the payment of the national foreign debt.

6. In case of the failure of a bank, the bonds were to be sold to meet its outstanding notes, and any deficiency was to be paid by the government.

7. The name of the issuing bank was to be printed on the notes.[1]

The fundamental purpose of this law, of course, was to insure the convertibility of the paper currency: the guarantee was to be a double one, the stock of gold paid in purchase of guarantee bonds, and the bonds themselves. In addition, the law was intended to provide a uniform currency in all parts of the country. Though some approach to uniformity had already been effected by the measures of 1881–83, it was still true that the notes issued by the official bank of one province would not circulate freely and at the same value in other provinces. It was supposed that the new plan, by throwing the right of issue open to all banks which chose to avail themselves of it, under a well-defined system of guarantee, would bring about the desired uniformity.

Whether in fact the government was sincere in its defense of the law on such grounds as these is open to question. It will be remembered that prior to the passage of this law, the right of emission had been restricted to five banks, four of which were

[1] On the Law of Guaranteed Banks, see:

Anuario Pillado, p. 56 *et seq.*

P. Agote: *Finances of the Argentine Government*, Ed. V, 1889.

I. Grinfeld: *Monetary Experiences of Argentina*, P. S. Q. (Col. Univ.), xxv, No. 1, 1910.

E. Lorini: *La Republica Argentina e i Suoi Maggiori Problemi di Economia e di Finanza*, i, 1902.

Emilio Hansen: *La Moneda Argentina*, 1916.

semi-official, and subject to some measure of government control; and that the amount of notes which these banks might maintain in circulation had been rigorously defined, together with the reserve of specie which they must maintain. According to an executive decree of December 24, 1886, the legal maximum of circulation of inconvertible paper was 85,294,000 pesos and the gold reserve 27,300,000 pesos. On December 31, 1886, the actual circulation was 80,251,380 pesos, and the specie reserve was 44,965,969 pesos.[1] The banks had apparently kept well within the terms of the law. Yet despite these restrictions upon note issue the currency was depreciated by reason of its redundance. To supplant the existing system by another less restrictive, by a system which threw open the privilege of issue to *any* bank fulfilling the conditions of the new act, could obviously have no other effect than to increase the already over-liberal issue. It is difficult to believe that the government was blind to so obvious a fact.

The uses to which the new system was put increase one's suspicion. Twenty banks availed themselves of the privilege of emission. Of these, thirteen were provincial institutions, whose capital was supplied by the provincial governments; one was the Banco Nacional, the financial agent of the national government; and six were private banks. Some of the provincial banks were banks only in name. Several "banks" that were declared incorporated into the new system "did not exist on the date of the decree authorizing their incorporation, and were only projects that were hatching in the portfolios of some of the provincial governments." [2]

To obtain the gold for the purchase of the guarantee bonds the provinces contracted foreign loans. There were nine such loans in 1888, for a total of 47,243,000 pesos (gold). These loans for the establishment of the new banking system form one of the chief items in the program of borrowing which contributed so largely to the Baring Panic.

[1] P. Agote: *Finances of the Argentine Government*, Ed. IV, p. 346.

[2] This statement applies to the "banks" of Santiago del Estero, La Rioja, Mendoza, San Juan, Catamarca, San Luis, and Corrientes. (See "Revista Económica de 1891," by Ricardo Pillado, published in *La Prensa*, Número Extraordinario de 1 Enero de 1892.)

Notwithstanding these borrowings, however, the fact appears to be that very few of the provinces paid for the bonds which they acquired as guarantee for their note issue. In the case of some of them the payment was deferred. Others seem never to have paid anything at all, payment being accredited to them by the federal government for book-keeping purposes. The Banco de la Provincia de Buenos Aires, for example, which made the largest emissions under the new act, 50,000,000 pesos, had as guarantee of this emission 50,000,000 pesos of gold guarantee bonds, of which 32,958,574 were acquired with gold, and 17,041,425 with "pagarés," or promises to pay. The Bank of Córdoba, President Celman's province, acquired 15,553,796 pesos of bonds, of which only 8,696,653 were paid for in gold, the rest with "pagarés." All in all, 196,832,590 pesos of bonds were delivered to the banks as guarantee of a like quantity of bank notes: the actual amount of gold paid for them was 76,500,000 pesos, or less than 40 per cent of the total value of the bonds.[1]

There is plenty of additional evidence of malpractice. Some of the banks used their power of note issue to make advances of paper money to politicians. The Report of the Caja de

---

[1] How the Guaranteed Bank bonds were acquired:

(Thousand gold pesos)

1. Banco Nacional............................ 41,333
   (Bonds received gratuitously, in accordance with Article 42 of the Law.)
2. Provincial Banks........................... 115,183
   (Purchased with gold, 85,185
   "   "   pagarés, 29,998)
3. Private Banks............................. 5,250
   (All purchased with gold)
4. An extra emission of bonds in July, 1890, to cover illegal emission of bank notes by the Banco Nacional and the Provincial Bank of Buenos Aires in April of that year.................. 35,116
   (These were to be amortized at the rate of 5 per cent quarterly, but only two quotas were paid.)
   ___
   Total Emission of Bonds................ 196,833
   Part of bonds purchased with gold, 90,435
   Actual gold paid (at 85), 76,500

(See Balance Sheet of the Caja de Conversión, 1890; also, *Anuario Pillado*, 1900, pp. 58–62.)

Conversión in 1890 shows that the banks issued false balance-sheets and made rosy statements of perfectly imaginary dividends. The Bank of Córdoba (Celman's province) was found to have issued 33,000,000 pesos of notes, although its legal maximum was eight millions.[1] An investigation by the new governor of the province in 1892, showed that all-in-all the bank of President Celman's province had managed to dispose in illegal ways of no less than 70,000,000 pesos. Even the Banco Nacional was not exempt. The special correspondent of the London *Economist* wrote that more than one-third of the total capital of the bank (50,000,000 pesos) had to be written off for bad debts after the crash of 1890; and asserted that some two hundred individuals had managed to lay hold on considerably more than the whole capital of the bank.[2]

Even had the free banking system been honestly administered, however, an undue expansion of the currency would have been inevitable. The throwing open of the right of issue to all banks fulfilling the conditions of the act was bound to result in an increase of the paper currency, which even prior to the Guaranteed Banks Act had been redundant.

The effect of the Guaranteed Banks Law on the quantity of paper money in circulation, year by year, was as follows:

QUANTITY OF PAPER AND THE GOLD PREMIUM, 1885–91 [3]
(Thousand paper pesos)

Year	Paper in Circulation [4]	Gold Premium [5]
1885	$74,820	37
1886	89,197	39
1887	94,071	35
1888	129,505	48
1889	163,748	91
1890	245,100	151
1891	261,408	287

[1] In answer to the protest of the Caja de Conversión, the national government merely authorized the Bank of Córdoba to exchange the illegal emission for a new one more illegal still, termed "Agricola Bonds," which were nothing else than provincial paper currency; a plain violation of the Guaranteed Banks Law.

[2] See *Economist*, 1892, ii, p. 539: and *Anuario Pillado*, p. 63. In March and April, 1890, the illegal emissions of the Banco Nacional and the Provincial Bank of Buenos Aires totalled 35,116,000 pesos.

[3] *Extracto Estadístico*, 1915, p. 297.

[4] Quantity in circulation on December 31.　　　　　　[5] Yearly averages.

The table indicates the striking difference in the quantity of paper money issued before and after 1887, the year of the passage of the Guaranteed Banks Act. In the first three years, 1885–87, the increase is less than twenty millions. In the three years following the passage of the act, the increase of the paper in circulation is one hundred and fifty-one millions; in other words, the quantity in circulation is about trebled.

Depreciation began at once. From 1885, the year of the collapse of specie payments, to 1888, the first year following the passage of the Guaranteed Banks Act, the premium on gold had been virtually stationary, so far as the yearly averages are concerned. There had even been a slight decline, in spite of the increase of twenty millions in the quantity of paper. This decline may fairly be attributed to the fact that during these years the balance of international payments was increasingly favorable to Argentina, owing to the increasingly heavy borrowing of foreign capital. The decline of the premium was so slight, however, that were it the only instance it would perhaps have no significance: but taken in connection with the evidence afforded by other periods, as that of 1881–85, already reviewed, and the period following 1891, which we shall examine later, it offers additional proof of the fact that the balance of payments was an important factor in determining the value of the currency.

After the passage of the Free Banking Law the premium on gold begins to rise, at first slowly, and then more rapidly as we approach the crisis of 1891. The maximum was reached in October, 1891, when gold was quoted on the stock exchange at a premium of 364. After 1891, the premium falls, then rises again in 1894–95, and then falls steadily until 1899, when the system of conversion put an end to further fluctuation.

As is always the case under a régime of depreciated paper money, the premium on gold was popularly ascribed to the manipulation of gold speculators. There was a similar outcry in the United States during the Civil War. As regards the fluctuations of the premium over short periods there is considerable truth in the criticism. It is possible by "rigging" the gold market to bring about a rise or fall of several points in the premium, and to realize a considerable profit from the operation. As was pointed out by the London *Economist*,[1] such manipulation of the market by a "ring" was much more practicable in Buenos Aires than it had been a quarter of a century before in the United States, because the market was narrower and the amount of gold in the country smaller. The stock of gold held by the two great official banks, the Banco Nacional and the Provincial Bank of Buenos Aires, amounted at the beginning of 1887 to only 15,500,000 pesos. The sale of not a very large sum by the banks would send down the premium with a run, while, on the other hand, the locking up or exportation of some of the floating supplies of the metal would force up the premium to a high point. That much of the buying and selling of gold was of this purely speculative character is shown by the monthly gold clearings of the Buenos Aires Stock Exchange. The total clearings for the last six months of 1886 were 379,000,000 pesos; the clearings of October alone amounted to 121,000,000 pesos. Transactions so entirely beyond the legitimate commercial needs — transactions, too, performed with so slender a stock of gold — prove that there was much buying and selling of gold that had no other motive than the making of a speculative profit.

This speculative manipulation of the gold market, moreover, had frequently another purpose besides the making of a profit from the mere buying and selling of gold. The movements of the gold premium were sometimes arranged so as to affect seriously the market for securities. "Rigs" with this end in view were frequent during the whole period of depreciated currency; but they come most prominently to one's notice in the years following the panic of 1891, when European banking houses found themselves loaded down with great quantities of Argentine securities which they had underwritten during the boom years, but which after the collapse of 1891 were worthless. To make these securities more salable European syndicates shipped gold to Buenos Aires. The increase in the supply of gold would cause paper to appreciate for a time. The fall of the gold premium

---

[1] *Economist*, 1887, i, p. 362.

would create the impression that the paper currency was on the mend. People would take a more hopeful view of the situation in general, and Argentine securities would begin to rise in value.

Still another variety of manipulation of the exchanges was that practiced by the foreign holders of the famous "cédulas," or land-mortgage bonds. The full discussion of these cédulas must be postponed until we come to the general subject of borrowings. For the present purposes it need only be said that they were ,bonds issued by land-mortgage banks, and sold in very large quantities abroad in the late eighties, giving rise to a most extraordinary speculation in land. Since both the interest and the principal of these bonds were payable in Argentine paper currency, their value to the foreign holder depended on the exchange value in gold of Argentine paper. The fact that hundreds of millions of cédulas were held abroad made extremely difficult the adoption of measures to strengthen the value of the paper money, for the holder of the cédula was at liberty at any time to return his bond. Whenever paper money rose in value, therefore, the cédulas flowed back to Buenos Aires for sale. The result was a general disturbance of the exchange market. The selling of cédulas in large quantities increased the demand for exchange, wherewith to remit the proceeds of the sales to the cédula holders; exchange fell, the gold premium went up, and the paper money became more unstable than ever.

Finance Minister Varela in 1889 declared that fluctuations of exchange due to the continual ebb and flow of the paper cédulas between Buenos Aires and London made impossible any improvement of the currency situation.[1] Once again we may admit that the foreign operations in paper cédulas, like the manipulations of the gold speculators, were a cause of *short-time* fluctuations in the gold premium, while denying that they were a fundamental factor in the situation. As will appear later, even had the paper cédulas been converted into gold cédulas, as Minister Varela proposed, the effect upon the gold premium would not have been decisive. Indeed, it may readily be seen that had the paper cédulas been converted into gold at the premium obtain-

[1] *Economist*, 1889, ii, p. 958.

ing in 1889, 151 per cent, the burden of interest payment in 1891 and the succeeding years, when the premium ranged from 250 per cent upward, would have been enormously increased, and would have resulted in a still further elevation of the premium on gold.

The truth appears to be that the government did not understand the problem that faced it, or, understanding, would not or could not take the proper methods for its solution. In his message to Congress in May, 1889, President Celman expressed his conviction that "whatever may be the sacrifice occasioned by the depreciation, it is insignificant when compared with the advantages which the Republic has derived from the opening of the banks throughout the provinces, and from the stimulus industry has received thereby."[1] He and his finance minister acquiesced in the popular verdict that the depreciation was due to the manipulation of the gold speculators on the Stock Exchange. In March, 1889, by executive decree, gold dealings on the stock exchange were prohibited: though the leading newspapers of the republic combined in reminding the President that in every country where it has been attempted to arrest the depreciation of a forced paper currency by taking steps against speculators, the result has been a disastrous failure.[2]

After what has been said in Chapter II, we need not stop long to consider the reason for the failure of the law prohibiting gold speculation. Speculation could not be stopped without prohibiting gold dealings altogether; and dealings in gold were necessary for all persons engaged in the foreign trade, since bills of exchange were purchasable only in gold. Since dealings on the stock exchange were prohibited, and importers, railroad companies, cédula holders, and all others having remittances to make were now denied the opportunity of purchasing gold at will, they were forced to provide themselves with a stock of that

[1] *Los Mensajes*, IV, p. 322 *et seq.*

[2] The same monumental fallacy was committed by the United States in 1864. The Gold Speculation Act of that year enjoyed a brief existence of fifteen days. In this time the price of 100 gold dollars rose from about 200 paper to very nearly 300. So obvious was its evil effect that it was hurriedly repealed as a means of preventing further commercial disasters.

metal. The result was to reduce the supply of gold in the market; to intensify private gold dealings outside of the stock exchange. Naturally, the price of gold rose rapidly.

The supply of gold became so inadequate for the demands of foreign trade that the government found itself obliged to sell gold. The Banco Nacional was authorized to sell daily of its funds between 300,000 and 600,000 pesos in gold, at a rate fixed by the bank. This heroic attempt to supplant the operation of the law of supply and demand by an official rate; to control the gold premium and the rate of foreign exchange by official decree, was, of course, futile. The market ignored the official rate, and adopted that notified by the money-changers.[1] In May, 1889, the government released some five millions of gold, using for the purpose the gold funds which had been received in payment of bonds guaranteeing note issue under the Guaranteed Banks Law. It will be remembered that the law provided for the retention of this fund by the Banco Nacional for two years from January 1, 1888, at the end of which period it was to be used for the redemption of a part of the foreign debt. By disposing of these deposits the government jeopardized its credit abroad, and, because of the depletion of the gold reserve, rendered still more precarious the paper currency.

The prohibition of speculation in gold having thus proved a failure, the administration laid before Congress in May, 1889, a more elaborate project. This was the proposal for the creation of a national treasury with a conversion fund of $50,000,000 in gold and silver specie, the fund to be composed of the gold funds of the government in the Banco Nacional and the Provincial Bank of Buenos Aires, the specie reserves of the banks, and the proceeds of the proposed sale of Central Argentine Railroad shares held by the government, and of various national public works and railroads. Against this specie fund the treasury was to issue $50,000,000 of gold and silver certificates, to be redeemable at par in gold or silver. These certificates were to be issued in exchange for the depreciated guaranteed bank notes, at a rate of exchange to be fixed by the finance minister. The

---

[1] *Bankers' Magazine* (London), 1890, i, p. 777.

notes thus secured were to be used for the purchase of the
$40,000,000 of 4½ per cent gold Internal Bonds which (in
accordance with the Free Banking Law) guaranteed the note
issue of the Banco Nacional. Once purchased, these forty
millions of bonds were to be placed abroad, and the proceeds
in gold and silver were to be used to replenish the conversion
fund; and to be offered to the public in exchange for treasury
certificates. The certificates thus received would be used to
purchase paper cédulas, which were to be converted to 4 per
cent gold hypothecary bonds. These gold cédulas were then to
be sold abroad as a substitute for paper cédulas; and the proceeds were to be used to meet the foreign bills of exchange which
the government had periodically to purchase for the remittance
of interest charges on the foreign debt.

It is difficult to ascertain precisely what motives lay behind
this elaborate scheme. In so far as they may be gathered from
the explanations of Finance Minister Varela to the Congress,
the purposes were two: (1) to diminish the quantity of depreciated inconvertible National Bank notes, and to substitute in
their place convertible Treasury certificates; (2) to lessen the
possibilities of manipulation of exchange by the gold speculators,
by (a) eliminating a large part of the paper cédulas and thus
putting an end to fluctuations of exchange occasioned by the
continual ebb and flow of paper cédulas between Buenos Aires
and Europe, and (b) by providing the government with the means
of purchasing exchange for its foreign remittances, thus depriv-
ing the gold speculators of one of their chief customers.

As to the first of these purposes, the restriction of National
Bank notes, and the partial substitution of conversion, there
are grounds for doubting that the government harbored any
such intention. For, in the same month that the proposal was
submitted to Congress, another bill, also framed by the administration, proposed that a tax of 2 per cent be imposed upon the
deposits of all banks that did not issue bank notes. In other
words, at the very time that the finance minister was proposing
measures avowedly for the curtailment of the redundant paper
currency, he was putting pressure upon the banks to compel

them to swell the volume of the paper currency by making non-issue the reason for imposing upon them special taxation.

As to the conversion feature of the new plan, that too was of doubtful intent, besides being impossible of realization. If the government had really intended to provide a means of converting the paper currency, and thus giving it a more stable value, why should the issue of specie certificates have been resorted to at all? Why not use the specie fund in the National Treasury in direct exchange for National Bank notes? It is difficult to suppose that the public would consent to an exchange at par of specie certificates for specie, for the certificates could never be worth more than the specie, and, notwithstanding the promise of redemption at par, they might soon, in the light of past experiences, become worth much less. This general lack of confidence was apparently well understood by the government, for one of the clauses of the bill provides that the treasury must not issue certificates in excess of the specie fund in the treasury; and adds that the employees of the treasury are empowered "to oppose and resist any order from any authority whatever (even from the government!) to issue in excess of the specie held."

The provision for the purchase of paper cédulas has already been discussed. Had it been carried out it would have had the beneficial result of relieving the home market of its plethora of cédulas, and would have eliminated one source of disturbance of the exchanges. As we shall see presently, however, its effect would not have been decisive; and, on the other hand, the accompanying proposal to emit 4 per cent gold cédulas abroad would eventually have increased, rather than diminished, the burden of the foreign liabilities of the country.

This proposal for the emission of gold cédulas, taken together with the proposal for the sale abroad of the $40,000,000 of the $4\frac{1}{2}$ per cent internal gold bonds guaranteeing the notes of the Banco Nacional, appears to indicate the real object that underlay the government's currency legislation during this period. There were but two ways in which the government could raise the value of the paper currency. One, the obvious method, was to put a stop to further emissions of paper and to burn a portion of that already emitted. This the government at first would not, and finally could not, do. Not until November, 1889, was this solution suggested, and then the government had not the courage to act upon it; for by that time inflation had progressed so far that a curtailment of the currency would have caused a general scaling down of prices, and a breakdown of the extravagant speculation in land. Affairs were therefore left to take their course, until trouble from another quarter, the external liabilities of the country, brought about the collapse.

The second method of improving the currency was to contract new loans abroad, to maintain at a height equal to that of former years the flow of borrowings. The year 1888 witnessed the flood tide of foreign borrowings. From that date the tide receded, and in proportion as it did so, the gold premium mounted steadily and rapidly. And when, in 1890, the government could no longer obtain new loans, the whole fabric of inflated credit collapsed, perforce.

The proposals to sell guaranteed bank bonds abroad and to sell gold cédulas abroad, are indications of this pressing need of borrowings. A more amusing instance is contained in a decree of President Celman of October, 1889, ordering the sale in Europe of 24,000 square leagues of land at a minimum price of $2 gold per hectare. These lands were scattered about in six of the national territories. They were to be colonized by English, Spanish, Swiss, Italian, French, and German families, the amount of land to be purchased by the people of each nationality being carefully defined. Special offices for the sale of the lands were to be opened in the principal cities of Europe; and notices of the sale were to be published for sixty days in leading European newspapers. The important provision is contained in Article 12: "The $120,000,000 gold, which would be the minimum proceeds of the sale of these public lands, and whatever balance be over that amount, shall be deposited in the mint for the conversion of bank notes." [1]

In his message to Congress submitting this decree for approval, President Celman details the benefits that will accrue to the

---

[1] *Economist*, 1889, ii, p. 1390: and *Memoria de Hacienda*, 1889.

republic. He predicts that in three years the lands will have been taken up, and occupied by at least 700,000 settlers; and he dwells on the "grand ends,"—the conversion of the paper currency, the partial or total payment of the foreign debt, and the commercial development of the country, which are to be accomplished with the gold obtained by the sales.

This scheme, like the preceding ones, was impossible of realization. The 216,000 square miles to be offered for sale were at an immense distance from markets of supply, and were without means of communication. Much of the land, besides, was bad. The Buenos Aires *Standard* gave its opinion that it would take every dollar realized by the sales to carry out the colonization scheme. The plan, apparently, was not approved by Congress, for nothing more was ever heard of it.

Taken together with the previous proposals, however, it indicates how pressing was the desire to maintain the borrowings of foreign capital at full tide.

It is to the borrowings, then, that we must turn to understand fully the monetary situation and the nature of the forces that precipitated the Panic of 1891.

CHAPTER VI

BORROWINGS, 1885-1890

THE borrowings of the second half of the eighties differ from those of the first half, not so much in their source or purposes as in their magnitude. It was in this period that the "boom" reached its height. The warning afforded by the brief crisis at the end of 1884 was unheeded. It caused scarcely an interruption of the inflow of foreign capital; within a year borrowing had begun again on a scale of much greater proportions.

Many reasons combine to explain the great speculative outburst of the late eighties. Europeans were responsible for it no less than the Argentines themselves. The middle eighties mark the beginning of a world-wide expansion of British investment. In South Africa the gold and diamond discoveries of 1884-85 resulted in the formation of hundreds of mining companies. The South African boom seemed to be the signal for unhealthy inflation in other countries, notably in Australia and South America. In this period, too, German capital, as well as Belgian and French, began to find its way to Argentina, although in amounts insignificant as compared with the tremendous influx from Great Britain.

Internal circumstances, also, contributed to the same end. Already, in the earlier eighties, President Roca's conquest of the Indians in the South, and his establishment of a strong central government, had rendered foreign investments more secure. The effect is made evident by the rise in the market rate of government bonds in 1882 and '83. The increase in railroad mileage, besides, had opened up new territory, and prepared the way for the sale of new lands. Port works, already under way, offered the promise of increased facilities for commerce. Information offices established in Europe were publishing glowing reports on Argentine agricultural possibilities; colonization schemes, the

sale of land in small lots at low terms, the government appropriations to pay the passage of laborers from Europe, were giving an impulse to immigration, especially from Italy and Spain.

Most important of all, perhaps, was the change of government policy caused by Celman's accession to the presidency in
1886. The previous program of comparatively moderate development gave way to one of extravagant optimism. Railroad concessions were multiplied far beyond the legitimate needs of the
country. Land operations, fostered by official mortgage banks,
degenerated into mere speculation. This speculative spirit was
intensified by the currency situation. The intoxicative effect of
such an artificial elevation of prices as is caused by depreciating
paper is too familiar to need comment. The instability of a
paper-money situation, moreover, the constant shifting of the
gold premium, gave opportunities for speculative gains of which
Europeans, as well as the Argentines themselves, sought to take
advantage.

As regards government loans, the connection between paper
money and borrowings was even more direct. The provincial
loans were, as I have said, for the purpose of buying bonds to
guarantee note issue. The desire of the national government to
contract foreign loans had two motives, both arising from the
currency situation: one motive was to secure funds to meet its
liabilities, both domestic and foreign, which, by reason of the
rapid depreciation of paper, were requiring a greater and greater
paper expenditure; the other was to counteract the decline of
the paper by an influx of foreign gold, which would improve the
value of paper in the continual exchange of gold for paper and
paper for gold, necessitated by the foreign trade. The increase
of gold supplies, moreover, would bring nearer the so-often-
promised day of specie redemption of paper money, and by thus
creating confidence would contribute even more strongly to bring
down the gold premium.

These were the chief causes of borrowing. Our present task
is to show how large the borrowings were, and to classify them
according to their purpose. The magnitude of the speculative
boom of the eighties, and the general course of it, are indicated

by the statistics of new companies registered in the *Registro Público de Comercio* (*Public Commercial Register*). The figures have no precise value, since they represent merely the declared capital, not the actual capital invested. "Some companies could secure but one or two quotas of their stock; others did not succeed in finding any subscribers at all."[1] They represent, too, domestic capital rather than foreign, since most foreign companies were incorporated abroad and were not required to record their capital in the *Commercial Register*. The table does, however, furnish an eloquent description of the speculative fever, of when it developed, and when it reached its maximum of intensity.

NEW COMPANIES RECORDED IN THE *Registro Público de Comercio* 1882-91

(Thousand paper pesos)

1882-83	$19,000
1884-85	24,500
1886-87	129,000
1888-89	574,000
1890-91	203,000
	$949,500

It is difficult to state with exactness the real purpose of many of these companies, because behind the most varied and pompous titles were often hidden projects of exclusive speculation. The following classification, however, is given as substantially correct[2]:

(Thousand paper pesos)

1. Dealings in land, colonization schemes, cultivation....	$275,000[3]
2. Railroads, tramways, navigation..................	244,000
3. Insurance companies...........................	139,000
4. Banks..	137,000
5. Industrial and commercial enterprises, telephone companies, miscellaneous	154,000
	$949,000

[1] *Anuario de Estadística de la Ciudad de Buenos Aires*, 1891, p. 312 *et seq.*

[2] *Ibid.*

[3] In this and succeeding chapters the "dollar sign" ($) is used to denote pesos. This is the common practice in Argentina. As previously noted, the Argentine (gold) peso is equivalent to U.S. $0.965.

The table indicates that the main currents of investment were land and railroads. This classification is even more accurate for foreign capital than for domestic. Foreign capital in banks, insurance companies, and industrial enterprises was as yet comparatively unimportant.[1] Meat refrigerating-plants, at present so important an item, did not come till later.[2]

I shall therefore discuss foreign borrowings under the following classification:

      I.   Private Investment.
             A.   Land.
             B.   Railroad.
             C.   Other investments.
     II.   Government Loans.
             A.   National.
             B.   Provincial and Municipal.
    III.   Balance of Borrowings.

I. PRIVATE BORROWINGS

A. *Speculation in Land,—The Land-Mortgage Banks and their "Cédulas"*

As is well known, Argentine land speculation in the late eighties took the form of land-mortgage bank operations. The bonds, or "cédulas," of the mortgage banks became as well known and as ubiquitous a speculative security on European stock exchanges as Erie Railroad bonds in the seventies. There were two of these banks, the Banco Hipotecario de la Provincia de Buenos Aires, founded in 1872, and the Banco Hipotecario Nacional, established in 1886. The general conception of them seems to have been borrowed from Spain and Austria, where land-mortgage banks had long been of benefit to a needy agricultural population. The purposes for which they were estab-

---

[1] Precise figures of capital in foreign banks and insurance companies cannot be had, since their published figures were for total capital, and did not state the amounts actually on hand in the relatively small branches maintained in Argentina. I have, however, been able to secure authoritative estimates.

[2] Four small British plants were established between 1880 and 1900.

lished, and the manner of their operation, form an interesting chapter in the history of this exclusively agricultural country.

In idea the banks were excellent. Their purpose was to bring together more effectively lenders of capital and needy land-owners; and, by directing foreign and domestic capital to the land, to develop the agricultural resources of the country. Before the banks were established, loans on the security of land had been few. Land did not represent a sufficiently secure guarantee to tempt the investor. The state of abandonment in which the land had remained for many years, the risks as to the goodness of the title deeds, the difficulties in the way of correct assessment of land values, provoked uncertainties which made the lender wary. The result was very high rates of interest, and a demand for the return of the principal within a relatively short period. The short period of the loan, the high interest charge, in many cases greater than the yield of the mortgaged land, the reluctance to lend at all,—difficulties of this sort virtually shut off the land-owner from the use of credit, and impeded agricultural develop-ment. Particularly was the resort to foreign capital difficult, since the foreigner had no means of ascertaining the worth of the security offered.

The land banks were designed to remedy this situation. They were to make the mortgaging of land safer, and more attractive to both parties: to the land-owners, by offering to them loans for long periods, at lower interest rates than an ordinary banker or capitalist would accept, and redeemable grádually, by small periodic payments [1]; to the lender by substituting for the indi-vidual guarantee of the mortgagor, the guarantee of the bank, which, in turn, had behind it the guarantee of the government.

The method of operation was as follows: The mortgage bank performed the rôle of intermediary between the borrower and the lender. It eliminated the direct loan. The land-owner solic-ited the bank for a loan on a certain piece of land, assuming the obligation to repay to the bank the sum lent by means of annual

[1] The gradual amortization of the mortgage, the Banco Hipotecario Nacional still holds to be the "fundamental principle" of a beneficial national land-mortgage system. See *Banco Hipotecario Nacional, 1886–1916*, p. 6, published in Buenos Aires, 1916, by the Bank.

payments which should comprise the interest and amortization of the debt at compound interest. The period of redemption granted was long enough to permit him to fulfil his obligation without discomfort. The bank made the loan, not in cash, but in mortgage bonds, or cédulas, which the mortgagor then sold in the market for cash. These cédulas bore a fixed rate of interest (the maximum not to exceed 8 per cent), payable by coupon, which the bank bound itself to pay to the buyer, regardless of whether or not the bank had, in its turn, received its interest payments on the mortgage loans. The cédulas were to be redeemed by a cumulative sinking fund, the maximum of which was not to exceed 2 per cent; amortization was to be made by drawings at par.

The cédulas were payable to the bearer, an important condition, since it permitted the free transference of the bonds without expenses of any sort. As the *Banco Hipotecario Nacional* says: "This circumstance facilitated the transactions." It was indeed one of the chief causes of the furious speculation in cédulas in the late eighties.

These provisions rendered cédulas attractive to the investor. The rate of interest on all cédulas emitted until the late nineties (save two small issues of gold cédulas) was 7 per cent to 8 per cent, and the amortization 1 per cent. This interest was payable in paper money, to be sure, but that circumstance was of small importance until depreciation of paper set in so heavily toward the end of the decade. Moreover, the buyer of cédulas need not concern himself with determining the value of land; that work was performed by the bank before making loans to the landowners. The cédula-holder could, as I have said, at any time transfer his cédulas by sale, and thus recover his principal.

Only one other circumstance was necessary to insure the complete acceptability of cédulas in the eyes of the investor. He must have confidence that the bank could stand behind them. A number of clauses of the federal law of September 24, 1886, creating the Banco Hipotecario Nacional, are designed to insure the stability of the bank in the eyes of the cédula-holders:

1. The organization of the bank and its control by government are carefully defined. The bank was to consist of a central institution in the federal capital, and of branches in the capitals of the provinces and national territories, and in such other points as the directorate might designate. The directorate was to consist of a president and eight other members, appointed by the federal executive, with the concurrence of the Senate; the directors to hold office for two years, one-half of the board being removed each year.

2. By Article V, "the nation guarantees to the bearers the service of interest and amortization of the cédulas emitted by the bank."

3. The amount of cédulas in circulation should not exceed the amount of mortgage loans made by the bank.

4. The bank should emit not more than $50,000,000 m/n[1] of cédulas; this sum not to be exceeded save by express legislative sanction.

5. The emission of cédulas would be made by series which would be distinguished by letter, and put into circulation in alphabetical order. Those which bore the same interest and had the same sinking fund, and an equal term for their service, would belong to the same series. In opening the emission of a series, the board of directors of the bank would fix the interest and sinking fund of the same, and the periods of service, whether quarterly or half-yearly. Each mortgage bond would represent a sum not exceeding $1,000 m/n or less than $25 m/n. Cédulas should be exempt from stamp duty and from all national and provincial taxes.

Other measures are designed to insure the financial stability of the bank in its dealings with mortgagors. On these provisions must in large measure depend the prosperity of the bank, since it had no capital beyond a credit of $2,000,000 m/n from the government to cover preliminary expenses of organization and installation, and to insure the first payment of the interest on cédulas. To meet its obligations to cédula-holders it must be sure that the mortgagors could, in their turn, fulfil their obligations to the bank.

[1] M/n = "Moneda Nacional," *i. e.*, paper pesos.

6. To insure the bank a margin of safety against possible losses due to a fall in land values, it is provided that loans should not exceed one-half the value of the land offered in mortgage.

7. Loans were not to be made on the security of lands incapable of producing a rent. Loans could not be granted whose "annual interest and amortization charge exceeded the ordinary and permanent yield of the property."

8. The land offered in mortgage must be free of any prior lien. Its title deeds must be free from any flaw or legal defect; and the bank might, if it deemed necessary, require the title to be proved for thirty years back.

9. The board of directors could make no loan of less than $1,000 m/n, or of more than $250,000 m/n to any person, nor could the provincial councils grant loans of over $5,000 m/n, though if so authorized by the board they might grant loans up to $20,000 m/n.

10. Every loan was to be based on a valuation of the property to be mortgaged, to be made by one or more valuers appointed by the bank; all costs to be borne by the owner.

11. In the contract for loan would be stated the undertaking by the debtor to pay to the bank a certain sum per annum, divided into quarterly or half-yearly parts, on the nominal value of the bonds he received, and for the number of years which might be fixed in the contract, which would include the interest and quota of amortization of the respective series, and the 1 per cent of annual commission in favor of the bank.

12. When the debtor should fail to pay a quarterly or half-yearly installment, as the case might be, and sixty days should have elapsed without his having complied with his obligation, and paid in addition a penal interest of 1 per cent for the period of delay, the bank might proceed to the sale of the property or properties mortgaged in the manner determined by this law (public auction).

13. The debtor might, at any time, cancel the whole or part of his debt, paying in addition to the interest and commission owing up to the date of payment, a quarter's interest for the whole or part which he cancels. The payment might be made in legal

currency (paper) or in cédulas of the same series as the obligation for their nominal value.[1]

This summary of the law sufficiently describes the organization, functions, and manner of operation of the National Mortgage Bank. The Provincial Mortgage Bank was similar, save that it was controlled only by the province of Buenos Aires, and its cédulas had the provincial, instead of the national, guarantee.

In idea, the banks were good. Well managed they might have accomplished all that was expected of them.[2] The mechanism of their operations, however, was delicate and complex; not at all suited to the troublous times of the Celman régime. They had no capital. If payments to them on mortgages ran behind, they had not wherewith to pay, in their turn, the interest on the cédulas. It was the business of the banks, to be sure, to guard against this possibility. They were to value the land, to know what it would bring at auction in foreclosure proceedings. This was their central function, indeed. European lenders could not go thousands of miles to value land. Upon the honest and correct valuation by the bank everything depended. Yet it was in this very particular that the banks proved most defective. When the National Mortgage Bank was opened in November, 1886, the paper currency was already depreciated, and prices correspondingly inflated. Speculation in land had already begun, and land prices were rising fast. The law prohibited loans exceeding 50 per cent of the assessed value of the land offered in mortgage, to be sure, and this margin had doubtless been sufficient prior to the speculative fever; but advances made at a later stage, when land prices had artificially risen, were necessarily covered by a much smaller margin of surplus value. With the land boom under way, moreover, the banks had every temptation to keep it going, for a slump in land values would cut the ground from under their feet.

[1] See "Leyes y Disposiciones," *Banco Hipotecario Nacional*, 1916, pp. 10–23.

[2] In proof witness the present prosperous condition of the National Mortgage Bank, with its $512,987,075 m/n of cédulas, against $566,048,570 of mortgages (December 31, 1916). "Informe sobre las Operaciones Del Año, 1916," *Banco Hipotecario Nacional*.

The banks, too, were under the control of the governments, a wholesome and necessary provision in normal times. With Celman in power, however, government control was a distinct handicap. The banks were dominated by political cliques; the governing bodies took good care to favor their partisans; it was not a difficult matter for a supporter of the party in power to obtain loans on properties utterly worthless, in spite of the express prohibition of the law. "Swamps and salt plains had as good a chance as a flourishing farm, provided the owner were in the political ring." [1]

Numerous stories were rife in the late eighties and early nineties about the scandalous proceedings of the mortgage banks. W. R. Lawson said the banks valued property at three or four times what it would bring in a bona fide sale.[2] The Buenos Aires *Standard* of October 12, 1887, relates the following swindle to which the National Mortgage Bank, it alleges, was a partner: Some plots of land near Rosario were bought by a syndicate for $30,000. The bank sent out a "tasador," or appraiser, who valued the land at $12 per square meter. There were 56,900 square meters in all! On this valuation the bank made a loan of $500,000 of cédulas. The law says that the maximum loan shall be $250,000, and loans shall not exceed one-half the value of land pledged.

There are numerous tales of this sort. They may be taken with a grain of salt, of course. Those were years of considerable spiritual exaltation. Yet tales coming from such various and respected sources must travel in the general direction of the truth, even if many of them go beyond it.

It must be remembered, too, that the cédulas were *paper* mortgage bonds, that their interest was payable in paper, and that the Europeans who bought them paid gold. The government needed gold to bolster up its tottering finances. An influx of gold was the only thing, aside from the burning of paper money, which would hold back the rising gold premium. To the European the cédulas wore still a different aspect. Their

[1] John Procter in *Bankers' Magazine*, London, March, 1891, i, p. 457.

[2] "The Argentine Crisis: Its Financial Aspects," *Fortnightly Review*, liv, p. 456.

interest was payable in paper, to be sure; but the rate was high, 7 per cent. In the years before the debasement of paper became marked, the investment seemed a good one. It seemed even better than the bonds of the government, for the cédulas bore a double guarantee, the guarantee of the land mortgaged, and the promise of the government to stand behind all the obligations of the bank. In later years, when panic was threatening, when it was known that the government could with difficulty meet its interest payments on foreign loans, when paper was depreciated several hundred per cent, the situation was different. Cédulas dropped into the thirties. The fact that cédulas were payable in paper (and freely transferable) was undoubtedly the chief reason for the enormous speculation in them both in Europe and in Argentina. Cédula quotations rose and fell with every fluctuation of the gold premium. They were, therefore, an ideal betting proposition. Even when cédulas had fallen far below their par value there was still a market for them in Europe, because of the gambler's chance that a cédula selling today at $50 might sell tomorrow at $45 or $60.

Finally, though the law creating the National Mortgage Bank named $50,000,000 as its limit of emission of cédulas, to be surpassed only by sanction of special laws, this provision was no safeguard during an administration with whom "special laws" were a specialty. There was, in fact, no limit upon emission, except that set by the appetite of the purchasing public. Emissions of cédulas on a large scale began in 1886. Until then land-mortgage operations had been moderate. Although the Provincial Mortgage Bank had been in operation since 1872, it had emitted but $76,557,000 cédulas, of which only $49,745,000 were actually in circulation on December 31, 1885. In January, 1886, the Provincial Bank opened a new series,[1] increasing the total circulation of cédulas to $79,000,000 by the end of 1886.

[1] *Memorias del Banco Hipotecario de la Provincia de Buenos Aires*, 1886–91: Anexo lxxi. At the same time the provincial bank raised the interest rate. Series E and F, emitted in January, 1882, and January, 1884, respectively, bore 6 per cent.; Series G of October, 1885, bore 7 per cent. All subsequent issues of the provincial bank were at 8 per cent.

By this time the land boom was in full swing, and the printing presses of the two banks were vying with each other in turning out cédulas. Authorities agree that prior to 1887 the cédulas had reached Europe in only minor quantities. Before the end of the year they were circulating on every European bourse of any pretensions. This opening up of an apparently inexhaustible new market goes far to explain the outburst of cédulas in 1887. The National Mortgage Bank began operations November 15, 1886. The board of directors decided to emit a Series A of 20,000,000 pesos bearing 7 per cent interest, 1 per cent amortization, and 1 per cent commission, payable quarterly. There was an influx of applicants from the beginning: "no fewer than 1,890 applicants for loans were attended to in the head office in six months."[1] By June, 1887, the series had been exhausted. The great demand induced the Board to begin a new Series B, of $15,000,000, subject to the same interest, amortization, and commission as its predecessor, but payable half-yearly. On August 26, Series C, likewise for $15,000,000, was begun. Thus, within one year of its founding, the bank had issued the full amount of $50,000,000 authorized by the law. Sixteen agencies had been established in the provinces, 3641 mortgage loans had been made, 2042 of them in the federal capital, 649 in the rich wheat province of Santa Fé, and the others in the various provinces and territories.[2]

The lands mortgaged were appraised by the bank at $111,-506,605, so that the $50,000,000 of loans given in the form of cédulas represented 44.84 per cent of the value of the property. At this time, the bank appears to have favored a conservative policy. The board announced that, although applications for mortgages exceeded the $50,000,000 limit, no more cédulas could be issued.[3]

But the tone soon changed. The cédulas had been well received. Series A was quoted at 90, Series B at 84. Political pressure from speculators, partisans of the government, was at work to increase the emission. Applications for mortgages

[1] P. Agote: *Finances of the Argentine Government*, p. 144.

[2] *Memoria del Banco Hipotecario Nacional*, 1887, p. 13.   [3] *Ibid.*

continued to pour in. A law of August 2, 1888, authorized a further emission of 60,000,000 pesos.[1]

The bank at once began three new series: Series D and E, for 20,000,000 pesos each, at 7 per cent interest, 1 per cent amortization, payable half-yearly; and a gold Series A, likewise for twenty millions, at 5 per cent interest, 1 per cent amortization, with half-yearly service. By the end of the year Series D had been run up to $16,894,000, Series E to $5,570,000, and the gold series to $6,136,000. By the end of 1889 E had been exhausted, and Series A, gold, had mounted to $18,214,000. In three years the bank had emitted eighty-nine and one-half millions of paper cédulas, and over eighteen millions of gold cédulas. This virtually concluded the emission of the National Mortgage Bank for the time being; the emissions of 1890, amounting to some $2,000,000, completing the $110,000,000 of cédulas authorized by law.

Meanwhile the Provincial Mortgage Bank had been proceeding at a brisk pace. Series K was begun in July, 1887, and run up to thirty millions. In the same year Series I and J were completed, making a total emission for the year of $44,679,000. The year 1888 witnessed three new provincial series: L and M, for a total of fifty-four and one-half millions, and a gold Series A (at 6 per cent interest) of which only five millions could be launched.[2] The year 1889 brought two more paper series, M and N, each for $50,000,000. The panic of 1890 brought the end of the mad business, though not before a new Series P, begun late in 1889, had been run up to $69,000,000,— the largest series of the lot! [3]

The emissions of the Provincial Bank in the four years from 1887 to 1890 had amounted to $275,000,000 in round numbers.[4]

---

[1] "Leyes y Disposiciónes," *Banco Hipotecario Nacional*, 1916, p. 39.

[2] Twenty millions were authorized, but the market would not take them. *Memorias del Banco Hipotecario de la Provincia de Buenos Aires*, 1886-91, Anexo xii.

[3] *Ibid.*

[4] Paper cédulas	$268,103,000
$5,096,000 gold cédulas (at $1.48)	7,542,000
Total in paper	$275,645,000

Adding the national cédulas,[1] which reckoned in paper come to $126,500,000, we get a total emission of over $402,000,000 m/n.

In comparison with the Provincial Bank, the operations of the National Mortgage Bank seem moderate. The effect is seen in the market quotations. Though the quotations of national cédulas fluctuated violently, in sympathy with the premium on gold, rising as high as 112[2] and falling as low as 73,[3] the general range was from 80 to 90, until as late as April, 1891, the worst year of the crisis.[4]

Provincial cédulas, naturally, fared much worse. They enjoyed merely the provincial guarantee. The enormous scale of emission was not calculated to produce confidence. Series M began in July, 1888, at 81; Series N, in December, at 76; Series O, in April, 1889, at 76. By then warnings of the inevitable panic were being sounded by the more prudent at home, and by the financial journals in Europe. Series P started in November, 1889, at 67.' The general average for 1890 was not above 60. When in 1891 the panic had burst, the Provincial Bank had gone under, and the province of Buenos Aires had defaulted, the bottom dropped out of the cédula market. By June, Series P was quoted at 30; the gold series A, at 28. No provincial cédulas were above 44.[5]

---

[1] Total of national cédulas = 90,000,000 pesos of paper cédulas
    and   20,000,000 "   " gold   "
Below the gold cédulas are calculated in paper:

1888.......	6,136,000 (at gold premium of 48) =	$9,081,280 paper
1889.......	12,078,000 (" " " " 91) =	23,068,980 "
1890.......	1,786,000 (" " " " 151) =	4,382,860 "

$36,533,120 paper

Total national cédulas stated in paper = 126,533,120 pesos.

[2] Series A, December 10, 1889.   [3] Series E, December 15, 1888.

[4] The national gold series, naturally, did not fare so well, falling heavily in proportion as the gold premium rose. The series starts at 80, November 23, 1888, descends to 74 in March, 1889, rises to 89 in June, 1889, then plunges downward to 62 in December, 1889. In February, 1891, it stood at 49. (See *Memoria del Banco Hipotecario Nacional*, 1890, p. 6.)

[5] *Memorias del Banco Hipotecario de la Provincia de Buenos Aires*, 1886–91, p. lxxxv.

The following table gives the total annual emission of cédulas, the amount actually realized thereon, and the annual payments made by the banks for interest and amortization:

YEARLY EMISSIONS OF CÉDULAS AND ANNUAL SERVICE, 1887–90 [1]

(Thousand paper pesos)

Year	Nominal Value	Realized Value	Interest and Amortization
1887	$94,679	$82,211	$8,239
1888........................	93,618	92,951	15,616
1889........................	153,894	116,681	23,167
1890........................	59,987	38,699	35,033

It is not possible to say with precision what part of this great mass of mortgage bonds went to Europe. Competent opinion, however, is agreed that it was by far the greater part. It is worth noting, again, that the great outburst of cédulas began simultaneously with the appearance of the bonds in European markets, and that the chief reason for organizing the banks was to attract capital from Europe to Argentine land. Necessarily, in a young country, with a population of less than 4,000,000, home capital was lacking. We may note, too, the statement of the finance minister in 1884 that virtually the whole of the public debt, internal as well as external, was in Europe.[2] Direct evidence on cédulas is afforded by the statement of the president of the Banco Hipotecario Nacional, that in 1900, "except for small lots existing in the home market in the hands of speculators, which might amount to $1,000,000 of the Series A to F,[3] and to $3,000,000 of Series G,[3] all cédulas might be considered, the paper ones as well as the gold, as being

[1] The statistics of nominal value of emissions and of interest and amortization are compiled from official data from the annual *Memorias*, or reports of the mortgage banks. The "Realized Value" has been obtained by computing each series of cédulas according to the market rate at which issued and totalling the results. The market quotations are also given in official reports. The gold series (provincial and national) have been converted into paper, at the average gold premium of the years in which issued, and added to paper cédulas to obtain the yearly totals of emission in terms of paper pesos.

[2] *Memoria de Hacienda* for 1883, i, p. 4.

[3] Series F not issued till 1895, Series G in 1897–98, Series H in 1900.

in Europe." [1] Inquiries made by the Argentine statistician, Sr. A. B. Martinez, in 1900 and again in 1904,[1] of the eminent Argentine banker, the late Sr. Ernesto Tornquist, whose services were of such value to the government during the reconstruction days of the nineties, brought the same reply: Broadly speaking, Series A to F were in their entirety in Europe; of Series G there might be some millions in the country, and likewise of Series H.[1]

To avoid exaggeration I take 90 per cent [2] as the portion of the annual emissions that went abroad. The following table gives the annual amount of cédulas sold to Europe, and the interest and amortization annually paid thereon. These figures are in gold pesos,[3] and they express the market value, that is, the amount actually paid for the cédulas.

FOREIGN CÉDULA BORROWINGS AND ANNUAL SERVICE THEREON, 1887-90

(Thousand gold pesos)

Year	Amount Realized on Cédulas Sold Abroad	Interest and Amortization
1887	$54,138	$5,492
1888	46,621	9,498
1889	55,885	10,981
1890	13,975	12,716

B. *Foreign Capital in Railroads*

The years of land speculation were also the years in which railroad construction reached its maximum of intensity. There is no need to discuss the causes, already reviewed: the artificial atmosphere of prosperity caused by rising prices incident to the depreciation of the currency, the over-confident policy of an extravagant administration, and the eagerness of British investors for new outlets for their capital. Virtually all of the capital invested in railroads during this period (and indeed to the present day) came from England.[4] Though in amount it

[1] *Censo General de la Ciudad de Buenos Aires*, 1904, chapter on "Los Valores Mobiliarios de la República Argentina," p. 491 *et seq.*

[2] Except for the two gold series, of which the whole went abroad.

[3] To get gold figures I have converted the figures for paper cédulas into gold at the average premium of the year in which the emissions occurred.

[4] An important exception was the French railroad in the Province of Santa Fé, as mentioned below, p. 86.

was much greater than the capital invested in cédulas, and therefore more important in an investigation of borrowings, its description is a simpler matter.

One fact, however, must be noted,— the change in the policy of the government. In Roca's time the building of state railroads had been encouraged. In 1885 45 per cent of the total capital in railroads was in state-owned lines, either national or provincial. By 1890 the state lines represented only 10 per cent of the total capital. In part the change was due to the financial difficulties of the provinces. In 1890 Buenos Aires sold the Western Railroad to a British syndicate. The province of Santa Fé leased its line to a French company, which eventually assumed the ownership. In part, too, the change was a characteristic result of the Celman régime. The presidential messages of 1887 and 1888 [1] dilate upon the advantages of private ownership over government ownership. Viewed as a part of the general policy of the administration, however, there can be no doubt that the chief motive for the change was that of the spendthrift, the desire to turn the state lines into ready money.[2]

The statistics of new railroad mileage give some idea of what was actually accomplished during this period by private enterprise. The entire decade of the eighties was one of unusual railroad building. From 1881 to 1886, 2500 miles were built. In the next five years the new construction amounted to 4150

[1] See *Los Mensajes*, Celman's message of May, 1887, iv, pp. 179 *et seq.*; and iv, p. 209, Celman's message of May, 1888.

[2] In 1887 the Andino road was sold to an English company (for $12,300,000 gold), and a portion of the Central Norte leased. In the nineties there was some tendency toward a return to the policy of state-owned roads. Capital in state roads showed a considerable increase. But that Celman's acts of alienation of state roads represent a distinct, permanent break with the past is evidenced by the fact that at present state railroads represent but 18 per cent of the total railroad mileage and 10 per cent of the total capital in railroads. There are now two state lines, the Central Norte and the Andino; their total capital is $122,-000,000 gold, and their length is 4,033 kilometers. The total capital in private lines is $1,210,000,000 gold, and the total length, 27,427 kilometers. These are the figures for 1913. (See *Estadistica de los Ferrocarriles en Explotación*, xxii, 1913: Dirección General de Ferrocarriles.)

miles, doubling the total mileage of the republic.[1] Taking the decade of the eighties as a whole, the increase is 6650 miles, as compared with 1040 built in the seventies, and 2770 in the nineties.

The figures, however, fail to do justice to the situation. They convey but a faint impression of the enthusiasm of the time for railroad expansion. Though the government had begun to alienate its own roads, it had not lost interest in railroad construction. It stimulated the formation of new companies by the liberal guarantee[2] of interest on the cost of construction. Guarantees of interest had been granted in earlier years, but not on the munificent scale of the late eighties. Railroad concessions were granted without regard to the present and future needs of the nation, the terms of one concession often having a destructive effect on another previously granted.[3]

Concessions were "frequently granted for some political purpose, or else as a means of remunerating people who, although

[1] GROWTH OF ARGENTINE RAILROADS, 1861-1911

By five-year periods

Year	Kilometers	Year	Kilometers
1861	39	1891	12,475
1866	515	1896	14,461
1871	852	1901	16,907
1876	2,033	1906	20,560
1881	2,516	1911	30,059
1886	6,689		

Estadistica de los Ferrocarriles en Explotación. Dirección General de Ferrocarriles, 1913, p. 400.

Figure for 1919 is 35,629 kilometers (22,141 miles).

[2] The terms of guarantes varied, being defined in each concession granted. In general, however, they were as follows: a certain annual rate of interest, usually 6 per cent to 7 per cent, was guaranteed on a construction cost not to exceed a certain prescribed amount per kilometer; the guarantee to run for the number of years named in the concession, usually twenty years. Interest was calculated on the basis of a division of the gross receipts of the road, as 60 per cent to count as costs, the rest as net earnings. Should these net earnings fall below the interest guaranteed on the total capital, the government made up the difference. Should the road another year earn more than the guaranteed interest, it must return all of the excess, or a portion of it as defined in the concession, to the government, and continue so to do till the full amount received as guarantee from the government had been refunded.

[3] President Pellegrini's Message, May, 1891, *Los Mensajes* v.

perhaps not entitled to any direct payment, had strong claims which it was well to satisfy in an indirect manner." [1] However this may be, it may at least be said that the general inflation had blinded the government to the serious liabilities incurred in granting subsidies to lines which were likely to prove unprofitable, while the eagerness of British investors to absorb Argentine securities of all kinds was a strong inducement to promoters to obtain guaranteed concessions wherever possible.

The mania for concessions reached its height in 1887. The following is the work of the Congress of that year: concessions were granted for the building of 6460 kilometers of railroad, whose maximum cost should not exceed $150,270,000, and whose annual guarantee was to be $7,513,500 gold. This is the "record," but it is closely seconded by the Congress of 1889, which granted concessions for 4553 kilometers, to cost not more than $131,184,200, with an annual guarantee of $6,559,175. Add to these the guaranteed concessions granted prior to 1887 and we have a total of 15,443 kilometers, with a maximum cost of $369,167,072 and an annual guarantee of $21,260,175 gold. [2]

Fortunately, the greater part of these lines were not built. Had they been, the burden of the guarantees, greater than the charge for the internal and external debt combined, would have put the country in a much worse plight than that in which it found itself in 1891, when the government was unable to meet its charges on the foreign debt.

Yet in the presidential message of May, 1888, we find the statement that by adding the proceeds from the sale of state railroads to the gold being received from the banks in payment of the bonds guaranteeing their note issue under the law of November, 1887 (see Chapter V, pp. 56-61), "the external obligations (of the republic) can be extinguished in eight years." This

[1] *Economist*, 1888, ii, p. 1378.

[2] In addition, the Congress of 1887 gave guarantees to Houston for a shipping line, and to Tornquist for sugar refineries, amounting to $461,720 gold, annually; and guarantees for mining projects, steamship lines, and cable service granted in 1889 represent an annual expenditure of $955,000 gold. The total annual guarantees (had they really been paid) would have come to over $22,600,000 gold.

naïve statement, obviously a mere excuse for disposing of the railroads, becomes doubly interesting in the light of what actually happened to the foreign debt within the eight years mentioned.[1]

The railroad guarantees caused a deal of ill-feeling between the government and the railroads, the former maintaining (often with truth) that the roads were simply resting on the guarantee. Some roads were built with no other purpose than that of obtaining the 6 per cent or 7 per cent of interest promised them in their concession.[2] Complaints were made, too, that such guaranteed roads as did prosper did not return to the government their profits in excess of the interest guaranteed, in quittance of guarantees paid in former years, as required to do by law. President Pellegrini in 1892 declared that the government had in all paid out $16,000,000 gold without a cent of it having been returned.[3] A detailed discussion of the railroad policy is beyond our province. We may leave the subject with some eloquent figures from J. J. Castro, showing the stir that was created in railroad circles by the policy of indiscriminate concessions. When the panic came the situation was as follows:

STATE OF RAILROAD CONSTRUCTION IN 1892 [4]

	Kilometers
1. In operation..	12,994
2. In active construction...........................	528
3. Construction almost paralyzed..................	500
4. Construction completely paralyzed.............	3,699
5. "Studied"...	4,089
6. "Being Studied".................................	61
7. "To be Studied".................................	7,794
Total....................................	29,664

[1] *Los Mensajes*, iv, p. 244.

[2] The special correspondent of the London *Economist* says in 1892 that "the guaranteed railroads seem to possess little intrinsic merit; their future depends on the ability . . . of the state to meet its obligations " (*Economist*, 1892, i, p. 697).

[3] *Los Mensajes*, v, p. 66.

[4] J. J. Castro: *South American Railways*, p. 180 *et seq.*

Our task is to note how this policy of railroad guarantees [1] increased the foreign liabilities of the government; and to describe the effect that it had, combined with the other causes previously mentioned, on foreign investments in railroads.

The investments of foreign capital in railroads in this period were extraordinary. According to the *Economist*, the total capital in privately owned railroads at the end of 1885 was about $76,500,000 (gold).[2] Finance Minister Hansen's report in October, 1892, says that the total capital of the private roads was $312,500,000.[3] The increase was thus about $236,000,000. About three-fifths of this, or $141,000,000, represent the railroad investments of two years, 1888 and 1889, the years when the "boom" reached its maximum.[4]

As every one knows who has attempted investigation of this sort, it is very difficult to determine precisely the amount of capital in so large an industry as railroads, to distinguish the declared capital from that actually invested, to assign to each year the amount invested in that year. Martinez has truly said that such an investigation is a "veritable labyrinth." Particularly is it difficult in a country like Argentina, in so remote a period as the late eighties, when Argentine statistical investigation was in its rudimentary stages. The figures that I shall give, however, are based on a comparison of many sources, the most important of which are given in the footnote. It may be fairly said, too, that in a study of this sort, which deals with general tendencies and broad principles, small errors are of little con-

---

[1] The guarantees actually paid by the government were as follows:

RAILROAD GUARANTEES PAID, 1887–90

(Thousand gold pesos)

| 1887 | $840 | 1889 | $3,738 |
| 1888 | 838 | 1890 | 2,919 |

From *Memorias de Hacienda* (*Annual Reports of Finance Minister*).

[2] *Economist*, 1886, i, p. 106.

[3] *Memoria de Hacienda*, 1891, i, and *Exposición sobre el Estado Economico y Financiero de la República Argentina*, 1893, p. 149.

[4] Year Book of London Stock Exchange, 1890; *Financial News*, 1888.

sequence. What we are seeking is a substantially accurate statement of the round sum annually borrowed by Argentina, of
the interest payments thereon, and of the effects of these
financial dealings on the monetary situation and the balance
of trade.

The yearly investments of foreign capital in railroads were as
follows: [1]

FOREIGN INVESTMENTS IN ARGENTINE RAILROADS, 1885–91

(Thousand gold pesos)

1885	$11,543	1889	$51,897
1886	15,993	1890	20,000
1887	37,812	1891	5,736
1888	89,419		

C. *Other Private Capital*

The amount of foreign capital other than that invested in
cédulas, railroads, and public loans is much more difficult to
get at. I cannot claim for my figures anything more than that
they represent the result of a comparison of statements coming
from a number of respected sources. The inability to obtain
precise data, however, is the less important in view of the fact
that these miscellaneous branches of investment were of much
smaller amount than the three main streams already cited. It
is for this reason, indeed, that the data are less ample. Various
careful estimates of this miscellaneous capital, however, have
been made, even for the period as early as that of my study.

[1] Sources: These figures are compiled from Report of the Dirección General
de Ferrocarriles, 1913, p. 424; the London *Economist; Financial News;* Year
Book of London Stock Exchange; report of Finance Minister Hansen for 1891;
Exposición sobre el Estado Economico y Financiero de la República Argentina,
Buenos Aires, 1893; Mulhall's *Handbook,* 1892; Louis Guilaimes's *La República
Argentina,* 1889, p. 348 (attaché to the Official Bureau of Information of the Argentine Republic); G. Canderlier's *La Vérité sur l'Immigration des Travailleurs et
des Capitaux Belges dans la République Argentine,* p. 33 *et seq.;* and a very valuable
collection of financial "Clippings" gathered through many years by the banking
firm of Tornquist & Co., Buenos Aires, which I have been permitted to consult in
their admirable private library.

Mulhall's investigation in 1878 showed the miscellaneous investments to be $21,000,000 gold.[1] The *Economist* puts mis-
cellaneous investments, exclusive of banks, at $27,000,000 at
the end of 1885; and the capital of the foreign banks at
$15,000,000. Adopting the practice followed by the Argentine
bankers, Tornquist & Co., in their inventory of 1904, we may
take one-half of the capital of the foreign banks as being in
Argentina. The total miscellaneous capital in 1885 was thus
$34,500,000. In 1892 we have the study of Domingo Lamas,
which, basing itself on a report of the British Legation in Buenos
Aires in 1891, puts the miscellaneous foreign capital at $85,-
000,000, exclusive of that in foreign banking establishments.[2]

It is clear from these statements that the miscellaneous investment was comparatively small, not more than $60,000,000
in the period of marked expansion we are now considering,
the late eighties. The items that are grouped under this head
of "miscellaneous" are various; banks, tramways, gas, colonization and land companies, and land-mortgage companies are
the chief. The only important omission is that of capital represented by farms and "estancias" owned by foreigners. This
item was undoubtedly a considerable one, but no data on its
amount are available for the period of my study. Moreover,
since most of the owners resided within the country, it does not
constitute an item of major importance in a computation of the
balance of external borrowings.

D. *Total Private Borrowings, Year by Year*

We may sum up, therefore, the yearly "private borrowings,"
as represented by cédulas held abroad, foreign investments in
railroads, and the investments in various minor fields. The
following table gives the annual influx of foreign "private"
capital, and the annual interest charge thereon:

[1] *The British in South America*, 1878, M. G. Mulhall, p. 640.

[2] Lamas, *Revista Economica*, November 5, July 5, 1892, p. 120 *et seq.* The capital
of the foreign banks in 1892 is given by Finance Minister Hansen as $20,000,000;
taking one-half of this we get a total of $95,000,000 (*Memoria de Hacienda*, 1891,
i, and *Exposición Sobre el Estado, etc.*, p. 149).

ANNUAL INVESTMENTS OF FOREIGN CAPITAL IN PRIVATE ENTERPRISE, 1885–91
(Thousand gold pesos)

Year	Capital	Interest Charge [1]
1885	$13,543	$5,563
1886	25,993	6,863
1887	106,950	14,996
1888	156,040	24,473
1889	122,805	29,300
1890	33,975	32,035
1891	5,736	23,486 [2]

II. PUBLIC FOREIGN BORROWINGS, 1886–90

A. *National Foreign Loans*

As related in Chapter IV, the increase in the public debt, national, provincial, and municipal, for the period 1881–85, was about $101,000,000. In the next five years the public debt was increased by double that sum. The national government alone borrowed $114,000,000,[3] by foreign loans. The largest loan was the 5 per cent "Public Works Loan" for $42,000,000, of which $20,160,000 was issued in January, 1886, and $21,-622,000 was issued in the following year. This loan supplanted the loans previously authorized for the building of the Riachuelo Port, and the sanitary works of the federal capital, which, it will be remembered, the government had not succeeded in floating in 1884. The other national loans of this period were the North Central Railroad Extension Loan, first and second series, issued in June, 1887, and April, 1888, for a total of $14,112,000 gold; the so-called "German Loan" of $10,291,000 gold issued in 1887 for the payment of the debt of the national government to the Banco Nacional; a 4½ per cent "internal"

[1] The interest and amortization of cédulas are official. The interest on railroad and other investments are reckoned at 5 per cent on the total capital in these enterprises at the end of each year.

[2] Full amount *owed* was much more than twenty-three millions; the decline is due to the bankruptcy of The Provincial Hypothecary Bank; it could not meet interest on cédulas (paid only $1,631,000 in 1891, though owing fully $10,000,000 gold a year). The National Mortgage Bank paid full interest on paper cédulas in 1891. (See Chapter VIII, p. 121.)

[3] This is the nominal value; the amount realized was $94,689,000 gold.

gold loan for $19,868,500, issued in London and on the continent of Europe in October, 1888; and finally, the famous Buenos Aires Water Supply and Drainage Loan, for $25,000,000 gold. It was this drainage loan that precipitated the panic, and forced Baring Brothers & Co., London, to close their doors in November, 1890.

The following table gives the annual emissions of national foreign debt, and the annual external payments made by the national government. To the annual service of the foreign debt is added 90 per cent of the interest on the internal debt, and the annual disbursements of interest guaranteed to railroads.

BALANCE OF BORROWINGS OF THE NATIONAL GOVERNMENT, 1886–90
(Thousand gold pesos)

Year	Loans		Interest and Amortization				Balance
	1 Nominal Value	2 Realized Value	3 Foreign Debt	4 Internal Debt (90 %)	5 R.R. Guar-antees	6 Total	7 (Cols. 2–6)
1886	$20,160	$16,128	$9,524	$2,634	$384	$12,542	+ $3,586
1887	38,465	33,744	10,403	2,678	840	13,921	+ 19,823
1888	34,787	31,750	10,321	1,604	838	12,763	+ 18,987
1889	13,246	13,067	11,677	1,162	3,738	16,577	− 3,510
1890	none	none	11,287	110	2,919	14,316	− 14,316

It will be noted that the interest charge on the internal debt (Col. 4) was steadily decreasing. There was no internal loan during this period, save the $4\frac{1}{2}$ per cent gold Guaranteed Bank bonds, of which I shall speak presently. The table indicates, too, that the service of the foreign debt (Col. 3) did not increase to the extent that one would expect in view of the large annual emissions of new debt (Cols. 1 and 2). The explanation is that a series of conversion loans in 1887–89 considerably reduced the interest charge on the old debt. Nevertheless, owing to the growing disbursements for guarantees of interest to railroads (Col. 5), the total burden of foreign payments (Col. 6) shows a sensible increase during the period. The last column of the table, the "balance," presents the situation of the government in the clearest light. It indicates that, on account of the heavy loans, the government was until 1889 receiving more from abroad than it paid out. In other words, the government could pay the interest on old loans out of the proceeds of the new ones. But in 1889 the situation is reversed. Interest charges exceed new loans. This reversal goes far to explain the anxiety of the government to raise new foreign loans; it confirms the view already given that the real purpose behind the complicated projects for new currency legislation in 1889 was to maintain the stream of foreign borrowing. In 1890, with access to foreign lenders shut off entirely, the full weight of the foreign debt falls on the government, with the result that the government is forced to confess that it cannot meet its foreign liabilities.

Two other circumstances, not indicated in the table, are necessary for a complete understanding of the difficult position in which the government found itself in 1890. The first is the $4\frac{1}{2}$ per cent gold internal loan of 1887. It will be remembered that this loan was specially issued for the guarantee of bank notes, under the Free Banking Law of November 4, 1887. It was to buy these bonds that the provinces borrowed so heavily from abroad, although there is evidence that in several instances the provinces acquired the bonds on the strength of a promise to pay in gold at some later date, rather than by actual purchase. All in all, $196,882,886 (gold) of these bonds were emitted by the national government; and one of the troublesome problems of the nineties was the cancellation of them. By 1890 their annual service was a heavy charge upon the government, the amount paid for their interest and amortization in that year being $4,066,000 gold. Since the provinces had borrowed from Europe the capital with which to purchase the guarantee bonds, the prompt payment of the interest to the provinces by the national government was as essential as the payment of the interest on the foreign debt itself, for should the national government cease the payments of interest to the provinces the latter, in their turn, must cease payments to their foreign bondholders.

The entire fabric of the public credit, therefore, rested on the ability of the national government to meet its obligations, internal as well as external; and the government's ability to do so rested, in turn, on its ability to maintain the stream of foreign loans at the height attained in 1887 and 1888. When the stream ebbed in 1889, and dried up in 1890, both the nation and the provinces were bankrupt.

The other circumstance which made more difficult the situation of the government was the fact that it received its revenues in paper money, which was rapidly depreciating in value. In such a situation, during the period when depreciation is manifesting itself most markedly, revenues must inevitably fall behind the expenditures; for some sources of public revenue are more or less fixed in character. Assessments for the land tax, for example, cannot be revised from week to week, yet paper money is falling in value from day to day. Moreover, the official valuations of the imports, on which the import duties are based, are not even today more than loosely accurate. They cannot reflect the continual price changes going on from week to week. How much less could they have done so in so unstable a period as that of 1889 to 1891, when the gold premium shot up from 55 in March, 1889, to 364 in October, 1891, a rise of 314 per cent, accompanied by violent fluctuations all along the way.

The result was a marked increase in government expenditure, a continual lagging of revenue in the race to catch up, and in consequence, a constant scramble to find external means, foreign loans, with which to make ends meet. The heavy expenditures of government in this period were in part, of course, due to extravagance; in part, however, they were the inevitable accompaniment of a rapidly rising gold premium.

Still other difficulties of the government grew out of this combination of heavy foreign borrowing and a depreciating currency. The heavy borrowings of 1886, '87, and '88, by increasing the supply of foreign exchange would tend to keep up the rate; and the result would be seen in a falling gold premium. This appears to have been the reason why the premium remained low during those years, notwithstanding the pouring of considerable amounts of paper currency into an already redundant circulation. The government would naturally be anxious to continue this state of affairs by keeping up the flow of foreign loans, for not only would the loans furnish it with resources wherewith to make its interest payments on the foreign debt, but by keeping up the rate of exchange and upholding the value of the paper money, they would enable the government to make its gold purchases, and buy its foreign exchange therewith, on more favorable terms. Once the ebb had set in, however, the situation rapidly changed for the worse. When loans ceased, the supply of exchange decreased. There being no decrease in the demand represented by interest payments, foreign loans, imports, etc., but, on the contrary, a continual increase, owing to the growing size of these interest payments, exchange fell. This condition of things, so unfavorable to a government having large foreign payments to make, was made worse by the speculators, who, having in their hands the gold which the government needed for the purchase of exchange with which to remit interest on foreign loans, could run up the price, temporarily, to almost any figure they chose. The interest payments on the national foreign debt in 1889 and 1890 cost the government $4,902,000 and $3,658,000 gold, respectively, because of these "differences in exchange."

The predicament of the government, it is clear, could scarcely have been worse. It is convenient, at this place, to point out once again that the bankrupt condition of the government was not due merely to its own extravagance and maladministration, as so often charged by Argentine writers. Extravagance and bad management there undoubtedly were; though these qualities were almost as ubiquitous during this period in private enterprise as in public enterprise. Everyone, lenders as well as borrowers, had for the time being succumbed to the fever of getting something for nothing. Many of the difficulties of the government, however, were inherent in the situation, in the combination of foreign borrowings and depreciating paper. Once these forces had begun to interact upon each other, it is difficult to see how national bankruptcy could have been avoided, especially when it is remembered that Argentina was a young country with a small population and practically no capital of its own. Without special arrangements with foreign bondholders such as were made in the nineties, designed to lessen the weight of the foreign debt, it is difficult to perceive how even the wisest statesman could have avoided the crash of 1890 and 1891.

This brief description of the special problems of the government indicates clearly enough the nature of the interrelation between foreign borrowings and depreciated paper money. The difficulties of the government, however, are after all but a secondary consideration. What chiefly concerns us is the study of the interrelation of these factors in the wider field, in the economic life of the country as a whole. It is for that reason that I am summing up in this chapter the total of borrowings, both private and public. We may continue with the summary.

B. *Provincial and Municipal Foreign Loans*

Until now, I have spoken only of the national foreign loans. The provincial loans amounted to a sum only slightly smaller. From 1886 to 1889, inclusive, the provinces emitted foreign loans totalling $99,759,000, nominal value, on which the sum realized, computed at the market rates at which the various loans were floated, was $86,801,000 gold.[1] In the early eighties the chief purpose of provincial borrowing had been the building of provincial railroads and other public works. In the latter half of the decade loans for this purpose continued, though not to so great an extent. From 1885 to 1890 there were five provincial railroad and public works loans, amounting in all to $20,970,000 gold. The chief cause of provincial borrowing in this period, however, was the Guaranteed Banks Law of 1887. No less than nine provinces made foreign loans for the purpose of securing gold with which to buy the national gold 4½ per cent bonds to guarantee their note issue. These loans, eleven in number, amounted to $50,975,000 (realized value $44,556,000). Of these nine loans a total of $47,243,000 was emitted in 1888.

In addition, we must include a series of municipal loans. Most important are the two foreign loans of the city of Buenos

[1] As compared with the provincial loans of 1881–85, which totalled $55,903,000 nominal value, or $50,371,000 market value.

Aires, issued in 1888 and 1889, the first a 6 per cent paper loan [1] of $10,000,000, sold by the city to the Banco Nacional, which negotiated it with a syndicate of European bankers for $6,949,-998 gold; and the second a 4½ per cent gold loan for $10,000,000 gold.[2] Both were for public works. Besides these, there were several small foreign loans,— two issued by the city of Córdoba, in 1887 and 1889, totalling $4,000,000 gold; three by Rosario, in 1887, 1888, and 1889, for $7,492,000 gold; two loans of the city of Parana, in 1889, for $2,068,480 gold; and one by the city of Santa Fé, in 1889, for $1,300,000 gold. The total of the municipal foreign loans, stated at the nominal value, was $34,860,000 gold; reckoned at their market value, they amounted to $29,238,000 gold.

C. *Total Public Foreign Borrowings*

All in all, then, the public foreign loans, national, provincial, and municipal, for the period 1886–90 were as follows:

TOTAL PUBLIC FOREIGN LOANS 1886–90

(Thousand gold pesos)

	Nominal Value	Amount Realized
National	$125,420 [3]	$106,109
Provincial	99,759	86,801
Municipal	34,860	29,238
Total	$260,039	$222,148

The effect of the reckless public borrowing of these years was to virtually double the total foreign obligation of the republic. The most careful statement of the public debt during this period was that made by Finance Minister Señor Emilio Hansen in March, 1892. It is based on a special inquiry in which considerable pains were taken to ascertain the extent of the pro-

---

[1] *Anuario Pillado*, pp. 115–116.

[2] For details of municipal loans see *Anuario Pillado*, p. 113.

[3] Viz.: Loans to government $114,000,000
Short-time loans of 1890 to Banco Nacional, assumed by
government in 1892 11,420,000

Total $125,420,000

vincial foreign debt, a subject on which information was meagre and inaccurate.

FINANCE MINISTER HANSEN'S STATEMENT OF THE PUBLIC [1]

FOREIGN DEBT ON DECEMBER 31, 1891

(Thousand gold pesos)

1. National.................................		$204,960
2. Provincial...............................		143,325
3. Municipal..............................		24,596 [2]
4. Back Interest:		
1. Provincial...................	$9,595	
2. Municipal...................	697	10,292
Total............................		$383,173

To this total should be added

5. 90 per cent of paper internal debt—		
stated in gold....................		$11,925
6. Guaranteed R.R.'s...................		81,800
Total public foreign liability.................		$476,895

III. BALANCE OF BORROWINGS

We may now draw up the table of the annual public foreign borrowings and of the annual interest charge, and strike the balance:

ANNUAL BALANCE OF PUBLIC FOREIGN BORROWINGS, 1886–90

(Thousand gold pesos)

Year	Borrowings				Interest Charge				Balance
	1 National	2 Provincial	3 Municipal	4 Total	5 National	6 Provincial	7 Municipal	8 Total	9 (Cols. 4–8)
1886	$16,128	$25,459	$ 0	$41,587	$12,542	$7,159	$200	$19,901	+$21,686
1887	33,744	10,912	1,892	46,548	13,921	8,043	345	22,309	+ 24,239
1888	31,750	48,810	11,200	91,760	12,763	11,610	677	25,050	+ 66,710
1889	13,067	1,620	16,146	30,833	16,577	11,733	2,192	30,502	+ 331
1890	0	0	0	0	14,316	11,733	2,157	28,206	− 28,206

[1] For Hansen's report see *Memoria de Hacienda* for 1891, i, pp. 207–231.

[2] His statement omits the $10,000,000 loan which the city of Buenos Aires sold to the Banco Nacional in 1888 and which was floated by the latter in Europe for $6,950,000. (See p. 99.)

It will be noted that total borrowings (Col. 4) show an increase to 1888, the borrowings of that year amounting to almost $92,000,000. In 1889 the borrowings diminish markedly, and in 1890 they come to a dead stop. Meanwhile, as shown in Column 8, the interest charge becomes steadily heavier. Column 9 shows the "balance" of public foreign borrowings. It indicates that to 1888 new borrowings annually exceeded the interest charge by a wide margin, but that in 1889 the margin is cut down to almost nothing, and in 1890, with borrowing at a stand-still, the full weight of the foreign debt charge falls upon the governments. As a result, they were unable in 1891 to meet their liabilities.

By combining the totals of private borrowings given in the table on page 93 with those just given for public loans we get the general balance of borrowings for the period:

BALANCE OF FOREIGN BORROWINGS, PUBLIC AND PRIVATE, 1886–91

(Thousand gold pesos)

Year	Borrowings			Interest Charge			Balance
	1 Public	2 Private	3 Total	4 Public	5 Private	6 Total	7 (Cols. 3–6)
1886	$41,587	$25,993	$67,580	$19,901	$6,863	$26,764	+$40,816
1887	46,548	106,950	153,498	22,309	14,996	37,305	+116,193
1888	91,760	156,040	247,796	25,050	24,473	49,523	+198,273
1889	30,833	122,805	153,612	30,502	29,300	59,802	+ 93,810
1890	11,420 [1]	33,975	45,395	28,206	32,035	60,241	— 14,846
1891	2,506 [2]	5,736	8,242	8,089	23,486	31,575	— 23,333

[1] Short-time loans of $11,420,000 made by European banking firms to the Banco Nacional, which shortly afterwards went into liquidation, the loans being assumed in 1892 by the national government.

[2] The part of the $100,000,000 (paper) internal "Patriotic" loan that went abroad. See Chapter VIII, p. 120. The total amount floated was $38,016,700. By 1900 the Banco de la Nación had retired all but $15,000,000 from circulation (*Anuario Pillado*, p. 172). Ernesto Tornquist later declared that the bonds of this loan "do not exist in this country (Argentina) except in very reduced quantity, except those held by the Banco de la Nación" (*Censo de Buenos Aires*, 1905, p. 501). I therefore take 90 per cent of $15,000,000 m/n ($13,500,000, issued at 75 equals $10,125,000 m/n, or $2,506,188 gold) as the maximum which went to Europe. It is probable, too, that the greater part of this found its way to Europe in later years, rather than in the panic year of 1891.

CHAPTER VII

THE INTERRELATION OF BORROWINGS AND PAPER
MONEY, 1885-1890

WITH the facts of monetary history and of borrowings before us, it is plain enough that the situation in 1890 was much the same as that of 1884-85, reviewed in Chapter III. The brief crisis that occurred at the end of 1884 was, as we saw, caused by over-liberal borrowings, which created an unfavorable balance of payments, drove foreign exchange to the export point, exhausted the reserves of the banks, and forced the suspension of specie payments. We found in that crisis a case in which depreciation of paper money was caused *solely* by heavy borrowing, there having been no increase in the paper money in circulation. The Baring Crisis affords an instance in which the liberal issue of paper goes hand in hand with heavy borrowings. The effect of these factors is heightened by enormous speculation in gold and in lands. In other words, *all* of the factors which tend to drive up the gold premium are operating together. Naturally, the effect was more pronounced; the depreciation of the paper money went to much greater lengths; the resultant crisis was much more spectacular and profound, and the subsequent depression of longer duration.

Before speaking of the panic itself, it may be well to point out more in detail the effect of the borrowings on the currency and the general situation. The first point to be noted is the extraordinary size of the borrowings. In five years, 1886-90, Argentina borrowed 668,000,000 pesos gold. The total of its foreign liabilities, including public loans and foreign capital in private enterprise, stood at the beginning of 1892 as follows:

TOTAL FOREIGN LIABILITIES OF ARGENTINA, JANUARY 1, 1892

(Thousand gold pesos)

Public loans and guaranteed railroads	$473,845
Railroads without guarantee	230,700
Cédulas	123,000
Miscellaneous	95,000
Total	$922,545

Stated in paper money, the total of the foreign capital in Argentina was $3,063,000,000.[1]

Fully 85 per cent of this capital had been borrowed in a single decade, 1880–90; and over 70 per cent of it in the last five years, 1885–90. As was shown in the last chapter, the climax was reached in 1888, the inflow of foreign capital in that year being almost $248,000,000 gold, or 27 per cent of the total Argentine borrowings to 1892. There are few instances in the history of foreign borrowings which surpass this record of Argentina in the late eighties.

Naturally the proceedings were watched with interest, and later with alarmed astonishment, by European bankers and the financial journals. The *Financial News* in its comment in 1888 says: Public loans are bad enough, but "that is nothing to the fun that the railroad concessionaires have had. Their insatiable maw has been stretched out eighteen distinct times, or at an average of once a fortnight in ten months. It has been sarcastically observed that the Argentine railways are just now the spoiled children of the money market. The authors of the sarcasm have very little idea how much truth there is in it. The city has had painful experience of prodigal borrowers; but in the whole history of foreign loans there has never been anything to compare with the above record. That the Argentine Republic is richly endowed by nature we readily admit; but if it were a first class European state, reckoning its tax payers by tens of thousands, and its accumulated wealth by millions, borrowing like that would be too fast for it. . . . Who among the most sanguine friends of the Argentine Republic will say that its four

[1] The gold premium in 1892 averaged 232 per cent.

millions of inhabitants are safe debtors for £25 per head? A burden like that would sober even a Maori financier." [1]

Such borrowing as this would in all likelihood have occasioned a panic even without the presence of depreciated paper. To my mind there can be no question that in this instance, as in that of 1884–85, the predominating cause of the crisis was borrowings, intensified, to be sure, by inconvertible currency, the depreciation of which was due quite as much to the collapse of borrowings as to over-issue of paper money. To demonstrate the effect of the borrowings on the currency one has only to note the general movement of the balance of international payments. It will be remembered that when, in the last chapter, the balance of borrowings alone was struck, it was found that down through 1888 the new annual borrowings exceeded the interest charge, but that when borrowings began to ebb in 1889, and interest charges to grow, the situation was reversed, so that in 1890 and 1891 the interest charge exceeded the new borrowings. When, instead of borrowings alone, we consider the *whole* balance of international payments, we find a similar state of affairs.

The following table presents the borrowings and interest payments, the exports and imports, and their sum for the years 1886–91, and strikes the balance:

ANNUAL BALANCE OF PAYMENTS, 1886–91

(Thousand gold pesos)

Year	Credits			Debits			Balance
	1 Exports	2 Borrowings	3 Total	4 Imports	5 Interest	6 Total	7 (Cols. 3–6)
1886	$69,835	$67,580	$137,415	$95,409	$26,764	$122,173	+$15,242
1887	84,422	153,498	237,920	117,352	37,305	154,657	+ 83,263
1888	100,112	247,796	347,908	128,412	49,523	177,935	+169,973
1889	90,145	153,612	243,757	164,570	59,802	224,372	+ 19,385
1890	100,819	45,395	146,214	142,241	60,241	202,482	− 56,268
1891	103,219	8,242	111,461	67,208	31,575	98,783	+ 12,678

[1] Tornquist's "Clippings."

There is no occasion at this point to enter into a discussion of exports and imports, since the foreign merchandise trade is to be considered in detail in a later portion of this study. It may be pointed out, however, that, taking the exports and imports by themselves (Cols. 1 and 4), we find a large excess of imports over exports. The imports show a rapid increase until 1889, then a moderate decline in 1890, and, finally, in the panic year of 1891, a most striking shrinkage to less than one-half the total for the previous year. The reasons for the abnormal expansion of imports, and the subsequent shrinkage, will be discussed later. The point to be noted here is simply that there is a pronounced excess of imports over exports down through 1890.

Relating this excess to the movements of foreign exchange, we should expect that, were merchandise trade the only item affecting foreign exchange transactions, exchange would run decidedly "against" Argentina throughout this period: for the demand for exchange represented by the imports is greatly in excess of the supply represented by the exports.

In fact, however, this was not the case, and the reason is to be found in the borrowings of foreign capital. From 1886 through 1888 the excess of imports over exports is more than offset by the heavy influx of borrowings, so that instead of a deficit in the balance of payments, we find a large and growing excess of the "Credits" account over the "Debits" account. The balance is decidedly "favorable" to Argentina. In 1889 we note a marked drop, which in 1890 develops into a large unfavorable balance. This, too, shows the dominating effect of borrowings in the balance of payments; it is the result of the cessation of new borrowings and the growth of the interest charge on the debt incurred in previous years.

Before going further with the analysis of the balance of payments, it should be pointed out that several items which of right should be included in the balance are omitted. The chief of these are immigrants' remittances and tourists' expenditures. How much was annually remitted to their native countries by the large number of immigrants in Argentina is unknown. I can find only two estimates for the period of my study, that of Mulhall in 1878 already mentioned in Chapter IV, which puts immigrants' remittances at $2,000,000 gold, and that of President Pellegrini in 1890, which puts them at $5,000,000 gold. Mulhall's estimate is based on an actual summing up of small remittances, on the basis of data furnished him by the banks. How trustworthy President Pellegrini's figures are, I do not know. President Pellegrini also gives $5,000,000 as the sum annually remitted to Argentine tourists in foreign countries. Of one thing, however, we may be certain. These items were small as compared with the two major items, borrowing and foreign trade. They were so small that their inclusion in the balance would not produce any essential change in its general trend. They in no wise contradict the assertion that borrowings formed the predominating factor in the balance of payments. For if we include in the balance given on page 104 the $10,000,000 of annual remittances mentioned by President Pellegrini as representing immigrants' remittances and tourists' expenditures we get the following results (I repeat the balance previously given for purposes of comparison):

(Thousand gold pesos)

Year	Balance of Payments given on p. 104 Borrowings and Merchandise Trade	The Amended Balance of Payments, including Immigrants' Remittances and Tourists' Expenditures
1886	+$15,242	+ $5,242
1887	+ 83,263	+ 73,263
1888	+169,973	+159,973
1889	+ 19,383	+ 9,385
1890	− 56,268	− 66,268
1891	+ 12,678	+ 2,678

The second column is the same as the first, except that an extra $10,000,000 gold a year has been included in the "Debits" account, as representing remittances by immigrants and those to tourists abroad. It is clear that their inclusion does not alter the general trend of the balance. It serves rather to accentuate the situation caused by the ebbing of borrowings in 1889, and their virtual cessation the following year. It cuts down the favorable balance of 1889 to an even smaller sum, and increases the deficit in 1890. Even should we double or treble the immigrants' remittances and tourists' expenditures, we should have virtually the same result, a slightly smaller favorable surplus in the early years, and a larger deficit at the end of the period.

There is one other item usually included in calculations of the balance of payments, which I have omitted — maritime freights. This omission is not due merely to an inability to find exact data, but to the fact that it ought not to figure in a computation of the Argentine balance of payments. The best proof is that, although in the past five or six years much interest has been shown in the balance of payments, and careful computations of it are now made annually, both by the noted Argentine banking firm of Ernesto Tornquist & Co. and by the Director General of National Statistics, Dr. Alejandro Bunge, the item of maritime freights is not included. The reason is to be found in the Argentine method of evaluating the imports and the exports.

The prices on which the values of exports are annually computed are the prices of the Buenos Aires market. They include the cost of transportation from the interior to the ports, but not the cost of ocean transport, for, as Dr. Bunge says, so far as exports are concerned, "maritime freight charges, which do not enter into our country because all the ships which transport our produce are owned abroad, are not paid by us; they are neither a credit nor a debit as between our country and the outside world, and must not figure as an item of value in our foreign commerce." [1]

The import prices, on the other hand, being likewise those of the Buenos Aires market, include the cost of maritime transpor-

---

[1] *El Inter-Cambio Economico de la República Argentina en 1916*, p. 13, by the Dirección General de Estadistica de la Nación. It should be said that the official import values are not strictly the market prices, but are based on "customs valuations" drawn up at irregular intervals, and loosely and often inaccurately revised from time to time. These customs valuations, however, are based on the import prices ruling in the Buenos Aires market at the time the customs valuations, or "tarifas de avalúos," are drawn up. They include maritime freight charges. Of the reliability of these official valuations of the imports I shall speak in the chapters on foreign trade. (See Chapter XII, pp. 178–80.)

tation. There is no occasion, therefore, for including maritime freights as a separate item in the balance of payments.

There can be no doubt, then, that the balance of payments as presented on page 104, the simple addition of the borrowings and the merchandise foreign trade, tells with substantial accuracy the story of this period. We may continue the consideration of the effect of the borrowings on the value of the paper money.

And first we must note the effects of the borrowings on foreign exchange. In the chart on the following page the movement of the rate of exchange on ninety-day sterling bills is shown for the period from January, 1888, to May, 1889,— a period which covers approximately the export season (November to May) of 1887–88 and that of 1888–89, together with the "off-season" winter months (June to September) of 1888.[1] In general, the

BALANCE OF PAYMENTS AND BALANCE
OF BORROWINGS
1888–1889

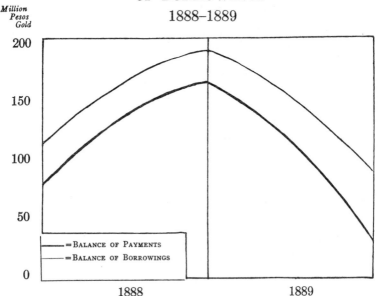

[1] For description of the Argentine trade year, and discussion of the effects of alternating "busy" and "off" seasons on exchange and the gold premium, see Chapter VIII, p. 196.

RATE OF EXCHANGE
FOR NINETY-DAY STERLING BILLS, JANUARY, 1887, TO MAY, 1889.

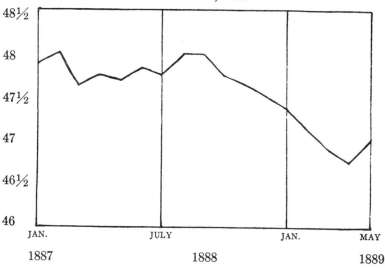

rate is high in 1888. But in October it begins to fall markedly. The fall is rapid and steady until April, 1889. And it is to be noted that the fall occurs in the export season, when, because of the increased supply of exchange occasioned by the sale of the exports, one would normally expect exchange to rise.

The explanation would appear to be that the increase in the supply of exchange from the exports was more than offset by the ebbing of the tide of foreign borrowings and by the growing interest charges, which, as has been described, were beginning to assume alarming proportions. In the lower half of page 108 is given the balance of payments in the years 1888–89, and in addition, the dominant item in that balance, the balance of foreign borrowings. Comparing the two diagrams, one finds readily enough the explanation of the fluctuations of exchange. The generally high rate of 1888 corresponds to the increase of borrowings in that year. The subsequent fall of exchange [1] is matched by the descent of the curve in the balance of payments, which in turn is due to the ebbing of borrowings, as represented by the descending line of the balance of borrowings in 1889.

The result of the movement of exchange was a large import of gold in 1888 and a large export of gold in 1889:

IMPORTS AND EXPORTS OF GOLD, 1886–90 [2]

(Thousand gold pesos)

Year	Imports	Exports	Balance
1886....................	$20,636	$8,358	+$12,378
1887....................	9,747	9,877	— 128
1888....................	44,810	8,735	+ 36,075
1889....................	11,750	28,431	— 16,681
1890....................	7,151	5,284	+ 1,867

The movements of gold, it will be seen, were erratic. Since gold movements were subject to so many influences besides that considered here, to the calculations of gold speculators in Argentina, to European syndicates seeking to manipulate the gold premium in order to render Argentine securities more salable abroad, to interest rates on call money and short-time paper, no consistent gold movement over a period of years is to be expected. The table does indicate, however, a general trend that is in keeping with the balance of payments. In the earlier years, when the balance was favorable there is a heavy import of gold; in 1889, when borrowings were rapidly ebbing and the interest charge was growing to alarming proportions, the current sets in the other way; gold flows out. And these movements of gold, as shown by our chart, are in accord with the movements of the foreign exchange rate.

One other fact is to be noted. The heavy gold movements,

[1] Toward the end of 1889 exchange rises again, and a generally high level is maintained in 1890 and 1891, exchange rising even as high as 49 and 50, in the face of the panic conditions of those years. This apparently paradoxical state of affairs is chiefly ascribable to the manipulations of gold speculators and the European syndicates, who sought to maintain an artificial rate by shipping gold into Argentina, for the purpose of unloading Argentina securities with which they were burdened. These manipulations and their significance are discussed in Chapter VIII. (See pp. 142–145.)

[2] *Extracto Estadistico*, p. 203.

totalling about $155,000,000 in the five years, and the fluctuations of foreign exchange in sympathy with the changes in the balance of payments, indicate plainly enough, as stated in Chapter II, that, so far as exchange operations were concerned, there was no essential difference between Buenos Aires exchange and any other. Although the currency of the country was depreciated paper, the exchanges were operated on a gold basis, exchange was bought and sold for gold, and gold moved into and out of Argentina in obedience to the mechanism of the "specie points." There was no "dislocation" of exchange, no paper exchange; but gold exchange operating in the same way as in gold-standard countries.

There was, however, a difference between the Argentine case and that ordinarily considered by the theorist of international trade. Though there was not a paper exchange, the currency of the country in all internal transactions was inconvertible paper money. And the value of this latter, as we have said, was affected by changes in the balance of payments quite as much as it would have been had the Buenos Aires exchange been a paper exchange rather than a gold. There is no need again to go over the ground already covered in the preliminary discussion of principles. (See Chapter II, p. 13 *et seq.*) What we must note here is what actually happened in the period of 1885–90.

The following table gives the circulation of paper money, the gold premium, the balance of payments, and the balance of gold imports and exports year by year for 1884–90.

Year	Paper Money in Circulation (Dec. 31)	Balance of Payments	Balance of Gold Imports and Exports	Gold Premium
	(Thousand paper pesos)	(Thousand gold pesos)	(Thousand gold pesos)	%
1884	$61,739	— $13,856	+ $391	Par
1885	74,820	+ 6,179	— 2,137	37
1886	89,198	+ 15,242	+12,378	39
1887	94,071	+ 83,263	— 128	35
1888	129,505	+ 169,973	+36,075	48
1889	163,648	+ 19,383	—16,681	91
1890	245,101	— 56,268	+ 1,867	151

It was in January, 1885, it will be remembered, that specie payments were suspended, owing to a fall of exchange late in 1884, caused by an unfavorable balance of payments, which was the result of over-liberal borrowings in earlier years. The gold premium remains low until 1889. It is lower in 1887 than in 1885. The rise of the premium in 1888 was slight, though the paper money in circulation was increased by 36,000,000 pesos. Meantime the balance of payments shows a heavy and a growing surplus in favor of Argentina. This surplus is reflected in the movements of gold. The export of gold occasioned late in 1884 and early in 1885 was soon checked by the renewal of borrowings. The year 1885 shows a favorable balance. Thereafter, the movement of gold is on the whole toward Argentina, until 1889. When one considers the events of 1884, already reviewed in Chapter IV, when an *unfavorable* balance of payments forced the suspension of specie payments, there having been no increase whatever in the quantity of paper in circulation; and notes, besides, that in the four subsequent years, 1885–88, when the balance of payments was increasingly *favorable* to Argentina, the gold premium scarcely rose at all, in spite of an increase of about 68,000,000 pesos in the paper money circulation, the conclusion appears warranted that the balance of payments, dominated as it was by borrowings of foreign capital, exercised a dominant effect upon the gold premium.

As regards the mechanism through which the balance of payments worked this effect, that subject has already been discussed in Chapter II. When, in 1884, borrowing declined and the balance of payments consequently became unfavorable to Argentina, demand for exchange exceeded supply, and exchange fell to "export point," giving rise for a demand for gold for export. The increased demand for gold, appearing coincidently with a decrease in its supply due to its exportation, drove up its price; specie payments were suspended, and gold was sold in the market at a premium. In the succeeding years, the balance of payments exercised the contrary influence on exchange. The excess of supply, represented by the borrowings and the exports, over the demand for exchange, represented by the imports and interest charges, drove up the rate of exchange to the gold import point, and gold flowed into Argentina, over $82,000,000 of gold in the four years (as against gold exports of about $35,000,000). Since, as already noted, the value of the paper money depended not merely on the condition of supply and demand for paper, but quite as much on the condition of supply and demand for gold, the increased gold supply during these years undoubtedly contributed heavily toward keeping the gold premium within moderate limits.

In 1889, 1890, 1891, the gold premium rises rapidly, from 48 per cent, the average for 1888, to 287 per cent, the average for 1891. In these years all of the factors that may bring about the depreciation of the currency are operating together. Because of the Guaranteed Banks Law of 1887 the quantity of paper money in circulation increases to an extraordinary degree. Meantime, borrowing of foreign capital first ebbs and then ceases; while interest charges are growing constantly larger. The balance of payments begins to run heavily against Argentina, showing in 1890 a deficit of some $56,000,000 (gold). Gold pours out of the country. The speculation in land has reached its maximum, and is on the point of collapse. The national government and the provinces are burdened with foreign liabilities which they cannot meet except out of new borrowings, and European lenders, now thoroughly alarmed, refuse to grant them.

This was the situation out of which there came in 1890–91 the Baring Panic.

CHAPTER VIII

THE PERIOD OF THE BARING PANIC, 1890-1895

I. THE PANIC

THE decade of the nineties was the logical aftermath of the financial and monetary debauch reviewed in the preceding chapters. Its story is that of the Baring Panic, and of the long period of slow recovery from that most severe of Argentine crises. An adequate account of the Baring Panic would require a separate volume. I can give merely such a general sketch of events as is required for the purposes of our present problem, the interrelations of paper money and foreign borrowings.

The approaching collapse was already apparent in 1889. (It is evidenced by the numerous and futile schemes of the government to keep down the gold premium, the projects for currency reform, and the attempts to negotiate new foreign loans) After the failure to control the premium by official mandate, and the failure to prevent speculation in gold, events moved rapidly. When the Stock Exchange dealings in gold were prohibited in February, 1889, the premium stood at 55 per cent.[1] When gold dealings on 'Change were again permitted in September, the premium stood at 106 [1]: and the government had expended the Guaranteed Bank reserves in supplying the continued demand for gold of the foreign trade market. Finance Minister Varela resigned. There followed a succession of finance ministers, each one holding office but a few months. An eleventh-hour attempt to raise a new foreign loan met with the response that a loan would be granted only on the following conditions: [2]

1. Sharp revision by the lending syndicate to prevent the government's making any grants not immediately required.

[1] Monthly average.   [2] *Bankers' Magazine* (London), 1890, i, p. 778.

2. No fresh loan for ten years.
3. The government to issue no more paper money.
4. The government to give a promise of strict economy.

Argentina resented such control and the negotiations languished.

In April, 1890, the gold premium touched 209 per cent. So rapid and so marked was the depreciation of the currency that there occurred what the *Bankers' Magazine*[1] termed a "new and puzzling phenomenon to economists," namely, that while the gold premium was going up there was a positive scarcity of currency and a constant demand for more money. Such was the shortage of paper money that it was announced as early as December, 1889, that some banks could not meet small checks even of their depositors. All over the interior there was a cry for more paper, and some of the provincial governments were resorting to the issue of promissory notes for small amounts, in spite of the fact that by the Guaranteed Banks Law the provinces were forbidden to issue paper money. The extreme tightness of the money market was beginning to play havoc amongst the great crowd of new companies created during the preceding years. Many of them were being forced into bankruptcy, though wholesale liquidation did not occur until 1890.

There is nothing inconsistent in this apparently paradoxical combination of a shortage of money and a redundancy of the currency. It is the familiar case of a demand for money induced by prices rising rapidly under the artificial stimulus of a violently depreciating currency, creating a situation in which two pesos are needed to do the work previously done by one. It should be remembered, too, that the depreciation of the currency was not connected solely with its quantity, but was in part the result of the outflow of gold caused by the ebbing of the tide of foreign borrowings. In part, too, it was the product of distrust, especially in the panic years.

In April, 1890, there was a severe banking crisis precipitated by the suspension of specie payments for six months by the National Bank of Uruguay. In June the government was severely attacked by Senator Del Valle for having suspended the

[1] *Bankers' Magazine* (London), 1890, ii, p. 1259.

Guaranteed Banks Act the preceding April, and connived at a clandestine issue [1] of bank notes by the Banco Nacional and the Bank of the Province of Buenos Aires to stave off the crisis. The finance minister, Señor Uriburu, described the Banco Nacional and the Bank of the Province of Buenos Aires as the great "pillars of the state," and drew a parallel between the suspension of the Bank Act in England in 1866 and the action of the Argentine government in April, 1890, which he said had saved the situation.[2]

The minister nevertheless demanded the resignation of the government-appointed directors of the Banco Nacional and their replacement by others. President Celman first agreed, then changed his mind. Uriburu resigned, and with his resignation terminated the negotiations for the foreign loan. The gold premium, which had fallen to 118, jumped to 165 in a single day.[3]

By this time a wholesale liquidation of the new companies floated during the period of inflation was taking place. Land prices had fallen 50 per cent within a year; large tracts were being offered daily, but could not find purchasers on any terms. In June the Banco Nacional announced in a telegram to Baring Brothers & Co., London, the suspension of the quarterly dividend.[4] Popular feeling against the government was running high. In July there was free fighting in the streets of Buenos Aires, the last important revolution in Argentina. President Celman was turned out of office,[5] to be replaced on August 6th by Vice-President Pellegrini, one of the ablest of Argentine statesmen. Pellegrini chose as his finance minister an able financier, a former president of the Bank of the Province of

[1] The total illegal emissions of these two banks in March and April, 1890, was $35,116,000. A law of July 18, 1890, authorized the emission of an equal amount of Guaranteed Bank bonds, to be amortized by the two banks at the rate of 5 per cent quarterly; but the banks paid only the first two quotas. The result was to increase the Guaranteed Bank bonds in circulation to $196,832,000. (See *Anuario Pillado*, p. 62.)

[2] *Economist* (London), 1890, ii, p. 920.   [3] *Ibid.*, p. 920.   [4] *Ibid.*, p. 857.

[5] The *Economist* attributed the downfall of Celman to the failure to raise new foreign loans. "The chief ambition of Celman had been the raising of fresh loans, and when the recent negotiations with that object in view fell through it was evident there would be a disturbance" (*Economist*, 1890, ii, p. 983).

Buenos Aires, Doctor Vicente Lopez. Some degree of confidence was restored; the gold premium, which had risen to 214 [1] during the revolution, fell to 155.[1]

When Dr. Lopez took office the country was already in the throes of financial crisis. The Banco Hipotecario Nacional, the Municipality of Buenos Aires, and the Banco Nacional were all in a virtually bankrupt condition. The debt of the Banco Nacional was as follows [2]:

Owed to the government.................		$47,491,483 paper
	and	12,641,120 gold
Owed to foreign creditors...............		18,540,186 gold [3]
Owed to creditors in country............		11,644,000 gold
Total stated in gold.................		$51,825,306

To save these banks and the city of Buenos Aires, Dr. Lopez issued 60,000,000 pesos of treasury notes, declaring this large increase of the currency to be unavoidable in so great an emergency.

There remained the service of the foreign debt to be provided for, and for this a foreign loan was necessary. Dr. Victorino de La Plaza [4] was sent to London to arrange a moratorium for one year under the form of a loan of £4,000,000 in amortizable bonds guaranteed on the customs duties. The principal object of this proposed operation was to avoid the necessity of the government's discounting bills in the Buenos Aires market, and to prevent the exportation of gold, which would still further have depreciated the currency. This subject we shall have occasion to consider more at length presently.

Negotiations were entered into with the house of Baring Brothers & Co., with whom, as Dr. Lopez says, Argentina had

[1] Monthly averages for July and August, 1890.

[2] See *Memoria de Hacienda* for 1890, i, Dr. Lopez's Report.

[3] *Memoria de Hacienda* for 1892, p. lxxxvii. The Banco Nacional had secured in March, June, and July, 1890, when it was still thought to be solvent, three short-time loans totalling $11,420,000 gold from L. & R. Cahen D'Anvers & Co. and the Bank of Antwerp. These loans were assumed by the government in 1892.

[4] He served as President of Argentina in 1915–16.

"had always the most friendly relations since the first Argentine loan in 1825, and which had of late years been buying up enormous quantities of Argentine securities."[1] Between 1882 and 1890 the Barings had underwritten $101,093,800 (gold) of Argentine bonds.[2] Most notable was the Buenos Aires Water Supply and Drainage Loan of $25,000,000 (gold), which the Barings had underwritten in 1888 for $21,000,000 (gold), to be paid in three annual installments. The loan was a complete failure from the first. British investors, alarmed at the extraordinary frequency with which Argentina had been appearing in the loan market, refused to subscribe; so that in 1890 Baring Brothers were loaded down with unsalable Argentine securities.

In the midst of the moratorium negotiations, therefore, says Dr. Lopez, there came in November, 1890, "like a thunderbolt," the intimation that Baring Brothers must go into liquidation "unless the Argentine government came to their rescue by paying up outstandings and releasing them from the obligation to pay £1,460,000," the third installment on the Water Supply and Drainage Loan.

The news precipitated a collapse all along the line. Baring Brothers & Co. closed their doors. The Argentine national government had to confess its inability to meet its interest payments on the foreign debt; the fourteen provinces one after another made a similar plea; the municipalities likewise defaulted.[3]

The position of the national government was as follows:

REVENUE AND EXPENDITURE OF THE NATIONAL GOVERNMENT IN 1890 [4]

Revenue		$4,481,000 gold
	and	44,221,000 paper
Expenditure		$14,141,000 gold
	and	56,114,000 paper
Deficit		$9,660,000 gold
	and	11,893,000 paper
Deficit stated in paper		$36,140,000

[1] *Memoria de Hacienda*, 1890, i, Report of Dr. Lopez to Congress, May 5, 1891.

[2] *Economist*, 1891, ii, p. 1263.   [3] But see exceptions noted, p. 135, n.

[4] *Memoria de Hacienda*, 1890.

The province of Buenos Aires was in even a worse plight. For the three years 1889-91 its revenue barely averaged an annual six millions of paper pesos, while the ordinary expenditure was in each year over seventeen millions paper.[1] In 1890 the province succeeded in postponing disaster by the sale of the Western Railway to an English syndicate for $21,000,000 gold; but in 1891 payments on the foreign debt ceased.

This state of affairs, it must be repeated, was not due solely to extravagance in expenditure. It was inherent in the situation, the inevitable result of a currency depreciating at such a pace that, in spite of the multiplication of new taxes, expenditure was bound to run into higher paper money figures than revenue. The provincial finance minister proposed to increase the property tax 20 per cent, and to lay a heavy tax on wool, cattle, sheep, in fact on all produce, despite the fact that the latter was not constitutionally taxable by the provinces. The national government in 1890 passed an act requiring 50 per cent of the customs duties to be paid in gold.[2] The export tax, abolished in 1887, was revived in 1890, as a 5 per cent[3] ad valorem tax on beef, hides, wool, tallow, and several other national products, though cereals were allowed to go free. A 2 per cent tax was laid on the deposits of all foreign banks; a 7 per cent tax on all premiums collected in Argentina by foreign insurance companies.[4] In spite of the increased taxation, however, the annual finance reports continued to show deficits.

In April, 1891, came, at last, the hour of the official banks. There was a run on the Bank of the Province of Buenos Aires, especially by small Italian depositors. At the same time, the

[1] *Economist*, 1892, i, p. 104; and also, the Report of the Provincial Finance Minister for 1891.

[2] But in fact customs dues continued to be paid in paper: the government fixed a rate which was somewhat below the gold exchange rate of the day, and the duties were paid in paper at this fixed rate. See British Documents, LXXXI, No. 1000. The entire gold receipts in 1891 were only $497,121. (See *Extracto Estadistico*, 1915, p. 236.)

[3] Reduced a few months later to 3 per cent. (See *Economist*, 1891, i, p. 104.)

[4] It is worth noting that virtually all of these taxes are designed to make the foreigner pay the piper.

Banco Nacional, despite the emission of $60,000,000 of treasury notes the previous year to save it, again clamored for assistance. Two internal "patriotic loans," one in August, 1890, for $30,000,000 paper, and one in March, 1891, for $100,000,000 paper, designed chiefly to save the official banks, were failures. Of the second only $38,016,700 was taken, and of this a large part was paid for with checks drawn on the very bank for whose assistance the loan was issued! Both banks were declared in liquidation on April 7th.[1] A special investigating committee of the shareholders of the Banco Nacional reported in June:

(1) that more than one-third of the capital ($50,000,000) had to be written off in December, 1890, for bad debts;

(2) that one hundred and twenty-five persons had pocketed over $5,000,000 gold;

(3) that the bank had over nineteen thousand customers, whose bills it held to the amount of $50,000,000 gold;

(4) that two hundred and eight favored individuals had laid hold on considerably more than the whole capital of the bank.

False balance sheets had been issued; imaginary dividends had been declared; wildcat speculations had been got up in the shares of the bank; public officials had made free with the funds.[2]

In the summer of 1891 the panic reached high-water mark. From July 4th to October 18th a general moratorium was declared; and though it appears that many firms did not take advantage of it, the pressure on the gold market upon the cessation of the moratorium was sufficient to drive the gold premium to the highest point it ever reached, 364 per cent.[3]

From this point the premium recedes, though not without violent ups and downs. Though the effects of the crisis were felt for fully ten years, the worst phases of it belong to 1890 and

---

[1] See *Memoria de Hacienda* for 1890, Dr. Lopez's Report; also, British Documents, LXXXI, No. 1000, and *Economist*, 1892, i, p. 539.

[2] *Economist*, 1892, ii, p. 952.

[3] The premium was doubtless affected by the establishment of the new Banco de la Nación, October 16, 1891, on the basis of a new large issue of paper money, and in the face of almost universal protest. (See p. 131–132.)

1891. Even in these years measures of reconstruction were got under way. Before turning to them I shall give some figures to indicate the effect of the crisis on public and private securities.

National paper cédulas came off well. A grant of $25,000,-000 [1] of treasury notes was sufficient to tide over the Banco Hipotecario Nacional. Indeed, the bank received only $1,063,500 of this grant, because of the fact that the Banco Nacional, the depositary of the government funds, had suspended payments and gone into liquidation. To make matters worse, up to September 30, 1891, the bank had received in annuities from its gold debtors only $154,488 out of a total of $1,603,815 due to it.[2] In 1892 so many of the bank's debtors were in arrears that their aggregate indebtedness reached the remarkable total of $50,-000,000 paper; and 2,143 properties were ordered to be sold. The sale of nine hundred and one estates, on which $25,700,000 had been lent, produced only $2,000,000.[3] Nevertheless, by excellent management, and with a further grant from the government of 5,000,000 paper pesos,[4] the bank pulled through the crisis. All payments on paper cédulas were duly met. The service on gold cédulas, however, was suspended for two years, interest being paid during that period in bonds of a national internal gold loan of $2,000,000. As a consequence of the maintenance of payment of the paper coupons, national paper cédulas did not go below 50; and the mean quotation for 1891 was as high as 80.[5]

The provincial mortgage bank collapsed. On April 18, 1891, the bank was authorized by the province of Buenos Aires to pay cédula coupons in paper certificates. Part of the interest in April and July was paid in money, after which money payments ceased entirely. Provincial cédulas were quoted at 30 to 40 in

[1] Part of the $60,000,000 issued September 6, 1890. (See above, p. 117.)

[2] *Banco Hipotecario Nacional, 1886-1916*, official history published by the bank in 1916, p. 33.

[3] *Economist*, 1893, i, p. 568.

[4] Consisting of a special issue of government paper money for the purpose on October 29, 1891. See *Banco Hipotecario Nacional, 1886-1916*, p. 35.

[5] Gold national cédulas, however, fell as low as 30. See report of the Banco Hipotecario Nacional for 1891.

1891. In 1900 there were still some $150,000,000 of provincial paper cédulas drifting about, with quotations of from 9 to 13.[1]

Just what was the extent of loss on the capital invested in private industries and government loans it is impossible to say. President Pellegrini quoted a British estimate to the effect that Argentine railway shares suffered a fall of £20,000,000.[2] The *Economist*[3] says that national government securities, including cédulas, having in January, 1890, a value of £26,157,000 had fallen by June, 1891, to £13,379,000; that provincial cédulas whose market value had been £29,903,000 had fallen to £9,218,-000; and adds that "if we were to add the far longer, if individually smaller, list of railway, financial, trading, and other companies and loans, it is not too much to say that a depreciation of nearly double that amount would disclose itself."

EFFECT OF CRISIS ON STOCKS AND SHARES [4]

Date	Banco Nacional	Banco Constructor	Catalinas Moles, etc.	Provincial Cédulas	Price of Gold
1889, Aug.	347	150	265	74	175
1889, Oct.	257	108	71	72	200
1890, Mar.	105	25	28	51	260
1890, Dec.	105	8	18	50	320
1891, June	30	4	9	40	400

FALL IN GOVERNMENT BONDS AND RAILROAD SHARES

Date	Govt. Loan of 1889	Govt. Loan of 1884	Gt. Southern R.R.	Rosario R.R.	Central Argentine R.R.
1889, Mar.	92	100	220	185	219
1891, Mar.	53	54	153	120	79
1891, July	33	31	129	74	47

[1] *Anuario Pillado*, p. 181.

[2] Message to Congress, May 12, 1891; in *Los Mensajes* (Mabragaña), v, p. 54.

[3] *Economist*, June 6, 1891.

[4] See British Documents, LXXXI, No. 1000, p. 64 *et seq.*

II. Reconstruction Measures

Such, in broad outline, was the Baring Panic. It was the inevitable result of the policy of paying off old debts with new ones. When new ones could not be had the bubble burst. It is to be noted that the government played the leading rôle. The Guaranteed Bank notes were a government project; the mortgage banks were created and controlled by the government. The excessive issues of paper and the frenzied speculation in lands may therefore be laid squarely at the government's door. A great part of the foreign borrowing had been government borrowing; the worst phases of the crisis grew out of the government's failure to maintain the stream of its own borrowing with new loans. The collapse of the Barings was the direct result of their overloading with Argentine government securities.

The only way out of the situation, therefore, was to put the government on its feet, and for this purpose there appeared to be but one method, a moratorium of the interest and amortization of the foreign debt. The inability to secure such an arrangement in 1890, because of the Baring difficulty, had precipitated the general default of the national, provincial, and municipal governments.

There was a double necessity for a moratorium of the interest charge: (1) the lack of resources by the government, due partly to its own extravagance, and partly, as has been explained, to the rapid depreciation of the currency, which caused expenditure to rise more rapidly than revenue; and (2) the effect which the payment of its interest obligations by the government would have upon foreign exchange and the gold premium. Because of the cessation of borrowing and the consequent overturn in the balance of payments, exchange was already against Argentina. Should the government buy exchange wherewith to remit interest payments, the effect would be to increase still more the demand for exchange and drive the rate still lower. Should the government, instead, choose to remit the interest payments in gold, its difficulties would be none the less great, for in either case it must first go into the market to buy gold. The increased demand for gold would drive its price still higher, render its cost to government excessive, and intensify the depreciation of the paper currency. It is to be noted, too, that in so narrow a gold market as that of Buenos Aires, even a slight increase in the demand for gold might have a considerable effect on its price; a demand so great as that of the government, whose annual obligations for interest on the foreign debt and on railroad guarantees were over $14,000,000 gold, would have a pronounced effect. And the greater the effect on the price of gold, the more onerous, of course, the burden on the government. With gold at a premium of 100, the burden would be $28,000,000 paper; with gold at 200, $42,000,000 paper; and so on.

One must remember, too, how entirely the government was at the mercy of the gold speculators. Knowing when the half-yearly remittances of interest came due, the speculators laid their plans accordingly. By "rigging the market" they ran up the price of gold in preparation for the great event, so that the government found itself forced to pay a higher price even than that which would have obtained through the simple operation of supply and demand. Such manipulation of the gold premium by speculating rings, though but temporary, and in no sense, therefore, an explanation of the *long-time* movement of the gold premium, was common procedure, which rendered difficult the position of the government throughout the period of depreciated paper money.[1]

It was for this double reason, therefore, the lack of funds and the desire to keep out of the exchange market, that a moratorium of the interest charges on the foreign debt was necessary, until such time as increased national production, by augmenting the export trade, should swing the balance of payments into Argentina's favor. Not only the Argentine government, but European lenders had a motive for desiring such an

[1] An Argentine banker has told me that such "rigs" were the rule, not the exception. Should the government not succeed in laying in a store of gold in advance, it must pay practically whatever the speculating ring chose to demand.

arrangement, especially the banking syndicates that had under-written such large quantities of Argentine securities, which they were anxious to render salable.

The moratorium negotiations, therefore, interrupted by the failure of the Barings, were renewed by the committee, headed by Baron Rothschild, which was appointed by the Bank of England as receivers for Baring Brothers & Co. After going over the situation with Dr. V. de La Plaza, the Argentine representative, the committee reported to the governor of the Bank of England (date of December 3, 1890) that "the result of the liquidation of Messrs. Baring's affairs is dependent in very great measure upon the future value of Argentine securities and obligations; besides which, a much larger amount of British capital is engaged in Argentina, the value of which depends greatly on the rehabilitation of the exchange." The report details the deliberations of the committee, which I sum up as follows:

1. The committee first examined the finances of Argentina, and decided that if gold were at par the national government would be solvent.

2. They next examined imports and exports. The latter showed constantly increasing vitality, while the former showed that with the suspension of railroad construction a large diminution might be expected.

3. Dr. de La Plaza told the committee that if the government had to buy bills of exchange on Europe to pay its debts, the premium on gold would probably go up very considerably, which would make living unbearable, except for the richer classes, and might even cause a revolution.

4. The committee gave its opinion that the chief factor for solvency consisted in the reëstablishment of the currency on a sounder basis. That was also the opinion of the Argentine government, for it had sent Dr. de La Plaza over to try and borrow the money to pay the coupons for the next two years, so as to avoid having to purchase bills on Europe.

5. The representatives of Germany and France on the committee took a more sanguine view of the situation than the English, and wanted to make a temporary loan to enable Argentina to pay its interest coupons for the next six months, when, they thought, Argentina would be ready to make its payments on its own account. But the English members refused to accede to this, for they thought it probable that at the end of six months the Argentine government would be in exactly the same position as at present. The foreign representatives then withdrew from the committee.[1]

The result of the deliberations was the Funding Loan Agreement of January 24, 1891. Its main provisions were as follows:

1. The Argentine government to be relieved from the necessity of remitting to Europe for three years (save for exception noted below).

2. The committee to grant to Argentina a 6 per cent funding loan of £15,000,000, to be secured on the customs, whose coupons were to be receivable as gold in payment of customs duties.

3. From January 1, 1891, to January 1, 1894, all interest payments on railway guarantees, and on the national foreign debt, to be made in the bonds of this Funding Loan; exception being made of the 5 per cent loan of 1886.[2]

4. The government to pledge itself not to undertake any new liabilities during the three years, and that in any arrangements with the provinces it would not increase the national obligations.

---

[1] *Economist*, 1890, ii, pp. 1534–1535.

[2] This is the Public Works Loan for $42,000,000. This loan was excepted because it was specially secured on the customs, whereas other loans were secured simply on the general revenues,— a doubtful reason. Puerto Madero Bonds of 1882 were also excepted. Finance Minister Hansen gives the following figures:

1. Debt whose interest was covered by Funding Bonds. . . $147,244,038
2. Debt whose interest was not covered by Funding Bonds,   57,714,871

(See *Memoria de Hacienda*, 1891, i, pp. 207–231.)

5. The government to undertake officially to cancel bank notes to the amount of at least 15,000,000 pesos a year for three years, so long as and whenever the gold premium should be above 50 per cent.

The Funding Loan accomplished its immediate purpose. It removed from the exchange market nearly the full weight of the foreign obligations of the national government, and relieved the government, temporarily, of the chief burden upon its revenues. The remittances on the foreign debt and the railway guarantees were reduced from \$14,316,000 gold in 1890 to \$3,461,000 gold in 1891, the remainder being paid in funding bonds.[1]

Yet the funding arrangement had serious defects which rendered it from the first the subject of controversy, and brought its abandonment before the expiration of the three years that it was to have run. The authors of it had underestimated the gravity of the crisis, supposing that the temporary relief afforded by the loan would be sufficient to enable the government to assume the full burden of its foreign liabilities in 1894,—a burden that would be augmented by the addition of the interest on the funding bonds to the previous obligations. The Funding Loan was at best a palliative, conceived in the spirit of the old policy which had brought Argentina to financial collapse, the policy of paying the interest on old loans with new ones. When Dr. M. Saenz Peña assumed the presidency in October, 1892, therefore, and Dr. J. J. Romero [2] was for a second time appointed

---

[1] Though the Funding Loan was for \$75,000,000, only \$38,458,561 were issued, viz.:

1891............	£1,458,069	1894...........	£1,637,666
1892............	2,519,724	1895............	108,425
1893............	1,906,781		

Memoria de Hacienda, 1894, ii, p. 162.

[2] One of the ablest of finance ministers. As finance minister under Roca in the early eighties he was the author of the monetary reform measures of that period, including the adoption of specie payments in 1883.

finance minister, the funding plan was abandoned.[1] A more wholesome arrangement was substituted for it, the "Arreglo Romero."[2] Since Argentina could not pay full interest she was to pay a part, the rest to be suspended. From July 12, 1893, to July 18, 1898, Argentina was to pay $7,887,600[3] annually; from July 12, 1898, to July 12, 1901, she was to meet the full interest charge on the foreign debt, $11,169,902 a year. On the latter date, 1901, the amortization was to be assumed. The government was thus allowed eight years in which to take up, by defined stages, the full burden of the foreign debt.[4]

The "Arreglo Romero" proved a satisfactory arrangement. The full interest charge was in fact assumed July 12, 1897, a year before the time agreed upon.

III. The Currency and the Balance of Payments

On the basis of the preceding outline of events during the panic period we may proceed more intelligibly with the discussion of our special problem, the interrelation of borrowings and paper money. It should by now be clear enough that these two factors, and principally the former, were responsible for the panic. We wish now to know their effects upon each other during the panic period. The remainder of this chapter is devoted to that subject.

A. *Paper Money, 1890–95*

It will be remembered that an important feature of the Funding Loan Agreement of 1891 had been the government's promise to cancel bank notes to the amount of 15,000,000 pesos annually

---

[1] Romero called attention to the fact that funding bonds had fallen to 63 in London, proof that confidence in the efficacy of the arrangement had been lost. This fall added, by the way, to the burden of the government, which paid the service on the bonds at par.

[2] *Memoria de Hacienda*, 1893, i, pp. 146–172; also, *Exposición sobre el Estado Financiero y Economico de la República Argentina*, 1893, p. 79 *et seq.*

[3] To this must be added a monthly payment of £30,000 on the short-time loans made to the Banco Nacional in 1890, and assumed by the government in December, 1892. A first payment of £150,000 was made in December, 1892.

[4] The railway guarantees were converted into funded or "consolidated" debt, by means of guarantee rescission bonds in 1896 and 1898. (See Chapter VIII, p. 134 and footnote.)

for three years. In fact the entire funding loan scheme had been based on the assumption that the Argentine treasury, when relieved of the necessity of remitting gold in payment of interest and guarantees, would be able to meet all other expenditures out of revenue, and have a surplus to be applied to the cancelling of bank notes.

No better proof could be had of the weakness of that arrangement; nothing indicates so conclusively the failure to estimate adequately the gravity of the crisis. In 1890 and for some years preceding Argentina could not meet expenditures out of revenue. The fall of the gold premium would have to be great indeed to wipe out that annual deficit in 1891; and in that year, with the panic at its climax, no external arrangement could be expected to produce a miracle. In spite of a slightly favorable balance of payments, brought about by the funding loan plan, the default of interest payments by the provinces and the provincial mortgage bank, and an enormous shrinkage of imports, the average premium for the year was 287 per cent, one hundred and thirty-six points higher than the average premium of 1890, the year in which the funding loan plan was conceived.

It should be noted, too, that the Argentine government depends for its revenue chiefly upon import duties, which in 1890 constituted 65 per cent of the total revenues.[1] In spite of the new 3 per cent duty on exports, the customs revenue, by reason of the shrinkage of imports,[2] declined from $47,546,786 in 1890 to $15,053,991 in 1891. Total revenue and expenditure for 1891 were as follows:

REVENUE AND EXPENDITURE, 1891 [3]

Expenditure................................	$132,204,000 paper
Revenue......................................	75,461,000 "
Deficit..	$56,743,000 paper
Subtracting funding bonds emitted in 1891—$7,348,668 (gold).............	= 28,441,000 "
Net deficit........................	$28,302,000 paper

[1] *Extracto Estadístico*, 1915, pp. 236–274. In 1915 import duties formed 42 per cent of total revenue.

[2] Imports 1890, $142,240,812 (gold); 1891, $67,207,788 (gold).

[3] *Extracto Estadístico*, 1915, p. 236.

Instead, then, of the surplus of $15,000,000 which was to have made possible the burning of an equal quantity of bank notes, there was a deficit of about twice that amount. It is scarcely necessary to add that the promise to contract the currency was not kept. On the contrary, there was a very considerable expansion of inconvertible paper money.

To gather up the loose ends of the currency situation, we must return to the early months of 1890, when the crisis was in its incipient stages. It will be recalled that in March and April of that year the Banco Nacional and the Provincial Bank of Buenos Aires, with the connivance of the government, issued 35,116,000 paper pesos not guaranteed by bonds. With these operations the period of Guaranteed Banks may be considered as terminated. The official decree forbidding further issue of bank notes appeared in July, 1890.[1] Virtually all of the provincial banks, and the Banco Nacional, collapsed during the panic. The private banks, all foreign but one, turned in their guarantee bonds and withdrew their notes.[2]

The remaining history of the fatal Guaranteed Banks experiment has to do merely with the cancellation of the bonds that had served as guarantee of the notes. In a series of arrangements stretching over the next ten years, whereby the national government took to its charge the provincial foreign debt, the $196,882,886 of guarantee bonds[3] were gradually surrendered to the national Caja de Conversión and burned.

By a law of 1894 the state formally took over all bank notes, which thus became government inconvertible paper. This act, however, was merely the legal recognition of a situation which had existed since 1890. From the collapse of the Guaranteed Banks in that year the full burden of the paper money rested upon the government.[4]

[1] Law of July 18, 1890.

[2] Except the British Bank of South America, which in 1900 still maintained its emission of $250,000.

[3] In 1900 there were still in circulation $3,099,000 of these bonds. See *Anuario Pillado*, p. 111.

[4] J. M. Rosa: *La Reforma Monetaria en la República Argentina* (1909), p. 85.

In 1890, also, began the emission of government paper, frankly inconvertible. The privilege of emission was accorded to the Caja de Conversión.[1] A month previous, September 6, 1890, a law had authorized the emission of $60,000,000 of treasury notes, full legal tender, to assist the official banks and the city of Buenos Aires.[2]

In 1891 there was another large issue, so astonishing as to demand especial attention. After the Banco Nacional had gone into liquidation on April 7, 1891, a project for a new state bank was set on foot, resulting in the creation of the Banco de la Nación Argentina.[3] The bank was to have a capital of 50,000,000 paper pesos, to consist of 500,000 shares of 100 pesos each, which were to be offered to public subscription. Shares could be purchased with scrip of the 6 per cent "Patriotic Internal Loan" of April, 1891. After the failure of two internal loans within a twelvemonth, this project was daring indeed; but not so daring as some other features of this bank plan. Article 19 of the law orders the Caja de Conversión to *anticipate* to the bank the face value of the shares, in new paper notes issued expressly for that purpose. It goes on to say that the paper issue shall be redeemed by the sale of the bank shares, and destroyed. But, as must have been foreseen, the stock was not subscribed. The subscription remained open from April 7, 1892, to June 20th; of the total of 500,000 shares, but 56,476 were subscribed, and these were paid for as follows:

In paper money..............................	$10,975
In "Internal Patriotic" bonds..................	5,636,625
Total....................................	$5,647,600

[1] Created by law of October 7, 1890, this Caja de Conversión did not deserve its name. Such a conversion treasury or bureau is in theory designed to raise, or at least sustain, the value of paper money, by providing means for its conversion into specie. This one was, indeed, "given permission" to convert paper into specie and vice versa, when paper should reach par (!) but that never happened, and was not expected at the time. Even today the Argentine paper peso is worth but 44 centavos gold. This Caja de Conversión was simply an office for emitting more paper.

[2] See above, p. 117.   [3] Created by law of October 15, 1891.

The government ordered a return of these values to the subscribers. Despite the failure of the stock subscription, however, the "Caja" continued to deliver the paper money to the bank. In other words, the Banco de la Nación was established on nothing more than an emission of $50,000,000 of inconvertible paper, authorized in the midst of the crisis, with gold at 364 per cent premium and in spite of the protests of the press, the bankers, and the business community.[1]

With these emissions to the Banco de la Nación the issues of paper money came to an end [2] for the decade of the nineties. From 1890 to 1893 inclusive the increase of the paper currency was in round numbers 157,000,000 pesos. Of this amount $35,000,000 were bank notes,[3] and $122,000,000 government inconvertible paper. Allowing for the cancellation of some fourteen millions of bank notes in this period, we have a net increase of 143,000,000 pesos, giving a total circulation on December 31, 1893, of 306,743,000 pesos, the highest circulation of the decade. From that date to 1899, the currency was very slightly contracted, some 15,000,000 pesos being cancelled within the six years.

[1] The paper was delivered in portions, as follows (ooo's omitted):

to June 30, 1892	$12,000
in July, 1892	3,000
in August, 1892	9,000
in May, 1893	26,000
Total	$50,000

See *Banco de la Nación Argentina*, official publication of the bank on its twenty-fifth anniversary, December 1, 1916, pp. 7–15. See, also, *Anuario Pillado*, pp. 169–173, and *Economist*, 1891, ii, p. 1395. (In spite of its amazing beginning the Banco de la Nación has had a wonderful development. Its capital and reserves amount to 161,000,000 pesos (December 1, 1916); and it has one hundred and seventy-six branches throughout the republic.)

[2] Minor issues not mentioned in the text:
  1. Law of August 21, 1890—$6,000,000 of notes less than 1 peso.
  2. Law of September 29, 1891—$1,500,000 of notes less than 1 peso.
  3. Law of October 29, 1891—$5,000,000 delivered to the Banco Hipotecario Nacional.
  See *Anuario Pillado*, p. 68.

[3] The clandestine issues of March and April, 1890, already referred to.

The following table gives the paper money in circulation on December 31st of each year from 1889 to 1895. It indicates that in the four years 1890–93, in the midst of the panic, and in spite of the most solemn resolutions of currency contraction, there was an increase of about 90 per cent in the circulation.

PAPER MONEY IN CIRCULATION, 1889–95 [1]

(Thousand pesos)

1889	$163,648	1893	$306,743
1890	245,100	1894	298,703
1891	261,408	1895	296,743
1892	281,609		

B. *The Balance of International Payments, 1890–95*

The balance of payments will require but little further comment since many of its details are scattered through the preceding pages of this chapter. The outstanding facts are two: first, the virtual cessation of borrowing, resulting in an excess of interest charge over new borrowing; and second, the overturn of the trade balance from "unfavorable" to "favorable." We may consider first the facts of borrowings.

Government foreign loans there were none. These ceased, in fact, in 1889 for a period of fourteen years. There was indeed a very considerable increase in the figures of the foreign debt, viz.:

INCREASE OF THE FOREIGN DEBT, 1891–1900

(Thousand gold pesos)

December 31, 1891	$204,959 [2]
December 31, 1900	389,069 [3]
Increase	184,106

None of this large increase, however, represents new borrowings. It is simply the result of the numerous arrangements of obligations contracted during the eighties. The chief of these arrangements were the taking over of the provincial debts and

---

[1] *Extracto Estadístico*, 1915, p. 297.

[2] *Memoria de Hacienda*, 1891, i, p. 207; Finance Minister Hansen's report.

[3] *Anuario Estadístico del Comercio y de la Navegación*, 1900, p. 282. *Anuario Pillado*, p. 120, gives total circulation of foreign debt on June 30, 1900, as $386,003,665 (gold) and gives the total emission of Argentine foreign debt to that date as $413,836,544 (gold).

the rescission of railway guarantees by means of bond issues.[1] For our purpose, this increase of the foreign debt is of interest solely for the reason that it served ultimately to swell the annual service to be remitted to Europe. So far as new borrowing is concerned, the sphere is confined to internal loans,[2] government short-time loans, and private investment. All told, the amount was small, some $36,000,000 gold in the period 1891–95.

One would expect, therefore, to find a large deficit in the balance of borrowings. The deficit was indeed considerable, but owing to the numerous defaults of interest caused by the panic, not by any means so large as it should have been. As we have seen, a considerable part of the foreign capital invested in the late eighties became a dead loss in the collapse of 1890–91. Such especially was the case with provincial cédulas, the payment of

[1] The following is the list of these loans for the arrangement of debts previously contracted:

1. *Obras de Salubridad,* 1891, $31,874,976. Bonds given to creditors in payment and rescission of the contract for Buenos Aires Water Supply and Drainage Loan, underwritten by Baring Brothers & Co. in 1888. See *Memoria de Hacienda,* 1891, i, pp. 207–231.

2. Port of Buenos Aires Loan, 1892 (law of October 27, 1882). Emitted in 1892, £1,384,700, and in 1899, £615,300. Bonds delivered to Port Constructors, E. Madero & Sons, in quittance of construction costs. Later floated as a foreign loan, in April, 1903. See *Memoria de Hacienda,* 1898, pp. x–xi, and Tornquist's *Manual of Argentine Loans.*

3. 4 per cent Railway Guarantee Rescission Loans, 1896 and 1898, $58,-500,000. Tornquist's *Manual of Argentine Loans,* pp. 18–19.

4. Conversion of Provincial Debts; Laws of August 8, 1896, July 7, 1899, and January 5, 1900: total, $93,291,379. See Tornquist's *Manual of Argentine Loans,* pp. 20–26.

5. 4 per cent loan of 1898 for $7,700,000 (gold) to cancel obligations undertaken by the Banco Nacional in respect of the City of Buenos Aires Loan of 1884–88. See Tornquist's *Manual of Argentine Loans,* p. 21.

[2] Of internal loans there were two, the "Patriotic" Loan of 1891 and the Buenos Aires Municipal Loan for $25,000,000 in the same year. Following the usual practice of taking 90 per cent of these emissions as the part going abroad, we have the following, expressed in gold:

PART OF INTERNAL LOANS GOING ABROAD.

1891	$2,506,000
1892	1,992,000
1893	2,042,000
Total	$6,540,000

the coupons ceasing permanently. Until the end of the decade, provincial loans were in a like case; the list of the suspensions of interest began January 1, 1891, and by July 1 included practically all of the provincial loans.[1] The same thing occurred with municipal foreign debts, with one important exception, the $4\frac{1}{2}$ per cent Buenos Aires loan of 1888.[2] When we include the decrease of some $11,000,000 gold in the service on the national foreign loans and railway guarantees, because of the funding loan arrangement of 1891, we find that whereas the full interest charge on public and private foreign obligations should have been in 1891 some $60,000,000 gold, the actual payment was $31,475,000 gold. Yet in spite of this diminution of about one-half in the annual interest payment, the deficit in the balance of borrowings was considerable throughout the period.

The overturn in the balance of foreign borrowings in 1890 was followed in 1891 by an overturn in the balance of trade. Imports shrank from about $142,000,000 in 1890 to about $67,000,000 in 1891: meantime exports increased from about $100,000,000 to $103,000,000. The result was that the unfavorable balance of 1890, some $41,000,000 gold, was converted into a favorable balance of $36,000,000 gold in 1891. From that year to the present the trade balance has steadily shown an excess of exports over imports, except in one year, 1893.[3] This overturn, which was intimately connected with the cessation of borrowings, and the explanation of which forms one of the chief aims of this study, we must leave for analysis to later chapters devoted exclusively to foreign merchandise trade. Our present purpose

[1] In one or two instances "funding" arrangements were made, but soon lapsed; e. g., Entre Rios paid interest on its provincial and municipal debts in 1891 and 1892 in bonds of funding loans made in 1891, but in 1893 it suspended all service. Mendoza made a similar arrangement in August, 1892, with the same result. See *Anuario Pillado*, pp. 142–147.

[2] Interest on this loan was paid without any interruption, but amortization was not resumed till 1898. In 1891 and '92 amortization was paid in bonds of an internal municipal loan of 1891; thereafter amortization was paid in gold five years after due date.

[3] In a more recent year, 1911, the balance of trade was again unfavorable.

is to continue for the period of the Baring Panic the analysis of the relation between the balance of international payments and paper money, as reflected in the movement of the premium on gold; for it is upon the proof of the interrelation between these two factors that we shall base the subsequent discussion of the foreign trade.

The following table gives the balance of payments from 1890 to 1895:

BALANCE OF INTERNATIONAL PAYMENTS, 1890–95

(Thousand gold pesos)

Date	Balance of Borrowings 1	Balance of Trade 2	Balance of Payments 1 + 2
1890	−$14,846	−$41,422	−$56,268
1891	− 23,333	+ 36,011	+ 12,678
1892	− 15,873	+ 21,889	+ 6,016
1893	− 20,130	− 2,133	− 22,263
1894	− 30,577	+ 8,889	− 21,688
1895	− 20,952	+ 24,971	+ 4,019

C. *The Premium on Gold, 1891–95*

Given the facts of paper money and of the balance of international payments in the panic period, as just set forth, there remains to be determined the essential question, the relation between the two, as shown in the fluctuations of the gold premium. It should be said at the outset that in this period the situation is much less clear than in the earlier periods that we have reviewed. In 1884–85 the adverse balance of payments was the only possible explanation of the suspension of specie payments. Virtually all competent observers of the time, government officials and bankers, attributed the suspension to the fall of exchange, and counselled a restriction of borrowings as the solution of the crisis. In 1888–91 the situation was equally clear. Though some ascribed the rising premium solely to excessive issues of paper, while others emphasized gold speculation, and European observers pointed particularly to the large borrowings, the essential fact is that all of these factors worked toward the same end. Any one of them might drive up the premium. All together were bound to do so. I have given my opinion, based on an examination of all of these factors, that the *chief* reason for the depreciation of paper money even in that period was the cessation of borrowings, which brought a deficit in the balance of payments, drove down foreign exchange, and created a demand for gold for export.

This explanation, however, was not insisted upon to the exclusion of other factors. It may be admitted, without damaging the argument, that only a very large flow of borrowings sustained over a long period could have prevented the depreciation of paper money issued with the liberality which characterized the years of the Guaranteed Banks experiment. It is not intended, in any case, to deny that excessive issues of paper were an important cause of its depreciation, but merely to insist that it was by no means the sole cause, and that, contrary to the opinion of many Argentine writers, the balance of payments was also an important cause of currency depreciation,— in my judgment the most important single cause. And above all, the purpose of this first part of my study has been to make clear that there was an interrelation between paper money and the balance of international payments. It was no accident that large paper issues and large borrowings coincided in the decade of the eighties. They were but different forms of borrowing. And once paper had begun to depreciate, it was clear even to the government itself that disaster could be averted only by maintaining such a stream of borrowings as would bring gold to Argentina, and thus cause paper to appreciate in terms of gold. Our history of the panic has been mainly the story of the failure to maintain such borrowings, ending in the outflow of gold, the rapid rise of the premium, and the collapse of 1890 and 1891.

So far everything seems clear enough. But from 1891 on, the situation is much more complicated. In 1891 the premium on gold and the balance of international payments were not in accord with each other. (After a large adverse balance in 1890 we find a slightly favorable balance of payments in 1891, owing to defaults of interest payments and to the marked shrinkage of imports.) The discrepancy in that year, however, is scarcely a matter for surprise. The year 1891 was the worst year of the panic. The official banks collapsed, the governments defaulted. From July to October we have a general moratorium. The land-boom bubble had burst. Things seemed to have come to smash generally: the general feeling was one of "get-from-under." The high premium of 1891 [1] was the logical and inevitable result of the overhasty and speculative borrowings of previous years. Argentina had felt for the first time in 1890 the full weight of her external obligations, and the effect was too profound to be immediately counteracted, in the midst of bankruptcy and confusion.

We may accept the discrepancy between the gold premium and the balance of payments in 1891, therefore, without surprise. Our main concern will be to see whether *on the whole* the testimony of this period of panic bears out that of other periods by showing an interaction between the balance of payments and the value of paper money. In order to do so, attention must first be paid to other factors which might conceivably have dominated the movements of the premium; for in this period it is impossible to limit one's attention to any single set of forces. The situation was too complicated, too unstable, the ups and downs of the premium too violent and erratic to permit of a simple explanation. Every observer had a different theory. It is even difficult to discern the general trend of the premium. The yearly averages, obtained from the monthly averages published by the national department of statistics, were as follows:

YEARLY AVERAGES OF GOLD PREMIUM, 1890–95

1890	151%	1893	224%
1891	287	1894	257
1892	232	1895	244

The yearly averages indicate one thing clearly enough, that there was a clearly defined wave movement: a sharp rise to 1891 gives way to a considerable fall in 1892 and 1893; then there is a rise again in 1894, followed by another fall. Yet the yearly averages are in this period deceiving. They appear to indicate

[1] The yearly average of the gold premium in 1891 was 287 per cent, as compared with 151 per cent in 1890.

that in 1893 the premium was falling; that in that year, indeed, it reached its lowest point. Such was not the case. The general movement of the premium in that year was decidedly upward. On the other hand, the fall in 1892 was pronounced and continued. To get a more exact idea of the premium one must turn to the *monthly* averages, as shown in the chart on page 140. There it is seen that the premium reached its highest point in October, 1891, and that from that date through December, 1892, there is a marked decline; in 1893 and to the middle of 1894 the movement is upward; in 1895 the premium, though erratic, tends downward.

The explanation of this "zigzagging" is at first glance difficult. Some light is thrown upon it by foreign trade movements. The Argentine export season is roughly from November to June. The annual exports of the harvest, by increasing the supply of exchange, regularly tended during the season to raise the rate of exchange, and consequently to lower the gold premium. Since the exports were increasing relatively to imports, and therefore coming to play a more and more important part in the annual settlement of Argentine liabilities, there was to be expected a considerable fall in the premium during the export months, and a rise toward the end of the export season, or in the "off-season" months.

In a very general way, the chart is in conformity with these expectations, but only in a very general way. The chart indicates that the fall of the premium occurred usually before the export season had opened, as if in anticipation of it. In some years, moreover, as in 1894 and 1895, there is a pronounced decline of the premium in the mid-winter [1] months, when, the export market being entirely inactive, one would expect just the contrary. Here is proof enough that the Argentine commercial year of active and inactive seasons is not by itself a sufficient explanation of the movements of the gold premium.

Other explanations, and many of them, were given by observers at the time. The subject was one that interested the pocketbook of every business man engaged in international

[1] *I. e.*, June, July, August.

dealings with Argentina. And almost every theory advanced had some truth in it. When in February, 1892, it became known that Dr. M. Saenz Peña, a highly esteemed member of the Supreme Court, was to be the next President, the premium

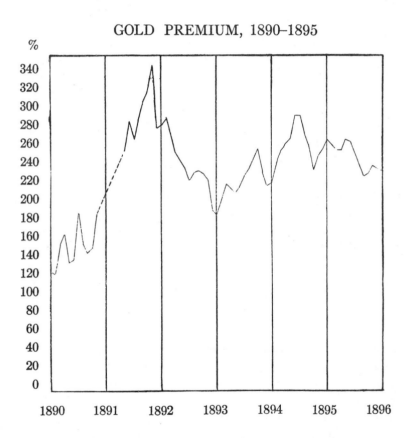

GOLD PREMIUM, 1890–1895

declined forty points within a month, and there were those who said that the gold premium depended simply on political conditions. Given a sound, honest government, the premium would vanish into thin air, and the paper peso be as good as gold. There was a grain of truth in this point of view. The paper peso would surely appreciate under wise political treatment; public confidence is a powerful factor in a depreciated-paper situation, though scarcely sufficient to make a paper peso worth about $0.25 become the equal of $1 gold without other forces coöperating. Concretely, the election of Saenz Peña did the following: it caused a deluge of gold to be thrown on the market, gold that came from the public hoarders of small sums who labored under the rooted delusion that politics is the main factor in currency matters.

Yet even about this election episode there is another side: for the correspondent of the London *Economist* said, "The tightness of the money market had at least as much to do with the fall of the premium as the announcement of Saenz Peña's candidacy." [1] He pointed to the fact that for two months, January and February, the Banco de la Nación had done no discounting, and that in addition there were private banks which "for reasons best known to themselves are not averse to seconding the views of the government by restricting their paper discounts when a fall in the gold premium suits the latter." [1] It appears from this, then, that the banks could cause paper to appreciate or depreciate, over short periods, by making it hard or easy to get; and that the government, through its official bank, played this game along with the private banks.

Then, there were the gold speculators, of whom we have spoken several times in this and preceding chapters. Working in so narrow a gold market as that of Buenos Aires, they could, by releasing or drawing in gold, seriously affect the premium temporarily; and this "rigging" was common practice, especially when it was known that the government must enter the market as a purchaser of gold in order to remit interest on its foreign liabilities.

This counterplay and interplay of forces is sufficient to explain why the rise and fall of the premium on gold should not have coincided with the movements of the export market. But these are only a few of many factors. There was the influence of the harvest: a superabundant harvest of wheat, or a good wool-clip, would give rise to optimistic hopes, which would be reflected in a fall of the gold premium. A poor prospect for the

[1] *Economist*, 1892, ii, pp. 416–417.

harvest would have just the contrary effect. Again, these fore-
casts of future conditions might not be connected in any way
with the harvest: they might be political, financial, or just a
vague feeling that things in general would get worse or better.
In any case, they affected the premium powerfully.

Thus the movements of the gold premium depended in part
upon what people thought was likely to happen to it months
hence. For instance, late in January, 1891, after the premium
had been rising all through 1890, the correspondent of the
Economist writes of "the conviction of our mercantile body (in
Argentina) that a further rise of the premium on gold this year
is inevitable. This conviction," he says, "is shared by the
public at large, especially by the producing classes. The wheat
farmers are steadily buying gold as they make sale of their crops.[1]
It is more than probable that the sheep farmers will do the same,
and thereby contribute to a further great depreciation of the
currency during the winter." [2] Such a conviction, natural enough
at a time when the panic was approaching its worst phases, was
the prevalent one in the business community. It was simply the
general desire to get hold of a sound money, since paper was
going to smash. It intensified the depreciation, already well
under way from other, more fundamental causes, and goes far
to explain why in 1891 the premium reached its highest point,
despite a favorable change in the balance of international payments.

The most powerful of these forces which exerted a temporary
influence upon the gold premium in this period, I have left till
the last: the operations of the European syndicates that had underwritten Argentine securities in the boom period. During the
panic, these securities were hopelessly depreciated; but a fall of
the gold premium would improve their salability. It would affect
paper-money securities, such as cédulas, directly, since the gold
value of these and of the interest payments upon them rose and
fell with the gold value of the paper money in which they were

[1] All transactions in cereals, wool, and the other exports took place in paper
pesos; chiefly in Buenos Aires and Rosario.

[2] *Economist*, 1891, i, p. 250.

payable. It would affect gold securities almost as much, though indirectly, by creating the impression that things were on the mend in Argentina, and that soon the government, the provinces, and the banks would be able to stand behind their obligations to their full extent. The opinion of the Rothschild Committee, receivers for Baring Brothers & Co., has already been cited,— that the solvency of Baring Brothers depended on the fall of the gold premium. The Barings had £5,818,662 of Argentine securities on their hands.[1] Other English and European houses were in a plight only less serious. The Funding Loan was intended to bring down the gold premium by taking the weight of the government's interest remittances off the exchange market. Other measures were also adopted, with a view to controlling artificially the movements of exchange and of the premium. Some competent observers regarded these operations by interested outsiders as the chief explanation of the movements of the premium in this period. The correspondent of the *Economist* inclined strongly at times to that opinion. In January, 1892, he says: "There is known to be on the way from England nearly a half-million sterling;" and he speaks of "the great noise made two months ago about the unlimited amounts of coin that the syndicate would send out." [2] A glance at the chart will show that the pronounced fall of the premium on gold began in November, 1891, coincidently with these rumors and shipments of specie. Shortly afterward, there was a pronounced rise in Argentine securities in the London market, increasing as the year 1892 went on.[3]

---

[1] *Economist*, 1892, ii, p. 1516: the official figures of the Rothschild Committee.

[2] *Economist*, 1892, i, p. 250.

[3] RISE OF ARGENTINE SECURITIES IN 1892

	Nov. 18, 1892	Lowest in 1892	Rise
1. Argentine 5% Customs Loan 1886....	72¾	58	14¾
2. Argentine 6% Funding Loan 1891....	72	49	23
3. Argentine 4½% Sterling Bonds......	41	27	14
4. National Cédulas (Series A gold)....	34½	20	14½
5. Buenos Aires 6% Loan 1884........	41	24	17

(See *Economist*, 1892, ii, p. 1447: Report of British Consul Bridgett.)

Reports of operations by European syndicates continued throughout the period. The comment of Mr. Bridgett, the British consul, was: "The European capitalists who are so deeply interested in the regeneration of this republic are making the same false move in applying their present stimulants to this country (i. e., booming Argentine securities in London) as they did in conceiving the three years' moratorium (the Funding Loan of 1891) now so generally condemned." [1] When the export market opened in the fall of 1892, "private bankers advanced several millions of gold pesos to speculators for the fall, to press down the market." [2] In the fall of 1893 it was reported that Baron Rothschild had opened a credit for the Argentine government of from £200,000 to £400,000, "to avoid the taking of large amounts of exchange at certain times of the year by the treasury, thus affecting the gold premium." [3]

These operations of speculators and European syndicates go far to explain the frequent and violent fluctuations of the premium in this period. They were undoubtedly the most powerful of the factors that exercised a *temporary* influence upon the value of the paper money. There appears to be no good reason, however, for assigning to them a more fundamental rôle. They do not explain that general zigzag movement displayed in the chart on page 140, the long fall to December, 1892, followed by almost as pronounced a rise to June, 1894. Were the activities of the European syndicate the dominant factor, one would expect the fall of the premium to continue; or at least one would not expect so pronounced a rise as that which we find to have taken place. The correspondent of the *Economist* whom I have quoted, himself expresses doubt at the end of 1892, in view of the protraction of the fall in the premium during that year, and remarks that "it is incontestable that in the past year affairs in Argentina have materially improved. Trade has steadily expanded, and financially the position has settled down to some extent."

Only a few months later, however, in the early months of 1893, the situation had again changed for the worse. The harvest was below normal. Exports in 1893 showed a decline; the trade

[1] *Economist*, 1892, ii, p. 940.   [2] *Ibid.*   [3] *Ibid.*, 1893, ii, p. 1535.

balance became slightly unfavorable. By the end of the year the foreign banks were shipping out gold.[1] Exchange was at a low rate, an unusual and anomalous situation at the moment when the busy export season was beginning; and it was being said in Buenos Aires that orders had been sent from London to the English banks to turn most of their large deposits of currency notes into gold. The premium had risen some sixty points in a twelvemonth, and, it was feared, would go higher. By June, 1894, the premium had risen to 289,[2] two points higher than the average of the panic year of 1891.

Yet the syndicate must have been as anxious as formerly to keep down the premium, and get the load of Argentine securities off their hands. The new credit of Baron Rothschild to the government late in 1893 is proof of the fact.

The truth of the matter appears to be that in 1892 the efforts of the syndicate were aided by the general improvement of conditions; or, to put the matter concretely, their efforts coincided with a favorable balance of international payments. In 1893 and 1894, on the other hand, the underlying conditions governing the exchange market were against them; the balance of payments had become unfavorable.

The movements of the balance of payments and of the gold premium were as follows:

BALANCE OF PAYMENTS AND THE GOLD PREMIUM, 1890–95
(Thousand gold pesos)

Date	Balance of International Payments	Gold Premium	
		Yearly Average	Trend
1890	—$56,268	151%	rising
1891	+ 12,678	287	rising
1892	+ 6,016	232	falling
1893	— 22,263	224	rising
1894	— 21,688	257	rising
1895	+ 4,019	244	falling

[1] *Economist*, 1893, ii, p. 1535: "One of the foreign banks here (Buenos Aires) has shipped home within the past week £70,000 to £100,000" (*Economist* of December 23, 1893).

[2] *Anuario de Estadistica del Comercio*, etc., 1896, ii, pp. 38–42.

The table requires little comment. With the exception of the panic year, 1891, the correspondence between the movements of the premium and those of the balance of payments is striking. The premium falls as the balance becomes "favorable," and rises as the balance becomes "unfavorable." We find in the balance of international payments a sufficient, and indeed the only, explanation of the fall of the gold premium in 1892, and of the rise in 1893 and 1894.

Before concluding, we must compare also the gold premium and the quantity of paper money. The large issues of paper and the circumstances that called them forth have been discussed. It will be recalled that the paper emitted was frankly inconvertible, consisting almost entirely of treasury notes. The following table shows the quantity of paper money in circulation on December 31st of each year from 1890 to 1895, together with the yearly averages of the gold premium:

PAPER MONEY IN CIRCULATION AND THE PREMIUM ON GOLD, 1890–95

(Thousand pesos)

Date	Paper Money in Circulation	Gold Premium	
		Yearly Average	Trend
1890	$245,100	151%	rising
1891	261,408	287	rising
1892	281,609	232	falling
1893	306,743	224	rising
1894	298,703	257	rising
1895	296,743	244	falling

It will be noted that after 1891 there is no correspondence whatever between the paper money in circulation and the gold premium. The fluctuations seem wholly erratic. An increase of some sixteen millions of paper pesos in 1891 is accompanied by an increase of one hundred and thirty-six points in the gold premium. But in 1892 and 1893 we have a much greater increase in the currency, some 45,000,000 pesos, accompanied by a decrease of sixty-three points in the gold premium. In the following year, 1894, the movements are reversed. Paper decreases eight millions while the premium increases thirty-three points. This period seems to offer the most ample proof that something besides excessive issues of paper money was responsible for these pronounced alterations in its value. If the excessive issues of paper under the Guaranteed Banks Law had brought on the state of affairs reflected in the high premium of 1891, as has been so often asserted by some writers; if, as declared by Martinez and Lewandowski, that high premium had nothing to do with the balance of international payments, how is one to explain the subsequent marked fall of the premium in spite of the large issues of government paper, frankly inconvertible, emitted in spite of the protest of the entire business community?

CHAPTER IX

THE SOLUTION OF THE PROBLEM OF PAPER MONEY

IN the closing years of the nineteenth century there was a slow but perceptible recovery from the effects of the Baring Panic. The export trade shows increasing vitality, though interrupted at times by locust pests, the bane of the Argentine farmer. The average annual value of exports in the five years 1896–1900 was 25 per cent greater than that of the first half of the decade.[1] Though the paper money in circulation remains about stationary, the gold premium shows a marked decline, from 257[2] in 1894 to 125[2] in 1899. Finally, by the Conversion Law of 1899, the problem of a shifting gold premium is definitely solved, and the paper peso given a stable value of $0.44 gold, which it has retained to the present day. In this period, we shall need to consider only such matters as bear directly upon the value of the paper money. We must explain, above all, the marked decline of the premium on gold.

I. THE BALANCE OF INTERNATIONAL PAYMENTS, 1895–1900

Among the early indications of recovery from panic conditions are the reports in the financial and trade journals of a renewal of foreign borrowings. European investors again turned toward Argentina, though in nothing like the stream of the preceding decade. The reports begin as early as 1895. The exact extent of the new investment is problematical, for the reason that its main direction was different from that of the earlier periods that have been reviewed. In those periods, as we saw, European capital went chiefly into government bonds and railroads; for which official data are available. In the nineties, on the other

---

[1] Average annual value of exports 1891–95: 107,000,000 pesos gold. Average annual value of exports 1896–1900: 134,000,000 pesos gold.

[2] Yearly average.

hand, there was not a single foreign loan,[1] national, provincial, or municipal. There was a large increase of the national foreign debt, as explained in the preceding chapter,[2] but none of it represented new borrowings. The increase was simply the result of the assumption of the provincial foreign debts by the nation, of the rescission of railway guarantees by means of bond issues, and of other similar arrangements of liabilities contracted during the preceding decade. The essential effect of these arrangements was to increase the interest charge on the foreign debt.

As to railroad investments, they show a moderate recovery, yet amount to only $48,500,000 (gold) in six years, 1895–1900. In the main, the new investment was in those various lines of enterprise which have in former periods been classed under the general head of "miscellaneous;" in tramways, gas and electric power and lighting, warehouses, drainage and water works, produce agencies, trading companies, and the like. It is to be noted, too, that the new capital does not come so preponderantly from a single source. The British financial and commercial supremacy in Argentina, though still very marked, begins to be challenged from the continent, and especially by Germany. The Banco Transatlántico Alemán was founded in Buenos Aires in 1893, with an authorized capital of 20,000,000 marks.[3] By 1900 it had branches in various parts of South America, in Valparaiso, Santiago de Chile, Concepción, Iquique, and Valdivia, all in connection with the Deutsche Bank of Berlin. In 1898 the Germans established the Compañia Alemána Transatlántica de Electricidad, with a capital of 10,000,000 marks, and the right to emit 1,000,000 marks of bonds. This company is today the chief provider of electric light and power in Argentina. In addition there were started a factory of meat extract, several factories of quebracho extract, the Hamburg-South American steamship line, and various commercial and in-

---

[1] There were some internal loans; and since 90 per cent of these went abroad, they will presently be taken into account. (See p. 151.)

[2] See Chapter VIII, p. 134, footnote 1.

[3] 12,800,000 marks was actually paid up by May, 1900. See *Anuario Pillado*, 1900, p. 184.

dustrial German houses. Señor A. B. Martinez [1] in 1904 stated that experienced bankers calculated the German capital employed in banks, commercial houses, "estancias" (cattle ranches), industrial establishments, and the like at $150,000,000 gold. He predicted a rapid increase of German capital, a prediction amply fulfilled since 1904.[1]

Less important, but considerable, was French and Belgian capital. An inventory quoted by Martinez puts the amount of this in 1904 at one hundred and eighty-five millions, including capital in government loans.[2] In addition, British capital shows a considerable increase. A very careful inventory of British capital made by the noted banking firm of Tornquist & Co. in 1900 puts the British capital in miscellaneous enterprise (i. e., outside of public loans and railways) at $102,000,000 gold.[3]

Year-by-year data on these miscellaneous investments are not obtainable; and, inasmuch as this capital constituted the chief item of borrowing in the last half of the nineties, it is impossible to draw up an exact balance of borrowings for the period. We may estimate, however, with a fair probability of correctness the average annual amounts on the basis of the inventories which I have mentioned. In 1892 we have Lamas' inventory and that of Finance Minister Hansen, which give for foreign capital, other than that in public loans, cédulas, and railroads, a total of $95,146,000 gold.[4] Comparing with the

[1] See *Censo General de la Ciudad de Buenos Aires*, 1905, p. 491 *et seq.* A. B. Martinez is Chief of the Bureau of Statistics of the city of Buenos Aires, and Director of the last National Census, begun in 1914; the author of several works on Argentine finance and the balance of payments in recent years, and, with Lewandowski, author of *Argentina in the Twentieth Century*, to which reference has several times been made in this study.

[2] *Ibid.*

[3] The same inventory gives the total British capital in Argentina in 1900 as $945,202,000, gold, distributed as follows:

Public loans	$366,215,000
Railroads	477,345,000
Miscellaneous	101,642,000

See *Censo General de la Ciudad de Buenos Aires*, 1905, p. 491 *et seq.*

[4] See Chapter VI, p. 92, and footnote 2.

computations of Tornquist in 1900 and of Martinez in 1904, we find an increase of at least $100,000,000 gold. Since little capital could have entered Argentina in the panic period, we may without danger of exaggeration estimate an annual investment in miscellaneous forms of enterprise of some $20,000,000 gold from 1895 to 1900. A verification of this estimate is afforded by that careful handbook, the *Anuario Pillado*.[1] A summing up of the paid-up capital and the bond issues of the foreign enterprises there mentioned as having been established in 1897 and 1898 gives the following results:

1897............................	$24,247,000 gold
1898............................	20,137,000 gold

The estimate of an annual "miscellaneous" investment of $20,000,000 gold, therefore, would appear to be no overstatement.

For the rest, the new railroad borrowings and the public loans, we have the official record. The railroad capital is given each year by the *Dirección General de Ferrocarriles*, which bases its figures on the annual reports of the railroads themselves. The public loans are, of course, officially recorded. Of these, there were only "internal" loans. Since, however, 90 per cent[2] of the internal loans went abroad, a word must be said about them before presenting the balance of borrowings.

The chief subject of interest in Argentina in the last five years of the century was the boundary dispute with Chile. In 1895 and again in 1898 the countries were very close to war. The dispute was finally settled by arbitration at the hands of Great Britain, but in the mean time the fear of war had occasioned large military and naval appropriations. Six cruisers, three destroyers, and three transports were added to the Argentine fleet in three years, 1896–98, at a cost of $17,855,000 gold.[3] The official reports of the finance ministry show a total of

[1] *Anuario Pillado*, 1900, pp. 176–182.

[2] See *Censo General de la Ciudad de Buenos Aires*, p. 491 *et seq.* The annual balance now computed by Tornquist & Co. also takes 90 per cent of the internal debt as held abroad.

[3] *Memoria de Hacienda*, 1898, p. 435.

"secret" appropriations for warlike purposes of $31,976,000 gold for the years 1895–98. The result was an annual piling up of budgetary deficits. By 1897 the deficit had reached $33,-458,000 paper and $13,407,000 gold.[1]

In part, this added burden was met by short-time loans contracted with bankers abroad.[2] A foreign loan of $30,000,000 gold was voted by Congress in 1898, but could not be floated on satisfactory terms, and was dropped. For the most part, the annual deficits were met by internal loans, of which there were four in this period, for a total of $86,000,000 [3] paper.

With so much of general detail, we may proceed to draw up the balance of international payments for the period from 1895 to 1909:

BALANCE OF INTERNATIONAL PAYMENTS, 1895–1900
(Thousand gold pesos)

Date	Balance of Borrowings			Balance of Trade			Balance of Payments (Cols. 3–6)
	1 Borrowings	2 Interest	3 Balance (Cols. 1–2)	4 Exports	5 Imports	6 Balance (Cols. 4–5)	
1895	$17,197	$38,149	—$20,952	$120,068	$95,096	+$24,971	+ $4,019
1896	37,144	39,863	— 2,719	116,802	112,164	+ 4,638	+ 1,919
1897	38,295	43,985	— 5,690	101,169	98,289	+ 2,880	— 2,810
1898	46,063	50,530	— 4,467	133,829	107,429	+ 26,400	+ 21,934
1899	24,966	54,698	— 29,732	184,918	116,851	+ 68,067	+ 38,335
1900	27,540	58,575	— 31,033	154,600	113,485	+ 41,115	+ 9,082

[1] *Memoria de Hacienda*, 1897, p. xxxvi *et seq.*

[2] *Ibid.* In 1897 there was an advance from Baring Brothers of £200,000; in 1898, one of £400,000; and in addition, a two-year 6 per cent loan of £800,000, to enable the government to redeem Puerto Madero bonds then in the hands of the constructor of the Buenos Aires harbor works.

[3] 1. Loan of 1894 for $15,000,000 (paper), subsequently increased to $22,200,000, and emitted in portions scattered over the next four years.

    2. Internal loan of 1898 for $45,818,000 (paper), to cover budgetary deficits.

    3. Loan of 1897 for $7,000,000 (paper), for the extinction of the locust pest, which caused havoc to the harvest of that year.

    4. Loan of $6,000,000 (paper) in 1898, for the payment of the debt of the National Government to the National Council of Education.

    5. Internal loan of the municipality of Buenos Aires, in 1897, for $5,000,000 (paper).

(See annual *Memoria de Hacienda*.)

The table indicates:

1. That, in spite of a renewal of borrowings, the balance of borrowings (Col. 3) shows a deficit, owing to the large and growing interest payments:

2. That this deficit is more than offset by the favorable balance of trade (Col. 6). Argentina is meeting her liabilities by the export of her agricultural and grazing products:

3. That upon combining the balance of borrowings with the trade balance we find that, with the exception of a single year, 1897, the balance of payments is favorable.

The unfavorable balance of 1897 is traceable to the diminution of exports in that year, owing to an unusually severe attack upon the wheat harvest by locust pests, which destroyed three-fourths of the crop.[1]

Granting that the balance of payments here given is imperfect, because of the necessity of relying upon estimates of "miscellaneous" foreign capital, there is every reason for thinking, nevertheless, that it represents the Argentine situation in this period with substantial accuracy. It is rather a remarkable fact that, with but one or two lapses of brief duration, exchange was above par throughout the period. In June, 1896, sterling exchange fell to 47; in May, 1897, to 47 7/16. Franc exchange fell below par only once, May, 1897, when it reached 4.97 francs, though in former years it was not rare, in the months in which the export trade diminished, to see it at 4.90 francs or even 4.85. Except in the mid-winter, off-season months of 1896–98, sterling remained steadily about 48, and francs about 5.[2] In 1889, sterling was as high as 48 7/16 in July, mid-winter. This fact of high exchange, as Dr. J. J. Romero[3] pointed out, "is a clear demonstration that the value of Argentine products sold in foreign markets has been superior to the consumption. In the word

---

[1] Wheat exported in 1897, $3,470,351, as compared with $22,368,900 in 1898, and over thirty-eight millions in 1898. The 1896 wheat exports were $12,830,027.

[2] *Extracto Estadístico*, 1915, p. 302.

[3] *La Nación* of May 27, 1905. Dr. Romero was twice finance minister.

'consumption,' I include not only the value of the imported articles, but also all that the country pays for the service of the
debt, the earnings of foreign enterprises, and the remuneration
of the capitals employed in all manner of exploitation. The
balances having been constantly favorable to us, foreign merchants have had to pay them in gold; and before our eyes exist
the quantities of gold arrived in the country during these latter
years."

The gold movement from 1895 to 1900 was as follows:

EXCESS OF IMPORTS OF GOLD OVER EXPORTS, 1895–1900 [1]
(Thousand pesos)

1895	$4,541
1896	3,884
1897	4,278[2]
1898	5,728
1899	1,744
1900	6,653
Net imports for period	$18,272

There was a considerable net inflow of gold in every year
except 1897, the only year when the balance of payments was
unfavorable. The generally high level of exchange and the
steady inflow of gold appear to me sufficient proof that a favorable balance of payments did in fact exist.

Under such favorable circumstances, a fall of the gold premium
was the logical expectation. The following table shows the balance of international payments, the premium on gold, and the
quantity of paper money in circulation from 1894 to 1900:

BALANCE OF PAYMENTS, GOLD PREMIUM, AND PAPER MONEY IN CIRCULATION,
1894–1900
(Thousand pesos)

Date	Balance of Payments	Gold Premium	Paper Money in Circulation (Dec. 31)
1894	—$21,688 (gold)	257%	$298,703
1895	+ 4,019	244	296,743
1896	+ 1,919	196	295,166
1897	— 2,810	191	292,704
1898	+ 21,934	158	292,047
1899	+ 38,335	125	291,342
1900	+ 9,082	131	295,166

[1] *Extracto Estadístico*, 1915, p. 203.   [2] Excess of exports over imports.

The quantity of paper money in circulation, it will be observed, was about stationary: yet the premium fell one hundred and twenty-seven points. On the other hand, in this period, as in the earlier ones that we have reviewed, the movements of the gold premium were in accord with the balance of international payments.

II. THE CONVERSION LAW OF 1899

The lowest point reached by the gold premium was 125 per cent. There is every reason for supposing that had matters been allowed to take their own course, paper money would have eventually come to a par with gold. Population has about doubled since 1890.[1] The export trade has steadily increased. In only one year, 1911, has there been an excess of imports over exports; in all other years there has been a favorable trade balance, ranging from $10,000,000 to $118,000,000 (gold), and averaging about $75,000,000.[2] This trade surplus has served to meet interest charges on borrowed capital. In addition, there has been a considerable inflow of new capital.[3] There is little doubt that in the great majority of years since 1900 the balance of payments has shown a considerable surplus in Argentina's favor. The subject has been one of great interest to Argentine financiers and statisticians; and a number of balances have been drawn up, all indicating a favorable balance of international payments.[4] Other indications support that view:

[1] Population is now about 8,000,000.

[2] In 1915, under abnormal war conditions, exports exceeded imports by $331,387,910 (gold). See *Extracto Estadistico*, p. 3.

[3] The Buenos Aires *Handels Zeitung*, 1908, calculated at $40,000,000 (gold) the new foreign capital annually invested in Argentina.

[4] Following are some balances of international payments calculated by Argentine statisticians and financiers in recent years:

1. A. B. Martinez: balance of 1904: shows a favorable surplus of $27,000,000 (gold).
2. A. B. Martinez: balance of 1908: shows a favorable surplus of $39,000,000 (gold).
*3. Tornquist's balance of 1914–15: favorable surplus, $159,000,000 (gold).
*4. Tornquist's balance of 1915–16: favorable surplus, $30,200,000 (gold).

* Sr. Tornquist's balances are for the economic year, October 1 to September 30; the other balances are for the calendar year.

the rates of exchange, almost always favorable to Argentina, and a steady net inflow of specie. The excess of imports of specie over exports for 1900–15 was about $290,000,000. In only one year, 1914, did specie exports exceed imports.[1]

Under such conditions, to repeat, paper money would eventually have come to a par with gold. Yet the gold premium of 125 was the lowest point that it ever reached. The explanation is to be found in the Conversion Law of 1899. This law was the result of a project formulated by Finance Minister J. M. Rosa,[2] and supported by ex-President Pellegrini and the well-known Argentine banker, Ernesto Tornquist. The plan was: (1) To fix a ratio according to which redemption of paper money should be made in specie; (2) to accumulate a metallic reserve sufficient to permit such redemption; (3) to maintain the ratio fixed upon by adding to the Caja de Conversión a bureau to act as a regulator of the currency, increasing or decreasing the amount of paper in circulation according to the amount of gold deposited.

Rosa's chief intention, it will be seen, was to put an end to the continual rise and fall of the premium on gold, so prejudicial to the commercial interests of the country: and to do so by establishing a system of conversion of paper into specie, not at

5. Dr. A. E. Bunge (Director General of National Statistics), balance of 1916: favorable surplus of $57,170,000 (gold).

6. Tornquist's balance of 1916–17: favorable surplus, $102,100,000 (gold).

7. Tornquist's balance of 1917–18: unfavorable surplus, $160,192,900 (gold).

The debit balance of 1917–18 was due to credit advances to France and England, and, to a less extent, to repayment of foreign capital invested in Argentina, as shown by the following figures:

	(Gold Pesos)
Loans to the governments of France and Great Britain,	$177,300,000
Reduction of foreign mortgage capital................	27,700,000
Repayment of short-term loans in the United States ...	20,000,000
Repatriation of Argentine securities..................	5,000,000

[1] For an analysis of the Argentine balance of payments and foreign exchange movements during the World War, see John H. Williams, "Latin American Foreign Exchange and International Balances during the War," *Quarterly Journal of Economics*, May, 1919, pp. 422–465.

[2] Finance Minister in General Roca's second term as President, 1898–1904. It will be recalled that Roca had been President from 1880 to 1886, during the period of monetary reform and the adoption of specie payments.

par, but at the then market rate; this ratio to be maintained without change from the day the conversion system should begin its operations.

The measure provoked a storm of controversy, such as perhaps has never been called forth by any other proposal or event in Argentine history. The speeches delivered on the subject in Congress fill six volumes. The plan was opposed by the press.[1] Five former finance ministers attacked it.[2] Dr. Frers renounced his ministry because of it. Dr. Terry, a former finance minister and professor of public finance in the National University, published a book against it. Petitions of merchants and industrials with four thousand signatures appealed to Congress to defeat the bill. Similar petitions were formulated by the Chamber of Commerce of the Stock Exchange, and by the Italian and French Chambers.

There is no occasion for our entering into the details of this conflict. It was argued that the conversion plan of 1876 had failed, owing to the fact that the metallic reserve had been violated to meet the pressing need of the government;[3] the same result, it was said, might be expected on this occasion. The earlier conversion system had merely served to increase the currency some 400,000,000 pesos, so that upon its failure in 1876 paper money was in a worse state of depreciation than ever. That, too, might happen again.

Moreover, conversion at the premium then existing would be a partial act of bankruptcy. Excluding amortizations, there had been issued between 1883 and 1891, 322,900,000 paper pesos. According to the premium on gold existing on the dates of the various emissions, this amount represented a sum of $187,324,000 gold. In converting the paper at the existing premium, 127 per cent, the Argentine government was a debtor only in the sum of $141,076,000, reducing thus its original debt by 25 per cent.[4]

[1] Led by the distinguished newspaper *La Nación*.

[2] Dr. Wenceslao Escalante, Dr. José A. Terry, Dr. Emilio Hansen, Dr. Victorino de La Plaza, and Dr. W. Pacheco.

[3] See Chapter III, p. 29.

[4] Jacques Lyons, *Mélanges Financiers* (Paris), p. 813.

This criticism is irrefutable. Yet its force is more apparent than real. The present holders of the notes were not the original ones, since the notes had passed from hand to hand for years. Conversion at the market rate represented no loss, from this source, to any namable person.

The chief objection made was that the conversion plan was artificial and therefore unsound, a violation of "economic law." Only by the increase of national wealth, it was said, and of population, by the natural process of "growing up to the currency," could a sound currency be obtained. Since, in the case of Argentina, increased national wealth is another term for increased foreign trade, the essential condition of development in all South American countries, what was really meant was that the fundamental condition of a sound paper currency was a favorable balance of international payments; and the contention was made that the currency would never attain a sound basis until this process had been allowed gradually to bring paper to par.

Dr. Terry advised conversion on a sliding scale, which should gradually approach par. Such a plan would have maintained the existing instability of paper money, and would have sanctioned, rather than solved, the essential difficulty,— that of a currency whose value was in a process of continual change.

There was no attempt to deny, on the part of Dr. Rosa and his supporters, the efficacy of increased national production in reducing the gold premium. It was, indeed, because of the very effectiveness of that process that the conversion measure was projected. For the marked decline of the gold premium in 1898–99 promised to be even more prejudicial to the economic interests of the country than had been its violent ascent in the years preceding the Baring Panic. Paper money had been debased for so long, and to so great a degree (the average premium for 1890–99 was 235 per cent), that the prices of goods and services, in fact the whole economic life, had become molded to the high premium. For paper money so markedly and for so long depreciated to be placed suddenly on a par with gold would have produced general perturbation. On the other hand, a rate of conversion according to the present market value of the paper would merely legalize the state of things which was then existing, and which had existed for so many years; and thereby would prevent the ruin of all the interests that had become bound to this situation.

The problem of a return to a specie basis under such circumstances is a fairly familiar one, and in no case where the paper money has been markedly and for a long period depreciated has the paper been redeemed at its face value. Russia in 1839 and more recently, Austria in 1811 and 1819, France in the past century, all returned to specie payments by fixing the premium on gold according to its market value.[1]

Fundamentally, this conversion controversy had its roots in a matter which will form the main theme of the final portion of this study,— the conflicting interests of exporters and importers. Exporters expended their costs in paper and sold the product abroad for gold. The prices of services were less sensitive to fluctuations of the premium on gold than were the prices of products. When the gold premium was rising, therefore, the receipts from the sale of their product abroad represented to exporters a margin of profit attributable to the rise of the premium. For instance, producers for export who expended their costs in paper when wages and domestic prices were by force of habit or inertia on the basis of a 200 per cent premium, and sold their product with gold at a premium of 250 per cent, profited to the extent of the difference. A fall of the premium would affect them in the contrary manner.

Importers were in just the opposite position. With a rising premium, they found the burden of paying for their purchases from abroad in gold more onerous; with a falling premium their purchases cost them less. In the same position as the importers were the industrial enterprises. They, too, were operating on a paper basis, the currency of the country. Their remittances abroad, however, in the form of dividends or of interest on bonds,

[1] Ordinarily the method has been to create a new gold coin having a less gold content than the old. Argentina has gone about it the other way: she has preserved her gold peso, as created in 1881; and has fixed the paper peso at the market rate of 1899, $0.44 gold (*i. e.*, gold was taken as at a premium of 127.27 per cent, or, as it is customarily expressed in Argentina, gold was at a price of 227.27 per cent paper).

were in gold. The gold value (the only value that matters to the foreign investor) of a 5 per cent railroad dividend, for example, depended on the gold value of Argentine paper money. With paper appreciating, the value would be more; with paper depreciating, the value would be less. The value of Argentine railroad or other industrial bonds would be affected in consequence of this necessity for comparison of the domestic paper currency and the international monetary standard, gold.

These two opposing classes of interests bulked large in the monetary controversy, and they go far to explain its virulence. Especially loud was the cry of the producers and exporters in 1898. In August, 1898, gold was at a premium of 176 per cent; in December of the same year it had fallen to 112 per cent. Such a pronounced decline, at the very opening of the export season, raised a cry of protest from the producers, who, having laid out their costs with gold a good fifty points higher than the premium reigning at the opening of the season, faced the prospect of being unable to compensate themselves by the sale of their products.

Dr. Rosa's measure was passed.[1] The government promised to redeem all paper money at the rate of 227.27 (44 centavos gold for a paper peso). The accumulation of a redemption fund was provided for, and a redemption bureau established in connection with the Caja de Conversión, which was to exchange gold for paper and paper for gold, at the rate mentioned, to any one presenting either gold or paper. A subsequent act has set the limit of the redemption fund at $30,000,000 in gold.[2] The accumulation of the fund has been steady; by 1910 the full limit set was attained.

The fund was intended solely for the redemption of the paper currency issued and in circulation prior to the passage of the

[1] On the Conversion Law of 1899 the best source is J. M. Rosa's *La Reforma Monetaria en la República Argentina*, 1909. See also Martinez and Lewandowski, *Argentina in the Twentieth Century*, p. 483 *et seq.*; and Emilio Hansen, *La Moneda*, 1916.

[2] Only once has the conversion fund been threatened. In 1902, when war with Chile again seemed inevitable, the government withdrew some $12,000,000, which it replaced (ten millions of it) in 1903. The danger which wrecked the first conversion attempt, that of 1876, has thus been avoided.

Law of 1899,— some $295,000,000. All subsequent issues were to be made by the new bureau in exchange for gold deposited with it. At present, the paper money circulation is $1,165,-278,000 (paper),[1] based on a conversion fund of $393,798,000 (gold), a guarantee of 76.8 per cent[2] of the total fiduciary circulation.

The Conversion Law of 1899 has definitely killed the fluctuating gold premium of former years. There is no more speculation in gold, no more buying and selling of gold on the Stock Exchange. Most important of all, industry and the business community generally are released from the state of uncertainty and instability which forms the worst feature of a régime of debased currency. Essentially, it mattered nothing to the business man whether the paper peso was worth $0.25 gold or a full gold peso *today*. The really injurious circumstance was that he had no means of knowing what it would fetch *tomorrow;* but had to allow always in his calculations for this unpredictable, always shifting factor of unstable currency. Since 1899 there has been no such problem in Argentina.

In conclusion, it may be pointed out that a prominent force in assuring the success of the Conversion Law has been the succession of favorable balances of international payments which Argentina has enjoyed. The increase of the gold reserve depends directly on that circumstance, and the maintenance of the conversion system itself depends upon the maintenance of that reserve. It is still conceivable that a succession of unfavorable balances, prolonged over as long a period as that of the favorable balances of the last twenty years, would, by draining off the gold reserve, again raise the problem of paper currency. Under such difficult circumstances one is permitted to wonder whether the specie in the Caja de Conversión would continue to be regarded as an inviolable fund.

But such a contingency is perhaps one of merely academic interest. There is no reason for anticipating any pronounced

[1] Ernesto Tornquist y Ca, *Business Conditions in Argentina*, No. 145 (1919).

[2] *I. e.*, of the *gold value* of the paper money, which is $512,728,000 (these are figures of July 31, 1919).

change in the balance of international payments; at least no succession of unfavorable balances.

It is interesting to conclude the consideration of this problem of the relation between inconvertible paper money and the balance of international payments with a quotation from Martinez and Lewandowski.[1] In commenting upon the conversion plan, they make reference to the criticisms made in some quarters at the rapid increase in the paper money circulation since the law went into operation, which has given rise to the cry that such large emissions may even yet bring back the old problem of debased currency. The reply of these writers is as follows:

> But it is easy to understand that those alarms are not justified, from the moment in which such emissions are guaranteed by a corresponding deposit in gold in the Caja de Conversión. Besides, if one reflects a little, one cannot do less than recognize that, the product of the surplus of the economic balance of the country being every day more important, this surplus will have an influence on the monetary situation, even though, instead of being conserved in the Caja de Conversión, the surplus should be found in the strong boxes of the private banks.

Evidently, a favorable balance of payments is recognized as a factor in maintaining the value of the paper currency, even though in a previous chapter it is denied by these writers that the unfavorable balances of the eighties and of the panic period were a factor in its debasement.

[1] Martinez and Lewandowski, *Argentina en El Siglo XX*, p. 499.

CHAPTER X

THE RELATION BETWEEN THE VALUE OF PAPER MONEY AND THE BALANCE OF INTERNATIONAL PAYMENTS: A GENERAL SURVEY

IN the preceding chapters we have reviewed the entire period of inconvertible paper money, from the suspension of specie payments in January, 1885, to the Conversion Law of 1899. It was convenient for the adequate description and analysis of the various special phases of the period to divide into three periods of about five years each. The first (1885–90) was the period of the "boom,"— of heavy borrowings, large issues of paper money, extravagant speculation in land and in gold. The second (1890–95) was the period of the Baring Panic,— of the cessation of foreign borrowings, the collapse of the National Bank system, the temporary bankruptcy of the federal government and of the provinces. Finally, we have reviewed the period (1895–99) of slow recovery from the crisis,— in which borrowing begins again on a moderate scale and the export trade shows signs of extraordinary development, and in which, at last, the problem of a fluctuating paper currency is solved by the Conversion Law.

In each of these periods we have considered principally a single problem, the relation between the balance of international payments and the value of inconvertible paper money; giving attention to the special phases of the problem as they manifested themselves under the peculiar conditions which characterized each period. It is convenient now, before turning away from this problem, to take a general survey of the whole period during which inconvertible paper existed (1885–99) and to trace through it the central idea of the preceding chapters. Such a survey may best be put in the form of diagrams.

The chart on the following page compares the quantity of paper money in circulation in each year with the yearly averages of the gold premium. It indicates at a glance to what extent the changes in the value of paper money (as shown by the movements of the gold premium) are ascribable to changes in its quantity, and to what extent they clearly are not.

No attempt has been made to draw the two curves to the same scale. A common unit of measure could scarcely be found for such unlike entities as quantity of paper and percentage of pre-

PAPER MONEY IN CIRCULATION AND GOLD PREMIUM, 1885–1899

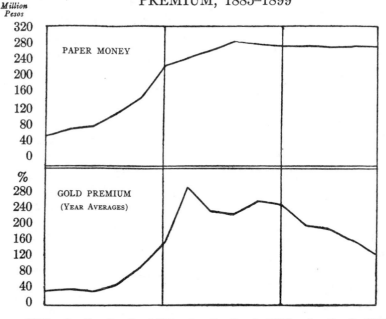

mium on gold; and in any case such a unit would have no significance, since it is not the relative degree of change in the two curves, but rather the direction of change which is significant. Quantity of paper is therefore represented in millions of pesos, and the gold premium in percentages.

Between 1885 and 1887 paper money increases some 20,000,000 pesos; the gold premium remains about stationary (declining from 37 per cent in 1885 to 35 per cent in 1887). Then comes the great expansion of the currency, beginning with the passing of the Guaranteed Banks Act in November, 1887. The rise of the curve of paper money is paralleled, up to 1891, by a rise of the premium on gold. But from this point on, agreement between the two curves ceases. Paper money continues to increase until 1893; but the gold premium falls sharply after 1891. In 1894, there is a slight contraction in the quantity of paper, but the gold premium rises to an average surpassed only by that of 1891. After 1894 the quantity of paper is about stationary; but the gold premium falls steadily to 1899.

It is in only one period, then, that quantity of paper money and the gold premium are in accord with each other, the period just preceding the Baring Panic. And in this period, as we have seen, *every* factor that could cause the premium on gold to ascend was operating.

We turn now to a comparison of the fluctuations of the premium on gold with those of the balance of international payments. On the following page are shown the curves of these two factors, the balance of payments being measured in millions of gold pesos and the gold premium in percentages. The line drawn through the center of the diagram represents the point at which total "credits" and "debits" are equal. Below this line the balance is "favorable" to Argentina; that is, credits (borrowings plus exports) exceed debits (interest charge plus imports). Above the line debits exceed credits.

The two curves display marked similarity with each other throughout the period. When the balance is "favorable" to Argentina (to 1888) the gold premium is low. When the balance turns against Argentina, reaching its climax in the large "unfavorable" balance of 1890, the gold premium rises sharply. The fall and the rise of the balance between 1890 and 1894 is matched approximately by a fall and a rise of the premium on gold. And the decline of the premium in the last five years (1894–99) is matched by a corresponding change in the balance of payments from unfavorable to favorable.

At only one or two points is there serious disagreement between the two curves. In 1891 the balance is favorable, but the premium rises. This divergence we have ascribed to the panic conditions of that year, which were chiefly due to the large borrowings of preceding years, which reached their climax in the large unfavorable balance of payments in 1890. It is worth recalling also the fact that the favorable balance of 1891 was entirely due to the de-

BALANCE OF PAYMENTS AND GOLD PREMIUM, 1885–1899

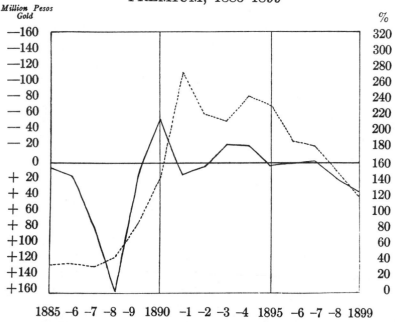

——— = Balance of Payments
- - - - = Gold Premium

faults of interest by the governments and the banks in that year, which reduced the interest from about $60,000,000 gold (the full amount owed) to about half that sum.

Again in 1893 there appears to be serious disagreement. The balance becomes unfavorable, but the premium falls. This divergence, however, is more apparent than real. The fall of the premium is due entirely to the use of the yearly averages.

The yearly average of 1893 is less than that of 1892. In fact, however, as was explained in Chapter VIII (see chart, p. 140) the premium on gold rose continuously in 1893 after having fallen continuously in 1892.

Viewing the general course of the two curves, without fixing one's attention upon specific years, the similarity between them stands out clearly, and appears to warrant the conclusion reached by more detailed analysis in preceding chapters, that the balance of international payments did in fact exercise a powerful influence upon the value of Argentine inconvertible paper money.

PART II

INCONVERTIBLE PAPER MONEY

AND

THE BALANCE OF MERCHANDISE TRADE

CHAPTER XI

SOME FURTHER DISCUSSION OF PRINCIPLES

AT the beginning of this study the thesis announced for investigation was international trade under a régime of depreciated paper money. Given a change in the balance of international payments, what is its effect upon foreign trade, and by what mechanism is that effect brought about? In Chapter II it was found convenient for purposes of exposition to divide the problem into two parts, for separate treatment:

(1) The relation of changes in the balance of international payments to the paper currency; and

(2) the relation of the paper currency to the balance of foreign merchandise trade.

In other words, a change in the balance of international payments effects, first of all, a change in the value of paper money. The changes in the value of the paper money effect, in turn, changes in exports and imports. Such, briefly, is the theoretical framework upon which the present inquiry is organized.

The first part of the process, the first step in the chain of consequences whereby a change in the balance of international payments affects the balance of merchandise trade, we may consider as completed in Part I. The particular change studied in the Argentine case has been that in the balance of foreign borrowings. Borrowings have been shown to have been of such great extent and so long continued as to dominate the balance of payments. And the balance of payments, in turn, has been shown to have dominated the fluctuations of the value of paper money.[1]

___

[1] Other factors, of course, were present and operative, notably the large issues of paper in the late eighties and early nineties. There is no attempt to deny their importance in the depreciation of the currency that occurred in that period. Excessive issues, however, do not explain the suspension of specie payments in 1885;

The first effect of Argentine borrowing operations, therefore, was upon the currency. We may proceed now to our second proposition: to consider how these borrowings, operating through their effect upon the currency, brought about changes in the balance of merchandise trade. Until now, the foreign trade has been passed over without comment. Such allusion as has been made to it has been merely what was necessary for the computation of the balance of payments. Nothing has been said as to the reasons for the fluctuations of exports and imports, and particularly for the overturn in the trade balance in 1891. Yet from the point of view of the theory of international trade under depreciated paper, this overturn constitutes the crux of the problem. Until 1891 Argentine imports regularly exceeded exports; from that date onward, except in 1893 and 1911, exports as regularly have exceeded imports. Why did the change come about? And more particularly, how, without the usual mechan-

---

nor the peculiar movements of the gold premium in the early nineties, which were just the contrary of what the facts of paper issue would lead one to expect; nor the fall of the premium in the later nineties, when the quantity of paper in circulation was stationary. All in all, surveying the whole twenty-year period, the balance of payments, and within that balance the borrowings, appears to have exercised a dominating influence upon the value of the currency.

Nor is there anything extraordinary in this conclusion. The phenomenon of the depreciation of paper money presumes the conversion of one money into another, the comparison of the domestic money with the international. That comparison is established almost exclusively, especially in the case of a country dependent on foreign commerce as is Argentina, on the occasion of external transactions. The balance of international accounts must equilibrate cost with cost. The country on a basis of "forced currency" must, if it is in a debtor position, find the means of meeting its foreign charges in a money acceptable to the foreigner. At the outset, at any rate, it must meet them in gold. The outflow of gold increases its price in terms of paper: the specie premium rises in consequence. Such was the position of Argentina during the two crises we have studied, in 1885 and in 1890–91, when an excess of interest charge over new borrowings produced an unfavorable balance of payments. A favorable balance, by bringing in gold and thus lowering its price, causes paper to appreciate. Such was the situation in Argentina from 1885 to 1888, when the premium remained almost stationary despite large emissions of paper, and in the late nineties, when the premium declined steadily despite the absence of any contraction in the circulation of paper. Throughout the twenty-year period 1880–1900, as we have seen, the movements of the premium on gold are in entire accord with the balance of international payments, and with no other factor.

ism presupposed in most discussions of international trade, could the change have come about?

It is not necessary to review again the entire theory of the case, which has already been given with sufficient fullness in Chapter II. It is enough to recall the statement there made that the explanation of the overturn of the Argentine trade balance was to be sought in an investigation of prices and costs. Let us note, therefore, the difference between the situation we are analyzing and that of gold countries, as regards money and price changes. It will have been observed that the shiftings in the value of money described in Part I were precisely the opposite of those that would occur in gold countries as the result of changes in the balance of payments. According to the theory of foreign trade between gold countries, a change in the balance of payments in favor of a country (such a change as new borrowings by Argentina) causes gold to flow to that country and raises the price level, with the result that exports are discouraged and imports encouraged. An unfavorable change, by causing gold to flow out, lowers the price level of the country, encouraging exports and discouraging imports. Exactly the opposite price changes are to be expected in paper money countries, says theory; and the present inquiry supports that conclusion. A favorable balance of payments causes paper money to rise in value, which is equivalent to saying that it causes the price level to fall; and an unfavorable balance causes the price level to rise, the extent of the rise being indicated with rough accuracy by the premium on gold.

In spite of this diametrical opposition in the direction of the price changes, however, the *same* result as regards foreign trade ensues as would occur in gold countries. With a favorable balance of payments, caused by new borrowings, the imports of the borrowing country are increased, and the exports discouraged; and with an "unfavorable" change in the balance of payments the contrary set of shifts occurs. Imports diminish and exports increase.

The explanation of these trade changes, then, involves a study of the price changes: of export and import prices as compared with domestic prices, and, most important of all, of export and import prices as compared with the price of labor and other costs. How does a paper currency, whose value is shifting under the influence of a change in the balance of payments, affect these various price categories? The answer to this question will be an answer to our second proposition: that changes in the value of paper money effect changes in the foreign trade.

The explanation of theory is that a depreciating paper currency operates like a protective duty. To the exporter it acts like a bounty; to the importer, as an added cost. The result is to encourage exports and diminish imports. These effects of depreciating paper on foreign trade grow out of the fact that the prices of commodities, and especially of those commodities that enter into foreign trade, are more sensitive to fluctuations in the value of the currency than are wages, rent, and other costs of production. To take the case of export prices: the Buenos Aires prices of wheat, wool, and other exports are reflections of the international prices of these products. Buenos Aires does not fix the foreign price; Argentine production is too small to control the world market. The Buenos Aires price is the international price, minus cost of transportation to the foreign consuming market. The international price is a gold price; the Argentine price is a paper money reflection of that price. Aside from transportation cost, therefore, the Argentine price represents a calculation in terms of paper, at the current premium on gold and the current rate of exchange, of the foreign gold price. It would seem obvious, therefore, that export prices would move in close accord with the premium on gold. When the premium rises, export prices rise; and vice versa. Costs, on the other hand, especially wages and rent, respond but sluggishly to fluctuations of the premium. When the premium is rising, therefore, the exporter and the producer receive an increased profit, represented by the difference between the increase in the paper price of their product and the much smaller increase in the paper price of their costs of production. In other words, to repeat, the exporting and producing classes receive, so long as their costs in paper remain unchanged, a "bounty" in consequence of the depreciation of paper money. The natural consequence is an increase of exports.

The importer is affected in the contrary manner. He buys abroad and must pay gold, or gold's worth by bill of exchange. The amount of his foreign payment, therefore, depends on the value of his paper money. When paper is at par, a bill of exchange for £1000 will cost him $5040. If paper falls 50 per cent, the bill will cost him $10,080. As the paper money depreciates, therefore, he must continuously advance the price of his imported goods; with a resultant falling off in sales. Moreover, the importer becomes afraid to buy abroad on credit, for he does not know what his bill of exchange will cost him in paper money when settlement day arrives. He is afraid, too, to sell on credit at home; for he cannot foretell what may be the value of the paper peso when the time comes for his customers to pay. The result is that some importers go out of business. Those who stay on are forced in spite of themselves to speculate on the ups and downs of the premium on gold.

A depreciating paper, then, is hailed with delight by the exporters, the farmers, the mining interests, by all those who, having little to import, expend their costs in paper money, and sell abroad in gold. They are enriched by a rising gold premium. The importers and those industrial interests, as railroads, who must make payment abroad instead of receiving payment from abroad, are injured.

When paper begins to appreciate in terms of gold, the situation is just the reverse. The exporting and producing classes find their "bounty" taken from them. If the appreciation is violent, they may find themselves forced to sell their products at prices which do not cover their costs. The importer, on the other hand, is in his heyday. His paper money buys more goods abroad; his home credits yield a greater sum. And unless he is strongly pushed by competitors, he will not lower his prices with the same prompt enthusiasm with which he raised them in the days when the gold premium was going upwards. The falling premium is a bounty to the importer, and a burden upon the exporter. Imports increase relatively to exports.

Such, in brief, is the theory. It will be noted that the *extent* of the depreciation of paper is not the significant matter. Whether the gold premium be high or low is of little importance, if only it will stay so, in order that all prices and costs may have time to mold themselves to the new situation; in order that wages, for instance, may catch up with the price of commodities. The bounty to the exporter, for example, consists not in a high premium on gold, but in a *rising* premium. In other words, this whole matter of the effect of depreciated paper on prices and foreign trade is one that concerns the "transition stage," of which mention has been made: the period between the old equilibrium of the balance of payments and the new one which will result from the shifts of exports and imports.

As regards this term "transition stage," however, one must be cautious of too precise statement. Experience shows that even in gold-standard countries transitions between states of equilibrium in the balance of payments may be of considerable duration. Their effects, too, may be so overlaid by other forces operating simultaneously that they are scarcely capable of precise, statistical definition. The difficulty of precisely delimiting or describing transition stages under conditions of inconvertible paper money is immeasurably greater than in gold countries. A paper money régime is in its essence abnormal. It is a state of flux and change. Values are unstable, their direction scarcely predictable from one day to the next. So long as paper is depreciated, so long as there is no machinery for its conversion into specie at a fixed rate of exchange, so long will it continue to fluctuate from day to day. Underlying the continual oscillation, however, there would seem to be a more or less definite value which might be described as its ruling norm. It is this norm that we have sought in striking the yearly averages of the gold premium, and it is this norm that we have compared with the balance of payments, year by year. Yet even the yearly averages show little tendency to "settle down." There is a more or less steady fall of the premium from 1891 to 1899 ; the likelihood is that if the paper peso had not been given a definite value in 1899 by the Law of Conversion, it would have continued to appreciate, under the influence of a succession of favorable balances of payments, until eventually it would have arrived at a par with gold. Short of conversion at a fixed rate, however, whether at par or at $0.44 gold as at present (it scarcely matters which), it would have been idle ever to expect the general level of values to settle. In other words, a "state of equilibrium" in an inconvertible paper money situation would appear to be an impossibility: at least it is impossible whenever and so long as paper money is depreciated below a par with gold, and no arrangement for its conversion at a fixed and permanent rate has been provided.[1] This matter of the inherent instability of a paper money situation, however, is perhaps too obvious to need much comment.

The theory of our problem has been stated with sufficient fullness for the purposes of this study. In the chapters that follow we shall seek verification of it in a study of the Argentine foreign trade in its relation to price and wage movements.

[1] Yet the serious losses occasioned by the pronounced fall of the premium in 1898 are proof that underneath the continual oscillation of the premium there was a more or less definite norm of value to which the economic life of the country had been adapted. For about fifteen years paper had been depreciated, and most of the time the yearly averages of the premium had ranged above 125; the country's business had molded itself to a high premium.

CHAPTER XII

THE FOREIGN TRADE : SOME GENERAL CONSIDERATIONS

MENTION has already been made of the importance of foreign trade in the economic life of Argentina. The activity of the republic is reflected in the figures of exports and imports. Its industrial enterprises, its railroads, its river traffic, its ports, its commercial centers, the finances of the government, all depend for their prosperity upon the fluctuating fortunes of the foreign trade.

In the period of our study Argentina was, and it still is, a purely agricultural and grazing couńtry. It has no coal and iron in workable quantities. The development of manufactures on any considerable scale, aside from the elaboration of its food products, appears improbable. Argentine economic life seems destined for a long time to come to continue in the channel that it has pursued in the past; namely, an exchange of its agricultural and grazing products, either in the raw state or as elaborated food products, for the manufactured products of the outside world. The volume and the terms of this exchange will continue to be the index of its economic wealth and growth.

Before attempting to make use of the statistics of foreign trade, something should be said as to their reliability and the method of their computation. Though trade statistics have been officially compiled since 1864, it is only in very recent years that care has been taken to insure their accuracy. It is a matter of common knowledge, much commented upon by Argentine writers, that the published statistics of "value of imports" are at best only a rough approximation to the actual market value. Martinez and Lewandowski estimate that the error has been usually on the side of exaggeration, the official figures sometimes exceeding the real figures, in their judgment, by 20 per cent.

On the other hand, some recent computations made by Dr. Bunge, the present director general of statistics, indicate that from 1910 to 1913 the official "value of imports" was from 8 to 18 per cent below the proper value, which Dr. Bunge has computed on the basis of the actual prices of the more important imported products in the Buenos Aires market. The divergence, as set forth by Dr. Bunge, was progressive; that is, the "value of imports" of 1910 understated the true situation by 7.8 per cent; those of 1911, by 10.4 per cent; 1912, 16.1 per cent; and 1913, 17.7 per cent. Under the abnormal price conditions of the war the divergence was much greater, attaining in 1916 the astounding figure of 68.4 per cent.[1] These discrepancies are an indication that while import prices since 1910 have been rising, the bases of the official computation have remained practically unchanged.

The bases of the official statistics of "value of imports" are the customs valuations. The Argentine government depends chiefly upon import duties for its revenue. The duties range at present from 5 to 50 per cent ad valorem[2]; and in addition there is a considerable resort to surtaxes, imposed and removed to suit the fluctuating exigencies of the national exchequer. A notable instance of the use of the surtax during the period of the present study was that of 1886, when 15 per cent additional was tacked on in order to make up for the loss of revenue occasioned by depreciation of the paper money.[3]

Duties are payable on the prices contained in the official "tarifa de avalúos"[4] (schedule of valuations). When this price

[1]

Nominal Value of Imports 1916	$217,409,322
Real Value of Imports 1916	366,130,571
Absolute difference	148,721,249
Relative difference	68.4%

Dr. A. E. Bunge: *El Intercambio Económico*, p. 17.

[2] About ninety-five articles are subject to specific duties.

[3] The Budget of 1886 estimated revenue at $41,197,500, of which $29,800,000 (three-fourths of the whole) was due from import and export duties. As a matter of fact, the duties yielded over $33,000,000 including the $6,405,000 resulting from the 15 per cent surtax.

[4] The "tarifa de avalúos" today enumerates and gives official prices for 3,699 articles; many of them have remained in force for years without change.

list is drawn up it is based on the actual purchase price abroad of the imported articles, plus transportation cost. According to the customs law in force up to 1900, the "tarifa de avalúos" was subject to annual revision. The revision, however, appears to have been spasmodic and partial, and conducted in the interests of government revenue rather than in those of the department of trade statistics. The result was that many of the official prices remained in force for years without change; others underwent frequent and rather startling alteration. Thus, Martinez and Lewandowski cite the case of coffee. In 1899 it was valued at 30 centavos gold, in 1900 at 20, in 1902 at 12. Granting that the price of coffee was experiencing a fall in those years, the decline indicated in the "tarifa de avalúos" appears to be an exaggeration. On the other hand, many of the customs valuations have for long periods been 20 to 30 per cent above the actual market price; and sometimes they have been purely fantastical. In fact, some of the articles listed as paying 50 per cent duty — textiles, furniture, shoes, perfume, lingerie, and similar articles — pay in some cases 100 per cent or more, owing to the arbitrary valuations placed upon them in the "tarifa de avalúos." [1]

The bearing of all this upon the official statistics of "value of imports" is but too apparent. They cannot be accepted as representing the actual state of things. As a statement of absolute values they are worthless. For purposes of general comparison of one year with another, however, they are generally thought to be serviceable. At any rate, they are all that we have to work with. In the period of this study, as it happens, the changes in the import trade were so large and clear-cut that conclusions from the official figures, when supported amply by other evidence, may be made with comparative safety.

The export statistics suffer from the same cause as the import statistics, though perhaps to a less degree. Until 1892 they too were based upon the official price tariffs rather than on the actual market prices. Since, however, export duties extended only to

---

[1] Martinez and Lewandowski, p. 299 *et seq.*

the grazing products,[1] and did not apply to cereals, which were coming to occupy a more and more important place in the exports during the period of our study, the extent of error due to imperfect customs valuations is perhaps, even for the period prior to 1892, less for the "value of exports" than for the "value of imports." Since 1892, the official valuations have pretty generally been based on the wholesale market price quotations in Buenos Aires, as published systematically in the *Boletín de la Bolsa de Comercio* (*Bulletin of the Stock Exchange*), and since 1913 in that of the *Bolsa de Cereales*.

To sum up, then, the statistics of imports and of exports are unreliable in so far as their absolute value is concerned. There is even some question as to their reliability for purposes of comparison of one year with another. Fortunately, however, in the period of this study the more significant changes in the import trade were so large and striking that conclusions may safely be drawn from the official figures, particularly in view of the abundance of other evidence which may be adduced in support of those conclusions. The changes in the export trade were much less marked; so that the drawing of conclusions from them becomes a rather delicate matter. It is generally admitted, however, that the statistics of quantities exported are accurate.[2]

The general course of Argentine foreign trade from 1866 to the present time is admirably shown in the following chart, drawn up by the Dirección General de Estadistica. Drawn to geometric scale, it indicates the proportional rate of growth and change in the successive five-year periods. The two broad phases in the history of the foreign trade stand out. To 1890 imports generally exceed exports. Thereafter the order is reversed. The absolute growth, also, is indicated. Imports increase from about

---

[1] The export duty was in effect from 1866 to 1887. Suppressed in the latter year it was reëstablished in 1890, year of the Baring Panic, to meet the needs of the Treasury. The duty was definitely removed in 1906. It was a 4 per cent *ad valorem* duty, chiefly upon hides, wool, tallow, ostrich plumes, horns, etc. On January 1, 1918, an export tax was again imposed on grazing products, as a "temporary" revenue measure, though the period of its duration was not defined.

[2] Bunge: *El Intercambio Económico*, p. 10. Whenever possible, therefore, we shall make reference to quantity as well as to value of exports.

COMERCIO EXTERIOR

VALORES ABSOLUTOS Y OSCILACIONES RELATIVAS (1)

GRÁFICO LOGARÍTMICO

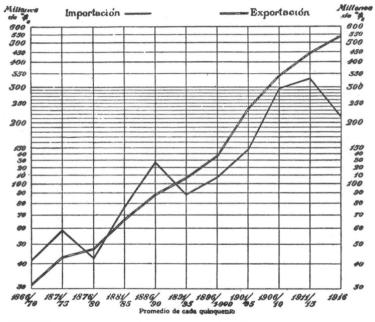

(1) En este cuadro las distancias que determinan las curvas son la expresión geométrica de los logaritmos de las cantidades. Las curvas revelan, en consecuencia, la razón del aumento ó diminución.

$32,000,000 gold, the average for 1866–70, to about 330 millions gold, the average for 1911–15. Exports increase from $42,000,000 gold to $450,000,000 gold in the same period. The effect of the recent war on the foreign trade is strikingly apparent. Imports for 1916 are $100,000,000 below the average for 1911–15: exports show an increase of about $100,000,000.[1]

[1] Exports for first nine months of 1917 were $414,028,386 and imports, $266,-787,767; representing, as compared with the corresponding figures for 1916, a gain in exports of $26,024,552, and a decline in imports of $8,681,138. The increase of exports would have been greater but for the falling off of cereals due to

Turning now to the period of our study, one's attention is
arrested by the extraordinary character of the fluctuations in
the foreign trade, as indicated in the chart on page 184, where are
plotted on the absolute scale the statistics of annual exports
and imports for the twenty years 1881 to 1900.

The following table presents the value of the exports and of
the imports, together with the balance of trade, for the twenty
years 1881 to 1900:

BALANCE OF TRADE, 1881–1900
(Thousand gold pesos)

Year	Exports	Imports	Balance
1881	$57,938	$55,706	+$2,232
1882	60,389	61,246	— 857
1883	60,208	80,436	—20,228
1884	68,030	94,056	—26,026
1885	83,879	92,222	— 8,343
1886	69,835	95,409	—25,574
1887	84,422	117,352	—32,930
1888	100,112	128,412	—28,300
1889	90,145	164,570	—74,425
1890	100,819	142,241	—41,422
1891	103,219	67,208	+36,011
1892	113,370	91,481	+21,889
1893	94,090	96,224	— 2,133
1894	101,688	92,789	+ 8,899
1895	120,068	95,096	+24,971
1896	116,802	112,164	+ 4,638
1897	101,169	98,289	+ 2,880
1898	133,829	107,429	+26,401
1899	184,918	116,851	+68,067
1900	154,600	113,485	+41,115

Particularly striking is the pronounced rise of imports between
1885 and 1890, followed by an abrupt drop from $142,000,000 to
$67,000,000 in the panic year of 1891. Exports on the whole
proceed more smoothly. The outstanding fact appears to be
that preceding and during the panic the growth of exports was
gradual and fairly steady, not to be compared with the upward
sweep that occurred just at the close of the century. In addition,

the poor harvest of 1916–17. Animal products showed a gain of $90,059,528.
whereas cereals fell off $41,220,314.

Exports in 1917 were $599,254,000 and in 1918 $756,638,000, as against imports of $258,750,000 and $479,397,000, respectively. (Figures are for the
"economic year," October 1 to September 30.)

VALUE OF IMPORTS AND OF EXPORTS,
1881–1900

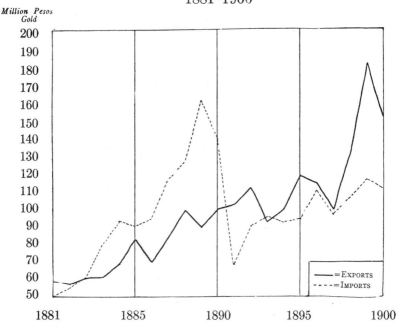

there is noticeable a distinct drop in the exports in 1893, which produced for that year a slightly unfavorable trade balance. On the whole, however, the overturn of the balance from "unfavorable" to "favorable" in 1891 is seen to have been followed by a growing excess of exports over imports. In 1900 the favorable balance was about $41,000,000.[1]

How far these changes of exports and imports are to be explained by price changes, arising out of the paper money situation; and how far they were due to other causes, such as bad harvests from locust pests or excess or deficiency of rainfall, conditions in foreign markets, ocean freight rates, and the like,

---

[1] Since that year it has been usually between 40 and 90 millions, falling below 40 millions in only three years, and being supplanted by an unfavorable balance in but one year, 1911. During the war the excess of exports was of course much larger: 277 millions in 1915 (Dr. Bunge's revised figures) and 207 millions in 1916.

is to be the subject of the succeeding chapters. Particularly do we wish to find the explanation of *how* the overturn of the trade balance occurred in 1891.

The *why* of the overturn, as was said in the preceding chapter, appears undoubtedly to have been the changes in the balance of borrowings. The relation between the borrowing operations and the foreign trade is shown in the following chart, which compares the trade balance and the balance of borrowings year by year from 1880 to 1900.

The chart shows the credits and debits of Argentina as regards foreign trade and foreign capital. The balance of borrowings represents the new foreign capital annually invested in Argentina minus the annual interest charge paid by Argentina on all foreign capital invested in the country. The trade balance represents exports minus imports.

The chart indicates that up to 1890 the new annual borrowings exceeded the interest charge. The course of the borrowing fever in the boom of the late eighties is indicated strikingly by the steep ascent of the curve between 1886 and 1888, and the even sharper fall from the latter year to 1890, when the Baring Panic virtually put an end temporarily to borrowing. Meantime, in the trade balance imports exceed exports. After 1890 the situation is reversed. Interest exceeds borrowings, and exports exceed imports.

Attention should be called to the remarkable similarity of form in the two balances. Almost invariably a change in the balance of borrowings is matched by a change in the contrary direction in the balance of trade. The most striking fluctuations in the trade balance appear to have occurred one year after the changes in the balance of borrowings. The great outburst of borrowings in the late eighties has its counterpart in an expansion of imports, which reaches its climax in 1889, one year after the borrowing operations attained their greatest magnitude. The overturn of the balance of borrowings occurs in 1890; it is followed in 1891 by the overturn of the trade balance.

That there is a lag of this sort, however, or that its duration is one year, need not, and perhaps ought not, to be insisted upon

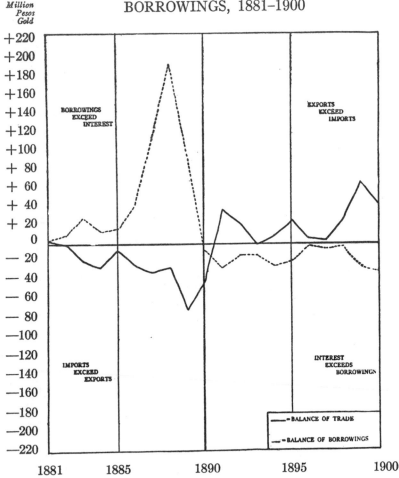

BALANCE OF TRADE AND BALANCE OF
BORROWINGS, 1881–1900

as indicating a principle. In fact, as we shall see later,[1] the lag
is attributable in the late eighties, to the *direct* connection between imports and borrowings; that is, to the fact that much
of the capital borrowed in England was straightway expended
there in the purchase of materials for railroad construction, and

[1] Chapter XV, p. 245.

the like. It was to be expected, therefore, that an increase of borrowing for railroad purposes in a given year would translate itself into an increase of imports of construction materials in the following year.

This direct connection, however, since it does not involve foreign exchange operations, and has therefore no immediate effect upon the paper money situation, is of secondary interest from the point of view of the theory of international trade under conditions of depreciated paper. What we wish to determine is to what extent the fluctuations in the balance of trade are attributable to what may be termed the *indirect* connection with borrowings; that is, to those borrowing operations which did give rise to exchange operations, thereby influencing the value of the currency in the manner described in Part I of this study, and thus producing, according to the assertions of theory, changes in prices and wages, which motivated the operations of exporters and importers, and thus produced changes in the balance of trade. This study of mechanism — of *how* borrowings, through their effect on the currency, influenced foreign trade — is the subject-matter of the succeeding chapters. But first of all it has been well to see, as shown in the chart under discussion, that there was indeed an inverse relation between the balance of borrowings and the balance of trade; that when borrowings exceeded interest charge, imports exceeded exports, and vice versa.

CHAPTER XIII

PAPER MONEY, PRICES AND WAGES, IN RELATION TO THE EXPORT TRADE

ANY investigation of a statistical character in Argentina, if it goes back of the past ten years, must struggle against the almost insurmountable defects and deficiencies of the material. We have seen that the official data on value of imports and of exports contain serious inaccuracies, so that they cannot be used except for purposes of general comparison, and even then only with caution and with constant appeal to other evidence. The obstacles presented by trade statistics are as nothing, however, compared with those that one encounters in an attempt to gather reliable data on wages and prices. Were it not that information on borrowings is to be had from more trustworthy sources than in most countries, owing to the fact that so large a part of borrowings and of interest payments pertained to the government, and are therefore officially recorded; and were it not that the changes in the quantity of paper money in circulation, in the gold premium, in the balance of payments, and in prices were so decided and spectacular as to be unmistakable, even in spite of the defectiveness of the statistics in certain fields, an investigation of the present character would appear to be foredoomed to failure, as regards the reliability of its conclusions.

Certain it is that prior to the past ten years wages and prices constituted the field in which Argentine statistics, even today in their infancy, were most lamentably lacking. The National Department of Labor was not established until 1907. Until that time little interest was taken in the collecting of wage data, or indeed in labor questions of any sort.[1]

[1] In 1904, there appeared *El Obrero en la República Argentina*, by Juan A. Alsina, which is much the fullest and most exact study of wages that had been made up to that time. In 1904, a two-volume work written by Dr. J. B. Massé, and pub-

In the period of this study, therefore, the wage data are meager, and for the most part unreliable. They refer, too, to city workers rather than to country workers, information concerning whom is most desirable for the purposes of the present inquiry. The most ambitious report on a single year is that of Señor Adrian Patroni,[1] a socialist, which gives wages for 1897 in some fifty occupations in the city of Buenos Aires. His thesis is that, whereas from 1880 to 1887 the workingman was in tolerable circumstances, from 1889 onward his condition became steadily worse. He points to the extraordinary increase of strikes in the nineties. The cause of the change he thinks to have been excessive immigration, occasioned by the reports which the Departamento General de Inmigración had spread broadcast by the thousands of pamphlets in Europe, designed, as Patroni says, to create the impression that a workman got such a high wage in Argentina that with his savings he could buy land which was so productive that in a few years he would become "un Señor Capitalista." One suspects that Patroni's data are prejudiced by his eagerness to depict the workman in all his abject misery. On the other hand, the pamphlets of the Department of Immigration, a prolific, if unsystematic, source on wages, may be suspected of having been in some measure guilty of the accusation which Patroni lays at their door. The department's business was to conduct propaganda; its pamphlets present rosy pictures, not all of which will bear serious examination. In any case, its method of presenting wage data was crude. The maximum and the minimum wage in a given occupation would be taken, and the average wage found by dividing the sum by two. Besides, the data furnished in these pamphlets of propaganda refer to different parts of the country in different years, as it was felt desirable to "boost" this, that, or the other district, and are therefore not comparable.

lished by the Minister of the Interior, Dr. Joaquin V. Gonzalez, gives a *Report on the State of the Working Classes in the Interior of the Republic* (*Informe sobre el Estado de las Clases Obreras en el Interior de la República*). These studies are evidence of the awakening interest that was to result, in 1907, in the formation of the Departamento Nacional de Trabajo.

[1] *Los Trabajadores en la Argentina*, 1898.

It has been necessary, therefore, so far as wage data are concerned, to rely mainly·on a single source, the admirable investigation conducted in 1896 by W. I. Buchanan, then United States Minister in Argentina.[1] Concerning his data, Mr. Buchanan says: "I have tried always to obtain the data at first hand, because I have believed that the result would be more satisfactory and would be nearer the truth than if I had relied on published statistics. I believe that the figures given in these pages are worthy of entire credence, because in each case I have sought for them in sure sources, and besides I have verified their exactitude with many persons."[2] Referring specifically to wage data, he explains that he had to "struggle against serious difficulties, the chief of which was the lack of statistics of wages in Argentina (except for government employments);" and that he was obliged "to resort to the original source," and adds: "I have encountered solicitous collaboration on the part of employers and workmen, to whom I am profoundly grateful."[3]

We may, then, rely upon Mr. Buchanan's wage data with some degree of confidence. With them I have constructed an index number based on wages in sixty-nine occupations, for the years 1886, 1890, 1892, 1894, 1896.

Wages constitute the chief difficulty. As regards export prices there is fortunately no difficulty whatever. The prices of the leading exports were quoted regularly in the bi-weekly bulletins of the Stock Exchange. They are the prices of the principal produce markets in Buenos Aires.[4] The index number here given

[1] "La Moneda y la Vida en la República Argentina," in *Revista de Derecho, Historia y Letras*, 1898, ii, p. 197 *et seq.* It appears also in United States Special Consular Reports, xiii, 1896–97, *Money and Prices in Foreign Countries*, as "Money, Wages, and Prices in Argentina in the Period 1886–96." Mr. Buchanan's study is warmly praised by Señor E. S. Zeballos, a former Minister of Argentina in Washington, and an authority on Argentine economic questions, especially agricultural problems; author of *La Agricultura en Ambas Americas*, Buenos Aires, 1896 (716 pages).

[2] *Ibid.*, p. 207.

[3] *Ibid.*, p. 208. I have myself come upon persons in Buenos Aires, merchants and shopkeepers, who recall Mr. Buchanan's personal visits to their establishments in search of wage and price data.

[4] The quotations which I have used are up to 1898 chiefly those of the Constitución market; from 1898 on, those of the new Mercado Central de Frutos.

is based on fifteen price quotations for nine products,[1] which comprised from 80 to 85 per cent of the total exports in the period of this study.[2] The remainder of the exports was made up of a larger number of insignificant items. The only important omissions from the index number are jerked beef (tasajo) and live stock, which together averaged from $6,000,000 to $10,-000,000 a year, but for which continuous, usable data are not available.[3] In constructing the index number of export prices care has been taken to include only the prices quoted during the export season. Attention has already been called to the fact that in the period here studied the Argentine commercial year consisted of a busy season and a dull season. The export market was active, roughly, from November to May.[4]

With so much of explanation of the data, we may proceed with the business of the present chapter, the comparison of paper money, export prices, and wages, with a view to ascertaining their effect upon the export trade. The following table presents the three factors mentioned in the form of index numbers. Both

[1] 3 for wool; 2 for woolly sheepskins; 2, cow hides; 1, mutton tallow; 1, horsehair; 2, wheat; 2, corn; 1, linseed; 1, wheat flour.

[2] (Thousand gold pesos)

Year	Total Exports	Exports Included in Index Number	Percentage of Total
1886	$69,835	$58,822	84%
1892	113,370	93,783	83%
1899	184,918	157,531	85%

[3] *Chilled and frozen meat*, which today ranks as a major export, along with wheat, wool, corn, and linseed, was a negligible item prior to 1900. The following figures give some notion of the growth of the refrigerated meat export trade of Argentina:

(Thousand gold pesos)

1890	$55	1900	$7,043
1895	1,754	1905	21,910
1899	2,665	1910	32,101
		1913	41,207
		1915	83,207

[4] The average price of each item for each export year has therefore been calculated from the price quotations of the following dates, November 15, January 15, March 15, and May 15; from these yearly averages the index number of each item has been calculated (on the base year 1886) and the general index number built up from the individual index numbers.

the arithmetic mean and the median are given. On the following page they are shown by chart.

INDEX NUMBERS OF PRICE OF GOLD, EXPORT PRICES, AND WAGES, 1886–1900

Year	Wages		Export Prices		Price of Gold
	Mean	Median	Mean	Median	
1886	100	100	100	100	100
1887	..	..	97	91	97
1888	..	..	93	84	106
1889	..	..	118	102	138
1890	125	120	165	133	181
1891	..	..	255	213	278
1892	138	133	232	213	239
1893	..	..	207	164	233
1894	146	146	209	176	257
1895	..	..	216	181	248
1896	161	161	204	153	213
1897	..	..	179	160	209
1898	..	..	177	157	186
1899	..	..	138	124	162
1900	..	..	154	143	166

The chart shows the striking upward sweep of the paper price of gold after 1888, culminating in the panic of 1891. The influence of a favorable balance of payments the following year, occasioned by the overturn of the trade balance and by the funding loan arrangement of the interest on the national foreign debt, is apparent in the descent of the price of gold after 1891; as also the effect of the abandonment of the funding arrangement in 1893 and the unfavorable trade balance of that year, which sent the price of gold upward again in 1894. Thereafter, we find a long steady fall, particularly marked in 1898 and in 1899, the year in which the fluctuations of paper money were at length curbed by the Conversion Law in force today.

As was to be expected, it is seen that export prices were exceedingly sensitive to changes in the price of gold. The fluctuations of the curves representing these two factors are in close sympathy. The rise of export prices, however, was considerably

PRICE OF GOLD, EXPORT PRICES, AND WAGES, 1886–1900

INDEX NUMBERS

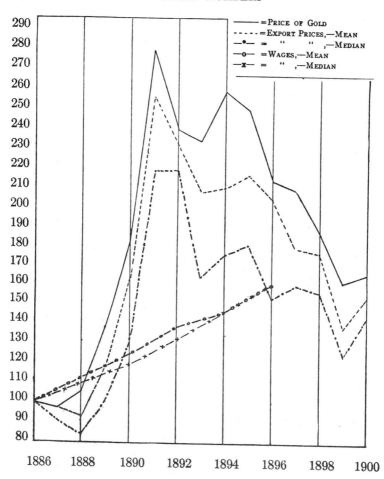

less than that of gold. Especially is this true of the median, a
better index for our purpose than the mean because not affected
so much by extreme fluctuations of individual price items.
Whether the more moderate elevation attained by export prices

is an indication that the general price level of Argentina did not rise so high as the price of gold, it is perhaps impossible to say. The price data are not sufficient for judgment. One would need to consider import and domestic prices as well as export prices, and to determine their relative importance. Import prices, as indicated by such data as are available,[1] appear to have risen higher than the price of gold. Domestic wholesale prices of exportable products, on the other hand, were probably dominated entirely by export prices. That at least is the conclusion to be drawn from such study as I have been able to make of domestic prices for cereals.[2] These latter rose and fell simultaneously with export prices, and to about the same degree. This state of things is quite in accordance with expectation, when one remembers the dominating position of the export trade in Argentina, and the insignificance of the home market (confined then chiefly to the cities of Buenos Aires and Rosario), a market so small that it could not affect, but merely reflect, the conditions operative in the export market.

In considering the general price level, the effects of depreciated paper upon it, and the significance of those effects for the general population, one would need to distinguish between city and country. For the rural peasant population the problem of de-

---

[1] See Chapter XV, pp. 251–252.

[2] INDEX NUMBER OF INTERNAL WHOLESALE PRICES FOR CEREALS

Year	Median	Mean
1887	49	50
1888	62	65
1889	71	71
1890	91	86
1891	179	181
1892	124	127
1893	131	126
1894	121	120
1895	110	107
1896	87	85
1897	108	119
1898	96	99
1899	64	70
1900	77	93

(Data from the *Boletines de la Bolsa de Comercio*.)

preciated paper money, in so far as it affected the cost of living, was much less significant than for the city population. The former lived directly upon the fruits of its "chacras" (small farms), buying but little, either of domestic or imported products. The city population, on the other hand, was dependent for its food on the country, and for virtually everything else upon imports. In the cities, therefore, the problem of debased currency was acute and ever present.

Putting aside these larger questions, however, we may confine ourselves to the specific problem in hand,—the comparative effect of debased currency on export prices and on wages. And on this point the evidence of the chart is unmistakable. Export prices moved in close sympathy with the price of gold; though they did not rise so high as the latter. The reasons why they did not, and the significance of the fact for our problem, will be considered presently. Wages, on the other hand, rose but sluggishly. The regularity of the upward movement is perhaps exaggerated by the curve of wages shown in the chart. It must be remembered that the curve is constructed entirely upon Buchanan's data, which refer to five years only, scattered over a ten-year period. What happened in the intervening years one can only surmise.

In an attempt to inquire further into the movement of wages, I have constructed an index number for twenty-one occupations, combining Buchanan's data with those of the Buenos Aires Census of 1887 and of Patroni for 1897.[1] It appears to indicate that in 1887 there was no upward tendency of wages, and that in 1897 the trend was downward. We may

[1] INDEX NUMBER OF WAGES IN TWENTY-ONE OCCUPATIONS, 1886–97

Year	Median	Mean
1886	100	100
1887	94	100
1890	126	120
1892	141	133
1894	151	144
1896	166	167
1897	141	145

(Data from *Censo de la Provincia de Buenos Aires*, 1887; A. Patroni, *Los Trabajadores en la Argentina*, 1897; W. I. Buchanan, "La Moneda y la Vida," 1898.)

conclude with probable safety that the rise of wages did not begin before 1888, the year in which the depreciation of paper money first set in markedly; that wages rose gradually from 1888 to 1896; and that for the next two or three years, when the gold premium was falling rapidly (the decline in 1898 and 1899 amounting to seventy-six points) the tendency of wages was downward rather than upward.

Of one fact, and that the essential one, we may be certain. The effect of depreciating paper money upon wages was much less marked than upon export prices. The rise of wages under the influence of a rising price of gold was much less rapid and much less considerable than was the rise of export prices. It may be pointed out, too, that even in 1896 when wages were at their highest point, whereas export prices and the price of gold were falling, wages, as measured in gold, were considerably below the level of 1886. In 1886 a paper-money wage of $1.39 a day would be equivalent to $1[1] gold. The equivalent of $1 gold in 1896 was $2.96 paper; but wages having risen only 61 per cent, the wage-earner got in 1896 but $2.24 paper. In the intervening years the position of the laborer was much worse, since the discrepancy between paper-money wages and the price of gold was then much greater than in either 1886 or 1896.

The chief defect of the wage data here presented is that they relate chiefly to city occupations. Rural wages, the wages that would most concern exporters and producers and would therefore be most apt for our problem, are unfortunately not available. Such scattered bits of information as I have been able to obtain, however, indicate that the rise of the wages of farm laborers was at least not greater than that of city workmen. Such general evidence as one can find points also in the same direction. Attention has once or twice been called to the statements of competent observers of the time that for the peasant population the paper-money problem was much less acute than for the city population. The laborer was fed and housed upon the farm. He purchased but little either of domestic products or of imports. A considerable part of the harvest, moreover, came from

[1] *I. e.*, the gold premium in 1886 was 39 per cent; and in 1896, 196 per cent.

small farms (the "chacras"), where there were no hired laborers and no money wages, for the most part; the farm being worked by the chacrero, his wife and children. Some of these families owned their own farms and machinery; but the greater part of them were renters, who paid their rental in produce, 10 to 20 per cent of their harvest going to the landlord.

Concerning wages on the "estancias," devoted to sheep and cattle raising, some evidence is given by Señor J. B. Justo, who says[1]: "In the rural establishments of Señor Lázaro Repetto, the monthly wage of a peón was from $12 to $16[2] gold in 1883–84 (when gold was at par); $25 paper in 1891–92 (when the price of gold was at about 350); and $30 paper from 1892 to date.[3] To shear 100 sheep in these same establishments a peón earned $3 to $4 gold in 1883–84, $5 paper in 1892, and now[3] $6 paper,— an exceptionally high wage, but not equal to that of twenty years ago. And each sheep today has more wool." Buchanan gives the wage of the farm laborer as from $15 to $45 a month with food and lodging, wages differing in different parts of the country. In Tucuman they were $25 to $35 a month. In the wheat district the majority of peóns did not get more than $25. For 1898–99 there are official data for rural wages[4]; the peón's wage in Santa Fé (the great wheat district) in that year is given as $30.[5]

If we accept these figures, and compare the percentage of increase in rural wages with that in the price of gold in the different years mentioned, we have the following:

Year	1883–84	1891–92	1896	1898–99
Price of Gold	par (= 100)	332	296	258
Rural Wages	100	179	214	214

The general result is seen to be the same as that shown in the chart on page 193. Rural wages responded only gradually to the rise in the price of gold.

[1] J. B. Justo, *La Moneda*, p. 37 *et seq.*

[2] F. Latzina (for many years Director General of National Statistics) gives wages of farm laborers in 1883 as $14 gold (£2 16s.). See *The Argentine Republic as a Field for European Immigration*, p. 9.

[3] 1903.

[4] *Boletín del Departamento Nacional del Trabajo*, 1913, No. 25, p. 1059.

[5] These are paper figures.

The figures just given refer to the permanent farm laborers. They do not include the large special class of migratory harvest hands, who came each year, partly from the capital, Buenos Aires, but chiefly from Spain and Italy, remained for the harvest (about four months) and returned home, repeating the journey year after year. The monthly wage of these harvest hands was much higher than that of the ordinary farm laborers. Buchanan puts it at $45 to $90 a month; the National Department of Labor gives it for 1898–99 as $3.30 for a working-day.[1] Just what was the effect of depreciation of paper on this class of wages it is perhaps impossible to say, except in one or two years. The pronounced rise of the gold premium in 1891 might have been expected to increase considerably the wages of harvest labor in that year, especially in view of the fact that in 1891 emigration for the first time in ten years exceeded immigration.[2] The cause of the large emigration was not far to seek: the depreciation of the paper peso, the consequent dearness of board and lodging, added to the fact that retrenchment was being made in many branches of business, especially in those relying on imports, and the fact that the rise in wages had only been about 25 per cent of the rise in the price of gold.[3]

The fact appears to be, however, that in spite of the large emigration and of the high gold premium, the wages of harvest laborers decreased rather than increased in 1891; for not withstanding the emigration, the supply of labor was well in excess of the demand, owing to the general business inactivity in the city. The railroads, too, dismissed large numbers of men. The result was a flow of laborers from the towns into the country.[4]

[1] These are paper figures.   [2] For statistics of immigration see p. 207.

[3] Mr. Arthur Herbert, of the British Legation, also estimated the rise of wages as only 25 per cent, an estimate that agrees precisely with that shown by our index number. See *Economist*, July 11, 1891, Trade Supplement, p. 9.

[4] *Economist*, 1891, i, p. 599: Mr. Vice Consul Bridgett reported from Santa Fé (the wheat district) that "contrary to expectations, the supply of agricultural labor has recently increased, and wages have become lower. It was thought that the falling off in immigration would lead to a scarcity of hands; but this has been entirely counterbalanced by the flow of laborers into the country from the towns, where it has been found necessary to reduce the staff in almost every branch. The railroad companies, too, have dismissed large numbers of men, who are seeking employment in the field."

The indications appear to be that the wages of harvest labor were no more responsive to the rise of the gold premium than were other classes of wages. One other important group of wage-earners should be mentioned,— the railroad employees. For them we have the evidence of Buchanan.[1] When gold was at par (1884), the unskilled workmen got about $1.25 per day. In 1896 the same personnel received $2 to $2.50 a day. The latter figure at the price of gold in 1896 (296) would equal about $0.85 gold per day. For the skilled operatives, engineers, firemen, conductors, brakemen, station masters, telegraph operatives, line inspectors, and the like, the railroads adopted a sliding scale, intended to make allowance for the major changes in the value of the paper peso. When the premium on gold first appeared, in 1885, the railroads increased wages by one-fourth of the premium. Later, as the price of gold rose, it was agreed that wages be increased by one-half of the gold premium whenever the premium should be above 180 and below 340. After the decline of the premium set in, in the nineties, the railroads that were accustomed to pay a part of their employees in this way, fixed upon 60 per cent of the premium on gold as the proportion by which wages should be increased. In other words, under this plan a man who had received $50 a month when gold was at par (1884), would get in 1896, gold being then at a premium of 196, $108.80, instead of $148, which would be the paper-money equivalent of the original gold wage.

The evidence from these special classes of wages supplements and confirms the data presented in the chart on page 193. There can be no doubt that wages responded less promptly and to a less degree to the movements of the price of gold than did export prices.[2]

[1] W. I. Buchanan, "La Moneda y la Vida," p. 213 *et seq.*

[2] To get a complete picture of the producer's cost of production, one should supplement the study of wages by an investigation of agricultural rents. Unfortunately the available data are not sufficient for that purpose. Buchanan, however, declares that rents underwent but little change during the period of depreciated paper. It should be noted, too, that most of the small farmers, the "chacreros," did not pay money rent; so that the factor of the effect of depreciating paper on rent did not enter into their costs. The landlord furnished the land, the tools, the seed; and received in payment a percentage of the harvest.

In other words, the conclusions of theory are borne out by the facts of the Argentine case. Depreciating paper created a gap between selling price and costs, which was equivalent to a bounty on exports. On the other hand, when paper money began to appreciate violently, notably in 1898 and 1899, the situation of the producer and the exporter was reversed. Export prices fell more rapidly than costs. The exporter found his "bounty" withdrawn. Wheat, for example, which sold at $12 (paper) per hundred kilos when gold was at 300, sold now at $8 (paper), gold being at 200; while wages were little if at all lower than in the former period. The result was that the producer, who in the early nineties was an ardent advocate of inconvertible paper, became in 1898 an equally ardent supporter of the campaign for conversion of paper money, which terminating in the Conversion Law of 1899 fixed once for all the value of the paper peso.

These conclusions based on the price and wage data are confirmed by the actual happenings of the times in the export market. It will be recalled, for example, that in October, 1891, the gold premium reached its highest point, 364 per cent. From that it fell violently during the remainder of the year and during 1892, reaching 185 in December, 1892. The fall, fundamentally due to a favorable balance of international payments, growing partly out of the funding arrangement of the interest of the national foreign debt and partly out of an excess of exports over imports in both of these years, was enhanced by the operations, already described, of the European syndicate, which, to affect an artificial rise of Argentine paper money and thus of the Argentine securities which they held, shipped gold to Argentina, and by other means, also, sought to control the exchange market. The effect of the fall of the premium on wool exports which came to market from October, 1891, to January, 1892, is related by the correspondent of the *Economist*, who says:

Those "estancieros" who can afford to wait for their money refuse to sell at the prices now offered and they have sent their wool to deposit, believing that the violent fall in the gold premium in October, having been produced by artificial means for the purpose of exchange operations, cannot last, and that they will be able to secure better prices before the new year is far advanced. So general is this belief that on Saturday last (December

19) there was the enormous quantity of five million kilos of wool of all qualities in deposit, whereas last year at this date the quantity in deposit was only half a million kilos.[1]

Buchanan also makes reference to this practice. "With the lowering of gold," he says, "the 'estanciero,' who gained by the rise, becomes a speculator, and holds his grains and his cattle in order to gain by a better premium." [2] In some years, in order to avoid loss occasioned by a falling gold premium, the farmer sold his wool on the sheep's back, or his grain in the fields, some months before the export season opened.[3]

The effect of the pronounced fall of the gold premium in 1898 and 1899 is related by the *Economist's* correspondent, who writes on October 31, 1898:

The downward movement of the premium continues. The movement has been so violent and rapid since the wool season opened, that it has completely upset the market for that staple, which is accumulating in the depots, as large growers are not inclined to accept present prices. One of them told me a few days ago that the fall in the premium had entailed on him a loss in comparison with his estimates of over $100,000.[4]

And in June, 1899, he writes of the effect of the low premium on the wheat producers:

The gold premium has been falling for a year. The farmer can no longer live; his expenses being the same in currency today as when the premium on gold was as 3 to 1, while he gets one-third less for the produce of his toil. The proof of this state of things is seen in the exodus of small farmers— all foreigners—who are leaving the country in numbers unheard of for many years.[5]

Without going further into details concerning the export conditions and operations of specific years, the conclusion appears amply warranted that so far as export prices and costs of production are concerned, the influence of inconvertible money in Argentina was entirely in accord with theoretical expectation.

[1] *Economist*, 1892, i, pp. 104–105.

[2] W. I. Buchanan, "La Moneda y la Vida," p. 221.

[3] The premium was higher in the "off-season" than during the export season, since export operations tended to drive up the rate of exchange, and therefore bring down the premium on gold.

[4] *Economist*, 1898, ii, p. 1728.   [5] *Ibid.*, 1899, ii, p. 1119.

Export prices were much more sensitive to fluctuations of the price of gold than were wages, with the result that when gold was rising, the producer secured an extra profit attributable to the circumstance that the price of his product had risen faster than his costs, and when gold was falling, his profits were cut down because of the fact that export prices fell more rapidly than costs of production.

One would expect, therefore, to find a decided expansion of exports between 1888 and 1895; for in these seven years the gold premium rose in rapid and spectacular fashion, mounting from 48 per cent [1] in 1888 to 287 per cent [1] in 1891, and maintained for the five years 1891–95 the high average of 249 per cent. On the other hand, for the last five years of the decade, 1896–1900, one would expect a considerable depression of the export trade, or at least such a change from the previous period as to indicate unmistakably the fact that in these five years the gold premium was undergoing a decline almost as violent as had been its rise a few years earlier. The gold premium fell from 244 per cent [1] in 1895 to 125 per cent [1] in 1899. Particularly noticeable, one would suppose, would be the restriction of exports in 1898 and in 1899, when, the premium having fallen seventy-six points in two years, the farmers and exporters were clamoring loudly for a system of gold conversion which would prevent a violently appreciating currency from reducing them to utter ruin.

Some such general movement of exports — a great outburst in the late eighties and early nineties, followed by a less pronounced growth, or even by some diminution, of exports in the later nineties is the expectation both of theory and of the facts reviewed concerning the price of gold, export prices, and wages.

When, however, one turns to the actual statistics of export trade, one finds awaiting him a considerable surprise. The movement of the value of exports is just the reverse of that expected. In the late eighties and early nineties exports increase but slowly: in the later period, the late nineties, there is an unmistakable expansion of the export trade. The diagram on page 203 gives the annual value of the exports from

[1] The yearly averages.

VALUE OF EXPORTS, 1884–1901

THREE-YEAR MOVING AVERAGE

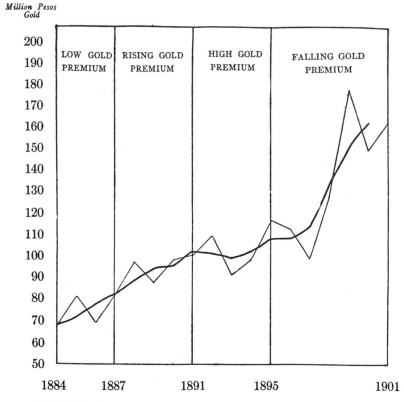

Million Pesos Gold

LOW GOLD PREMIUM — RISING GOLD PREMIUM — HIGH GOLD PREMIUM — FALLING GOLD PREMIUM

━━━ = Moving Average
──── = Annual Figures

1884, the year in which gold was at par, to 1901, when because of the Conversion Law the fluctuations of the gold premium had definitely and permanently ceased. The general trend of the value of exports is also shown, seasonal fluctuations being eliminated by the employment of a three-year moving average. The period of our study has been divided into four parts, intended to facilitate the comparison between the major movements of the gold premium and the general trend of the value of exports. In the first period, after the rise of the premium from zero in 1884 to 37 [1] in 1885, the premium was about stationary, being 39 per cent in 1886 and 35 per cent [1] in 1887. In the second period, we have the spectacular rise of the gold premium,— 48 per cent in 1888, 91 per cent in 1889, 151 per cent in 1890, and 287 per cent in 1891, a rise of some two hundred and fifty points in the four years 1887–91. In the third period, in spite of a considerable decline in 1892, followed by a rise in 1894, the general level of the premium is very high, 249 per cent. In the fourth period, the premium falls rapidly, from 244 per cent in 1895 to 125 per cent in 1899.

The periods of most interest for our purpose are the second and the fourth, the periods of the rise and the fall of the gold premium. As has been said in an earlier place, the stimulus to trade is not to be looked for from a high premium, but from a rising premium: from the fact that as the premium rises, export prices rise more rapidly than wages; the resulting extra profits for the producer giving a stimulus to exports. Likewise, the discouragement of exports would result not from a low premium but from a falling premium. One would expect, therefore, a pronounced expansion of exports in the second period, and a contraction, or at least a cessation of growth, in the fourth period.

But the outstanding fact displayed by the moving average in the diagram is that in the second period the growth of the exports was only moderate, whereas in the fourth period there was a sudden outbreak, marking a new stage in the Argentine export trade. And it is to be noted that the great expansion occurred in 1898 and 1899, precisely the years in which the gold premium fell most violently. In these two years exports increased $84,000,-000 gold (or 83 per cent) as compared with the bad harvest year of 1897, and $68,000,000 gold (or 59 per cent) as compared with the good year 1896.

Value of exports, then, did not act in accordance with theoretical expectation. And yet that the theoretical reasoning is sound has been shown by the study of export prices and of wages. We have proof, too, of its soundness in the complaint of the pro-

---

[1] All figures of gold premium on this page refer to yearly averages.

ducers at the fall of the premium in 1898, evidence that although, contrary to their assertion, the Argentine export trade was not being ruined but was in fact expanding notably, they recognized a falling gold premium as one source of loss to them, and marked its effect in the decline of export prices.

The difficulty is one common enough in economic investigation. "Other things being equal," the effect of a rising gold premium would have been to stimulate exports; and the effect of a falling premium would have been to discourage them. But other things were not equal. Other things were working at cross-purposes to the particular factor which the theory isolates: and they so overlaid it as to prevent its working out its logical effect upon the export trade.

One obvious circumstance, of great importance for the export trade, but over which monetary conditions could have no control, was the fluctuations of good and bad seasons. Rainfall in the rich cereal belt,[1] though amply sufficient on an average of seasons, varies extremely from year to year, with resultant losses from drought or excessive rainfall.[2] Much more serious was the locust pestilence, ever present in some degree but differing widely in its effect on the harvests from year to year. A rapid glance through the period of our study (see chart, page 203) shows the irregularity of exports, occasioned in large measure by these purely natural conditions. From 1886 to 1888, for instance, exports increased over $30,000,000 gold, or 41 per cent.[3] The rise appears extraordinary, and much was made of it at the time. But 1886 was a poor year. If one compares the preceding year, 1885, when the harvest was unusually good, with 1888, the increase is only some $16,000,000 gold, or about 19 per cent. Even this is considerable, however, and inasmuch as it occurs entirely in a single year, 1888, the first year in which the gold premium displayed any marked upward tendency, it is

---

[1] The cereal belt comprises northeast Argentina, including Santa Fé, Entre Rios, the northern part of Buenos Aires, and the eastern part of Córdoba.

[2] The lack of facilities for storing grain awaiting transportation to the seaboard contributed seriously to losses from excessive rainfall.

[3] Exports 1888.................................... $110,112,000 gold
1886.................................... 69,835,000 gold

encouraging from the point of view of our theory. Yet in 1889 an ascent of the gold premium much more pronounced than that of the preceding year is accompanied by a decline of 10 per cent in exports, a decline attributable to the poor harvest of that year (1888–89 harvest). Wheat exports dwindled to about one-eighth the quantity exported the previous season. Again in 1891, the year when gold touched its zenith and when one looks for a great outburst of exports, value of exports is virtually stationary [1]; a condition partly to be explained by the almost total destruction of the corn crop of that year by locusts. The corn crop of 1893 was also a failure. Wool too was that year of poor quality; the result being that in 1893 for the only time (except 1911) since 1890 imports exceeded exports. Exports dropped from about $113,000,000 gold in 1892 to $94,000,000 gold in 1893, a decline of over 20 per cent; and a decline in no wise explicable by the movement of the gold premium, for during the export season 1891–92 the gold premium underwent a spectacular fall, whereas all through 1893 its tendency was upward. So again in 1896 and 1897 we find bad wheat harvests due to the inroads of the locusts. In 1897 the wheat exports dropped to the insignificant figure of $3,000,000 gold. [2] The result was the pronounced depression of the export trade in that year.

Fluctuations from this cause, irregular and unpredictable as they are, interfere profoundly with the operation of such a set of forces as that here studied,— depreciated paper money, fluctuating gold premium, price and wage movements, all resulting, *if unimpeded*, in an artificial stimulus to exports. Especially is this the case with countries like Argentina, whose exports are of a purely agricultural character, and therefore peculiarly subject to variations of weather and other natural conditions.

The computation of the moving average of exports, by combining three-year periods, minimizes, though it cannot remove, the effect of these fluctuations due to natural causes; and permits one to compare the general trend of exports, taking one

[1] The year 1891 shows an increase of only 3 per cent over the value of exports in 1888.

[2] Stated in quantity figures, the wheat exports of 1897 were only 102,000 tons, as compared with 1,010,000 tons in 1895.

year with another, good harvests with bad, with the major phases of the movements of the gold premium. Granted that occasional bad years interrupt the operation of the particular factors investigated, it might be expected, nevertheless, that *on the whole* a gold premium ascending in striking fashion over several years would have occasioned an increase of exports, and that a pronounced fall of the premium, continuing for several years, would have caused a decrease. That such was not the case, however, but rather the reverse, was shown by the diagram on page 203.

The fact is that besides the irregularities occasioned by natural conditions — climate, pests, and the like — there was a network of other factors, working sometimes for and sometimes against those arising out of the paper money situation, but on the whole tending so to overlay and obstruct the effects of these latter as to almost entirely nullify their force, so far as the export trade was concerned. The unprecedented construction of railroads in the eighties by opening up new territory and connecting the interior with the river fronts and the seaboard, was of course a major cause of the growth of exports in that decade, and particularly of the increase of the wheat trade, which is the outstanding feature of Argentine export trade during the late eighties and the early nineties. Closely connected therewith, also, is the factor of immigration. During this period, the immigrants,[1] chiefly Italian and Spanish, settled almost exclusively

[1] NET IMMIGRATION 1880–1900

(ooo's omitted)

1880	21	1890	30
1881	25	1891	—30*
1882	43	1892	29
1883	54	1893	36
1884	63	1894	39
1885	94	1895	44
1886	79	1896	89
1887	107	1897	48
1888	139	1898	42
1889	220	1899	49
		1900	50

* Net emigration.

(See *Extracto Estadistico*, 1915, p. 589.)

in the cereal district.[1] The particularly heavy net immigration [2] of the late eighties (466,000 in three years, 1887–89) was a natural accompaniment of the land boom of those years. More directly, it was the result of the campaign of propaganda then being conducted in Europe, accompanied by the lavish distribution of premiums, subventions, and passage money. It was undoubtedly a leading cause of the increasingly prominent position taken in this period and in the nineties by the agricultural products, as opposed to the "cattle products," wool, hides, and the like.[3]

A third factor affecting the export trade in the eighties was the land boom, and especially the activities of the mortgage banks. The extraordinary facility of acquiring land through the mechanism of these banks, combined with the growth of the railway net and the heavy immigration, is a sufficient explanation of the growth of the export trade between 1885 and 1888. On the other hand, in 1890 and 1891, when the land boom collapsed, land values falling at least 50 per cent within a few months, some of the land brought under cultivation by the artificial stimulus of the boom was thrown out again. In other words, mortgage-bank operations and the land boom constituted one of the factors which tended to nullify the influence on

---

[1] *I. e.*, Santa Fé, north of Buenos Aires, Entre Rios, east of Córdoba. This was the region most easily accessible, most fertile, offering the best conditions of land tenure. The southern half of Buenos Aires, though well adapted for wheat growing, did not attract the immigrant, chiefly, according to Lix Klett, because of the monopoly of the land by capitalists. The more remote parts of Argentina, the Chaco in the north, the Andino region in the west, and the southern plains, were less easily accessible, and owing to an insufficiency of rainfall, suited to grazing rather than to agriculture.

[2] The Law of Colonization, passed in 1876, stimulated immigration by the granting of free lands and special privileges.

INCREASE OF COLONIES OF IMMIGRANTS

1856	3	1880	74
1860	5	1890	257
1870	36	1894	365

See Carlos Lix Klett, *Estudios Economicos*, ii, p. 1159.

[3] As will be shown presently, however, wool retained its position as the premier export throughout the period. Today, with the growth of the frozen meat trade, the grazing products are well in the lead.

foreign trade of a rising gold premium during the period when that influence was most to be expected. It was in 1891 that the overturn in the trade balance occurred; it was in that year that the gold premium rose most strikingly (from 151 per cent in 1890 to 287 per cent in 1891). It is in that year, therefore, that one would most expect a decided increase of exports, from the greater influence of the gold premium on export prices than on wages and other costs. Yet in that same year we have the collapse of the land boom, a decrease of the area under cultivation, and an exodus of immigrants,— all of which would tend to decrease production [1]; and in addition we have the almost complete destruction of the corn crop by locusts.

These examples illustrate the complexity of the influences at work in the export trade, and the difficulty of earmarking the separate effect of a given factor, such as that of a rising gold premium. There were other factors, moreover, of at least equal importance with those just reviewed: there was the progress in agricultural methods, in the grading of wheat, in storage facilities, in preparations for shipment,—which would of themselves, quite independently of a rising or falling gold premium, affect both the quantities available for export and their values.

Finally, there was a set of factors which bore particularly upon the question of export prices, and are therefore of especial importance for the purposes of our study. The exporter bought his product in paper money in Buenos Aires, and sold it abroad in gold. *One* of the factors determining his demand price was,

---

[1] *Economist*, 1891, i, p. 599: A summary is given of a report by the British Consul, Mr. Bridgett, who mentions the great difficulty which existed in getting reliable information as to production, and warns against past official statistics on this head. (The Department of Agriculture was not established till 1898.) He says that as a result of reckless land speculation, in those parts of the republic where through fictitious values lands were most heavily mortgaged, the area under production decreased considerably at this time. "The interest on the mortgage loans has been in excess of the value of the crops the land was capable of yielding, and therefore large tracts have been allowed to fall out of cultivation, especially in the province of Buenos Aires, where within the past three years cultivated land has been reduced in area by 42 per cent." It may be well to recall here what was said in Chapter VII. about the National Mortgage Bank and its difficulty owing to the failure of mortgagees to make their annual payments during the panic period.

of course, the gold premium. That is, the exporter translated the gold price which he could afford to offer into paper pesos, at the current market price for gold. It is for this reason, chiefly, that export prices were so exceedingly sensitive to the price of gold. When paper was cheap, the exporter would give more paper for 100 kilos of wheat; when paper was dear, he would give less. Assume that the gold price upon which the exporter based his calculation had remained unchanged from year to year, and there is no reason why the paper prices paid for exports in Buenos Aires should not have risen and fallen to the same degree as the price of gold. In other words, reverting to the chart on page 193, so far as the effect of the gold premium on export prices is concerned, one would expect the curve of export prices to rise as high as the curve representing the price of gold; and, in fact, to be practically identical with it. If that had occurred only one thing could have prevented a considerable increase of the export trade during the period of the rising gold premium,— an absolute failure of the *quantity* of exportable products to respond to the stimulus afforded by so marked a gap between export prices and wages.

In fact, however, as we have seen, the curve of export prices, though strikingly sympathetic to the curve of the price of gold, rose considerably less than the latter. In other words, stated in terms of gold, export prices were really falling. The "value of exports" are in gold, as are all other items entering into the balance of international payments. What is required, according to the theory, is that the rising gold premium should so stimulate the export trade that the *gold* value of exports would be increased. But since, in the Argentine case, the *gold* export prices had declined, the increase of quantity exported (under the stimulus of the extra profit occasioned by the gap between *paper* selling price and *paper* wages) would have to be considerable. For example, a 10 per cent increase in quantity exported would not increase the total value of a given export if there had been a 10 per cent fall in its *gold* price.

We turn, then, to the factors, *other* than the premium on gold, which affected export prices. An exporter seeking to buy wheat, for example, in Buenos Aires, would base his buying price on four factors: on the price of wheat in the foreign market where he was to sell his product, on the cost of ocean transport, on the current rate of exchange, and on the current premium on gold.

Concerning the first of these factors, it need scarcely be said that Argentine exports, in any field, are too small a proportion of the world supply to dominate the world price. As regards their effect on the international price, wheat, wool, or any of the chief exports of Argentina, is in a position different from that of Brazilian coffee,[1] for example. Since Brazil supplies some 80 per cent of the world's supply of coffee, the conditions of supply and sale of Brazilian coffee control the price of coffee in the world's markets. Since Argentina, on the other hand, contributes but a small portion of the world's supply of wheat, wool, corn, linseed, and the like, the Argentine supply has but a small[2] effect on the international market price for those products. Argentina sells what it can at the international price. The price of wheat in Argentina, therefore, is but a reflection of the price ruling in the foreign markets in which Argentine wheat is sold, minus cost of transportation from Argentina to the foreign market. Calculated at the current rate of exchange, these two factors of international gold price and cost of transportation, over neither of which the special conditions obtaining in Argentina, whether monetary or other, have control, determined the gold price which the exporter could offer for wheat in Buenos Aires.

But wheat, and all other Argentine exports, was dealt in in inconvertible paper money in Buenos Aires, since paper was the currency of the country. And the paper was depreciated, gold standing at a premium. The exporter, therefore, converted his gold buying price into paper at the current premium on gold.

What we must consider, then, are the factors which controlled *gold* export prices. The readiest way to do so is to sketch the

[1] Or United States cotton.

[2] The reference is, of course, to the normal peace-time conditions of international trade, and particularly to the period of our study, when Argentine products formed a smaller portion of world supply than today.

course of the main Argentine exports in the period of our study. By considering the items separately one may check up statistics of value by those of quantity. Since, moreover, price conditions in foreign markets are not uniform for all exports, a brief separate study of the principal exports is scarcely avoidable. We may begin with the wool trade, passing on subsequently to the more important of the cereal products.

CHAPTER XIV

THE CHIEF EXPORTS, INDIVIDUALLY CONSIDERED

I. Wool

Until recent years, wool has occupied the first rank among Argentine exports.[1] During the greater part of Argentine history, wool has, in fact, been the backbone of the export trade. Some attention, therefore, may be given to the broad phases of its growth.

In Argentina practically all regions are suited to sheep-raising. The best breeding-grounds, however, are the Pampas, flat grassy plains, comparatively treeless, sloping from the Andes to the Atlantic. The Pampas cover the whole of the provinces of Buenos Aires[2] and Santa Fé, and most of Córdoba, as well as some other territory. To the north of the Pampas, the provinces of Corrientes and Entre Rios are essentially stock-raising. Finally, the great dry, windy plains of Patagonia in the south are being devoted more and more to sheep. Since about 1890 (and more particularly since 1904) cereal production has been driving out sheep-raising to a considerable extent in the most fertile portions of the republic,— northern Buenos Aires, Santa Fé, and eastern Córdoba — the region that lies along the Paraná River, the main tributary of the River Plate.

Such is the geographical distribution of the industry. Its historical development may be broadly sketched in a few paragraphs. Though the wool trade reaches back to about 1600, when Antonio Juan sailed for Spain with a cargo of 2425 pounds, the trade was small and spasmodic throughout the colonial period. Spain, having prohibited commerce between her South American colonies and other countries, was the only foreign

[1] Since 1904 wheat (and in some years corn) has exceeded wool exports; and since 1915, refrigerated meats.

[2] The predominance of Buenos Aires in sheep-breeding is shown by the Agricultural and Pastoral Census of 1908, when Buenos Aires had 34,604,972 sheep, and Entre Rios (second) had but 7,005,469.

market; and since Spain herself occupied a commanding position in the wool export trade, the outlet for South American
wool was practically closed.

Toward the close of the eighteenth century and during the
early nineteenth century, important importations of merino
sheep were made. But the long period of internal strife among
the provinces, including the twenty-five years of the tyranny of
General Rosas, prevented any considerable progress during the
first half of the nineteenth century. And although the over-
throw of Rosas by Urquiza and the establishment of the present
Argentine constitution in 1853 marked the beginning of a new
political era, the wool industry remained for some time backward. Flocks were neglected. In most years the sheep were not
even sheared.[1] They were, besides, of poor type, and much
afflicted with mange.

The years 1860–65 witnessed a wool crisis in Australia and in
Europe, as well as in Argentina. To this was added the prohibi-
tive United States tariff of 1867. Since the United States had
been taking about 20 per cent[2] of Argentine wool, exportations
decreased considerably. It was found more economical to kill
off the poorer sheep than to pay for their upkeep. Moreover,
since the United States tariff duties on sheepskins were lighter
than those on wool, exporting houses encouraged the killing of
sheep for their skins.[3] The general slaughter that took place
was ultimately beneficial to the wool trade. The thinning out
of the flocks, leaving only the best, had an excellent effect, and
within a decade the quality of Argentine wool had notably improved.

Coincident with this thinning out of the old stock, there was
a general reawakening of interest in sheep-breeding, stimulated
particularly by the Sociedad Rural Argentina, founded in 1865,
and by the English sheep-growers. European breeds were imported and experimenting was begun with crossings of foreign

---

[1] Shearing did not become an annual country-wide operation until about 1860.

[2] Exceeded only by France, which took about 25 per cent. See C. Lix Klett:
Producción, Comercio, Finanzas é Intereses Generales de la República Argentina,
1900, ii, p. 1207.

[3] C. Lix Klett, *ibid.*, p. 1207 *et seq.*

sheep with the merinos existent in the country.[1] The foreign importation and the cross-breeding experiments mark a new period in the history of Argentine sheep-raising.

The first of the foreign sheep to attain prominence was the "Negrette."[2] The Negrette yielded an exceptionally fine merino wool, which brought a high price; but the Argentine climate prove unsuitable to it. As a meat-producer, moreover, the Negrette was valueless, because of its small size and the difficulty of fattening. By 1890, therefore, it had disappeared.

Then came the Rambouillet,[3] imported both from France and Germany. This also was a merino, noted for the fine quality of its wool. Its propagation in Argentina increased steadily between 1860 and 1870, until at the latter date it constituted virtually the entire sheep production of the country.

Finally, we have the introduction of the English long-wool breeds, particularly the Lincolns. The importation of these had begun as early as the forties. The wet seasons of 1842, 1843, and 1845 developed foot-rot among the merino sheep, particularly along the Atlantic seaboard. Breeders looked for some breed less susceptible to the malady. Englishmen began experimenting with various English long-wool sheep. The Lincolns proved well adapted to the climate, prospered in dry lands or wet, fattened on any kind of Argentine grass. They proved especially adaptable to the low lands of the south.[4] The wool of the pure Lincoln, however, proved difficult of sale in the Argentine markets; and crosses with merinos were tried, in many instances with success. The Lincoln cross-breeds of 1880–86

---

[1] Notably with the "Criollo," a descendant of the Spanish merino.

[2] Originally a Spanish merino from the folds of the Conde de Negrette; but it attained its highest development in Germany, between 1850 and 1860. It was first imported into Argentina by a German, Thomas Chas, in the fifties. See C. Lix Klett, *ibid.*, pp. 1205–1284.

[3] First introduced by Don Domingo Olivera in 1855.

[4] The Rambouillets, on the other hand, require the tender pasturage of the northeast, and of the southwest of the province of Buenos Aires. The development of the merino in this region moreover, was favored in the eighties and nineties by the subdivision of rural property going on under the influence of the developing cereal farming, a circumstance which did not hurt the merinos, but virtually drove the Lincolns from that region, since they required more ample pasturage.

were particularly good, those from the south of Buenos Aires bringing a high price in this period.

For years, however, the Lincoln had to struggle against the prejudices of the local farmers, accustomed as they were to the fine fleece of the merino. A succession of wet seasons between 1877 and 1884, however, occasioned further serious losses of merinos by foot-rot, while the long-wool withstood the disease and increased. The lung-worm also greatly injured the merinos in 1886, 1887, and 1889, but left the Lincolns untouched. In the nineties the frozen-meat trade proved a decided stimulus to the Lincoln breeds. Merino sheep were of comparatively little value in this trade. Small of carcass and hard to fatten, they were easily surpassed as producers of mutton by the larger long-wools. The result has been that the Lincoln has become the mainstay of the Argentine sheep-breeder; and Argentine wool has undergone a change. The early predominance of the fine, short-fibered merino, suited for woolens, has given way to a preponderance of coarse, long-fibered wools, best adapted for worsted.[1]

From these general considerations concerning the growth and character of sheep-raising and the wool trade in Argentina, we turn to the statistics of wool exports in the period of this study, with a view to explaining the fluctuations of trade with especial reference to the state of prices. The following chart, giving in the form of index numbers the gold value of wool exports, the quantity exported, and the paper price of gold, for the periods 1886-99, demonstrates how little the wool trade was dominated by the fluctuations in the value of paper money. The outstanding facts are (1) that in the period when the price of gold rose most sharply, 1890 and 1891, and when the overturn in the trade balance occurred, wool exports were decreasing; and (2) that in the period when the price of gold was falling so sharply

---

[1] The distribution of sheep in 1900 was as follows:

Total sheep, 130,000,000: of which
75 per cent were Lincolns,
20 per cent were merinos,
5 per cent were Criollos and others.

C. Lix Klett, *ibid.*, ii, p. 1236.

as to make necessary the Conversion Law of 1899, exports of wool, far from being depressed thereby, increased considerably both in quantity and in value. In fact, the last five years of the nineteenth century form perhaps the most prosperous period in the whole history of the Argentine wool trade.

In spots, one can discern the influence of the gold premium, notably in the years 1886–89, when value of wool exports and the price of gold rose together. But even here other factors were coöperating; and they were of at least equal force with the depreciation of paper money. These were the years of greatest railroad expansion, of the land boom, of the operations of the mortgage banks,— all of which helped to bring much new land under cultivation. And all of these factors were affected but indirectly by the depreciation of paper. They are symptoms of the general "fillip" to commercial and industrial activity common to periods of abnormally extended credit and rising prices, which end characteristically in panics, and which occur quite as commonly in gold countries as in paper-money countries.

Moreover, as we shall see presently, there was a factor at work of at least equal importance with any of those mentioned, and which bore directly upon the value of wool exports through its effect on *gold* prices,— the state of demand abroad for Argentine wool. Foreign prices rose markedly in these years, and were reflected in the gold price of Argentine wool. It is this circumstance which explains the sharp increase in the value of wool exported in 1886–89, though the quantity increased to a much less degree.

In 1892, also, there was a rise in wool exports, both in value and in quantity, which is attributable to the gold premium. Mention has been made of the sharp decline of the gold premium in the closing months of 1891, just as the season's wool clip was coming to market; and of the effect upon wool exports. Great quantities were stored in warehouses to avoid shipment at the ruinous prices obtaining in consequence of the fall of exchange and of the price of gold. The result was an abnormally large shipment in 1892 (155,000 tons as against 139,000 tons in 1891), and a consequent increase in the value of wool exports in that year.

EXPORTS OF WOOL AND THE PRICE OF GOLD, 1886–1899

INDEX NUMBERS

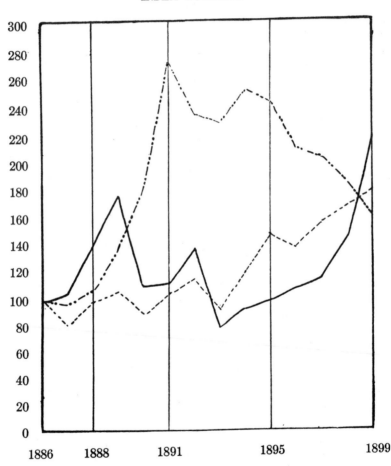

—— = Value of Wool Exported
- - - - = Quantity of Wool Exported
—••— = Price of Gold

Again in 1894 and 1895 there was an increase in the quantity shipped, and in consequence some slight rise in the value figures. And this, too, may be explained by reference to the premium on gold. The chart shows the sharp rise of gold in 1894; and, inasmuch as foreign gold prices for Argentine wool were falling, the increased exports are fairly attributable to the single factor of a rising gold premium, combined with good wool clips in those years.

Indications are not lacking here and there, then, that the gold premium did have the effect supposed by theory. The rising premium did at times stimulate wool exports, and the falling premium depress them. The general conclusion, however, viewing the period as a whole, is just the contrary of that expected theoretically; and this for the reason, already mentioned, that other factors so overlaid the particular ones here studied as to obstruct the working out of their logical effect.

The chief of these other factors, so far as wool was concerned, was undoubtedly that of the state of European demand, as reflected in the price offered for Argentine wool. The period 1890–95 was notoriously one of low prices in Europe; whereas, in the later period, 1895–1900, prices rose. This movement of European prices was just the reverse of that of the Argentine gold premium, and proved to be of far greater importance for the wool trade.

The year 1893 is a good instance of how European prices affected the Argentine wool trade. In 1889 a ton of Argentine wool brought on the average $400 gold; in 1892 a ton was worth $287 gold; in 1893, only $200 gold. The fall of price, combined with the fact that in 1893 the demand of foreign buyers was mostly for the finer grades, whereas the Argentine clip was predominantly of medium grade, and rather a poor clip, too, was responsible for the pronounced fall in wool exports in that year.

One factor tending to depress exports of wool after 1890 was the export duty [1] of 4 per cent ad valorem on pastoral products,

[1] Export duties were first applied in 1866; removed in 1887; reimposed in 1890; removed in 1906; reimposed January 1, 1918.

cereals being allowed to go free. The fact that the quantities exported show a considerable increase, however, despite such occasional bad years as 1890 and 1893, indicates that the duty, though probably a hindrance, did not greatly impede the volume of wool exports. The quantity figures indicate, too, by their greater evenness, that the factors of most effect on the wool trade influenced value rather than the volume brought to market, and point once again to the *gold* price of wool — the reflection of European prices — as the chief factor in the wool trade in this period.

The similarity between the fluctuations of the value of wool exports and the gold price of wool is shown in the following chart. The price data are those of Señor Carlos Lix Klett, probably the most eminent authority on the Argentine wool trade of this period.[1] The curves of wool exports and of the gold price of wool are in close accord with each other throughout,— in the rise to 1889, in the fall of the following years, and in the rise during the last four years of the period, 1895–99.

This latter period, 1895–99, is one of the high spots of the Argentine wool trade. Owing to persistent droughts in Australia, the merino flocks of that country were diminished, causing a decrease of about 100,000,000 kilos in Australian exports of merino wool during the period, or about 25,000,000 kilos a year.[2]

[1] C. Lix Klett: *Estudios sobre Producción, Comercio, Finanzas é Intereses Generales de la República Argentina*, 1900 (2 vols.). See ii, pp. 1205-1284, a study of wool-growing and the wool trade. For price data, see p. 1264 *et seq.* Señor Lix Klett was the official representative of the Argentine government at several conferences and expositions on the wool trade in Europe and in the United States.

[2] EXPORTS OF WOOL FROM AUSTRALIA, CAPE OF GOOD HOPE, AND ARGENTINA, 1895–99

(Thousand bales)

Year	Australia	Cape of Good Hope	Argentina
1895	2,001	269	513
1896	1,846	288	543
1897	1,894	274	550
1898	1,703	279	555
1899	1,641	267	540*

* The Argentine figure for 1899 is a decline in bales, but not in kilos. The decline in bales is due to a change from the old-style wool press ("de caballo") to hydraulic and steam presses, which increased the number of kilos per bale from about 400 to about 500. In fact, wool exports for 1899 were the largest in Argentine history. Lix Klett, *ibid.*, 1262.

GOLD PRICE OF WOOL PER TON AND VALUE
OF WOOL EXPORTS, 1886–1899

INDEX NUMBERS

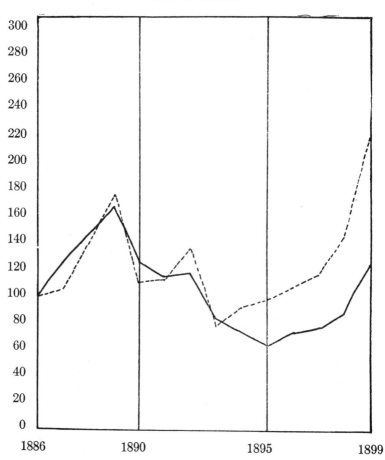

—— = GOLD PRICE OF ARGENTINE WOOL
EXPORTED
– – – = TOTAL ANNUAL VALUE OF WOOL
EXPORTED

This decrease tended to increase the price of Argentine merinos. The extraordinary rise of price in 1899 was due to an outburst of French and Belgian speculation in Argentine wool occasioned by the deficit in the Australian production, the impossibility of securing the South African clip owing to the Boer War, and the decrease in merino wool in all quarters, including Argentina.[1]

Only at two points, in 1892 and in 1894–95, is there disagreement between the curves of wool exports and of the gold price of wool. And these, as we have seen, are precisely the years in which the movements of the gold premium appear to offer a sufficient explanation of the movements of wool exports. Aside from them, "gold price of wool" and total "gold value of wool exported" move together, offering clear proof that the factor which dominated the gold price of wool, European prices,[2] dominated thereby the major movements of the wool trade. And inasmuch as European prices were moving in just the contrary direction from the Argentine gold premium during most of the period, the result was virtually to obliterate the effect of depreciated paper money on the exports of wool.

---

[1] C. Lix Klett, *Estudios sobre Producción, Comercio, Finanzas é Intereses Generales de la República Argentina,* ii, p. 1263.

[2] PRICE OF WOOL ON THE ANTWERP WOOL EXCHANGE, 1888–99

(For merino wool type "German B")

Year	Extreme Prices in Year
1888	4.64–5.67 francs per kilo
1889	5.10–6.20
1890	5.20–6.07
1891	4.40–5.55
1892	4.20–5.15
1893	4.30–4.94
1894	3.40–4.34
1895	3.22–4.49
1896	3.75–4.35
1897	3.58–4.03
1898	3.90–4.73
1899	4.73–6.75

C. Lix Klett, *ibid.,* ii, p. 1263.

II. Cereals

A. *The Wheat Trade*

From the wool trade we turn to cereals, the other main branch of Argentine foreign commerce. The outstanding fact of the export trade in the period of our study is the rapid rise of wheat. Until 1875 wheat was imported into Argentina. The exportation of 1878 was but 2547 tons ($105,350 gold). In the eighties the growth of the wheat trade was rapid, and in the panic period of the early nineties it was spectacular, reaching 1,600,000 tons ($27,118,142 gold) in 1894, about 27 per cent of the total export trade of that year. Since the period of the rise of wheat corresponds approximately with that of depreciated paper money, it is to wheat that one naturally turns for verification of the theory that a rising gold premium stimulates exports. Yet even here other factors obscure the workings of this particular one, and illustrate the difficulty of following through a single force in a complex situation made up of numerous forces, working sometimes in combination and sometimes at cross-purposes.

In the following chart are given in the form of index numbers the value and the quantity of wheat exported in the period 1884–1900, and, for comparison, the movements of the price of gold. One's first impression is one of meaningless irregularity. Both the value of wheat exported and the quantity — particularly the latter — rise and fall to an astonishing degree. The spectacular fluctuations are chiefly due to the irregular recurrence of bad seasons, and indicate the difficulty of attempting to apply a theory concerned solely with monetary and price conditions to agricultural products, which are affected so markedly by the uncontrollable vagaries of rainfall, climate, pests, and the like. The three bad seasons of 1886, 1889, and 1897 stand out sharply. Particularly marked is that of 1897, in which the wheat crop was almost wholly destroyed by locusts. In 1895 and 1896, too, the wheat crop suffered more than usually from locusts, so that the descent of the wheat export curves in those years is not ascribable to the falling price of gold. In proof, we have the

EXPORTS OF WHEAT AND THE PRICE OF GOLD, 1884–1900

INDEX NUMBERS

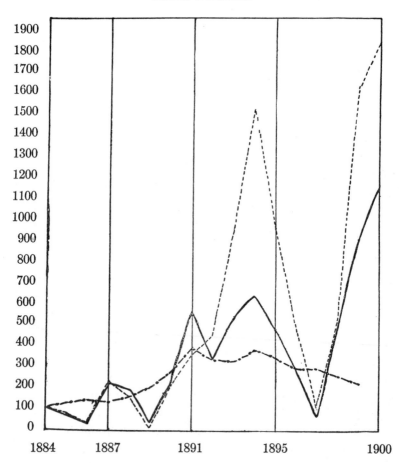

——— = VALUE OF WHEAT EXPORTED
– – – = QUANTITY OF WHEAT EXPORTED
—•— = PRICE OF GOLD

pronounced increase of 1899, a record year for the wheat trade, notwithstanding a decline of thirty-three points in the price of gold in 1898 and a further decline of twenty-eight points in 1899. Nor was the increase of 1899 due to any phenomenal rise in European prices for wheat, as was the case with wool. The increasing value appears to have been the result of the much greater increase in quantity exported, an increase which occurred in spite of the low price offered by foreign buyers. This again is an indication that in the cereal trade the main factor in determining the exports of a given year was the volume of the harvest. The year 1899 was a bumper-crop year; and, the home market being small, the farmer had no choice but to sell abroad at whatever price his wheat would fetch.

For wool the case was different. The large estancias devoted to sheep-raising were owned by men of means. Should prices in a given year prove disastrous the estanciero could warehouse his wool and await the next season. Such, in fact, was the common practice among wool-growers. The most notable instance, that of 1891–92, has been referred to. The decline of price in the closing months of 1891, due to a violent fall of the gold premium, caused the storing of some 5,000,000 kilos of wool, which went to swell the exports of 1892.

The wheat-growers, on the other hand, were small farmers of immigrant stock, dependent from year to year upon the sale of their harvests immediately after they were grown and reaped. Holding over a season for a better price was impossible, and in the absence of a home market the farmers sold to the foreign buyer, or to the representative of the large exporting houses in Buenos Aires, Rosario, or Bahia Blanca.

Granted, however, that the wheat farmer was thus mainly at the mercy of the vagaries of climate, and of the state of foreign demand, and that in some years his crop was eaten up by locusts which he was powerless to ward off, and that in others, having avoided locusts and the perils of the elements, he found himself forced to dispose of his abundant crop at ruinous prices, simply because in consequence of exceptional harvests elsewhere in the world, or because of a rise in ocean freight rates, the foreign buyer holding the whip hand offered a ruinously low price,—granting all this, it is of course true that, taking one year with another, the farmer made a comfortable profit, or he would have ceased to grow wheat. The fact that there were about 1,750,000 tons of wheat for export in 1899, and almost two millions in 1900 is proof that wheat-farming in Argentina "paid." And the fact that by 1894 wheat exports had reached 1,600,000 tons, as against 108,000 tons in 1884 (the best year in the Argentine wheat trade prior to 1887), is an indication that in the intervening ten-year period wheat paid handsomely. So marked an increase, the largest in any similar period in Argentine history, indicates that unusual forces were at work upon the wheat trade.

One of these forces, without doubt, was the ascending premium on gold. Barring the bad years 1886 and 1889, the curve of the paper price of wheat and of the value of wheat exports keep pace with each other. A rising premium is accompanied by increasing exports of wheat. Particularly marked is the increase in 1891, the year in which the price of gold rose highest, the first year in which total exports exceeded total imports; and again in 1894, when the price of gold rose thirty-three points.

The rising gold premium, however, was not the only factor stimulating wheat exports in these years, nor perhaps the most important factor. These are the years of greatest railroad expansion in Argentine history. They are the years of largest immigration; the years of the land boom; of the furor of cédula operations conducted by the official mortgage banks. All of these factors would tend to increase the area under wheat cultivation: they would affect wheat more than wool, for instance, or indeed even at the expense of wool. The immigrant acquired his small farm on easy terms, paying either a low annual money rent per acre, or a portion of the produce.[1] Sheep-raising, on the other hand, was a large-scale frontier operation. The railroads made the land easily accessible to immigrant settlers; the line of wheat culture advanced with the railroad and the immigrant

---

[1] This plan was especially followed in the numerous "colonization" schemes, designed with the purpose of attracting immigrants.

farmer; and before them the sheep-raiser retired west and north, and to the southern part of the province of Buenos Aires. The change in the character of the flock, from merino to Lincoln, hastened the process, the latter requiring greater pasturage, and thriving particularly on the plains of southern Argentina. By these means was developed the rich cereal belt of northeast Argentina, comprising Santa Fé, the north of Buenos Aires, Entre Rios, and the east of Córdoba.

It is for these reasons that the wool trade failed to expand, that the wheat trade sprang up in a decade, and by 1904 had become the chief of Argentine exports. Still another factor tending to increase the export of wheat was the improvement in agricultural methods and in methods of shipment. Even in the nineties harvesting methods were still primitive, the wheat being left on the ground or in stacks without proper protection from the weather, and when threshed put into bags without attempts at classification. Since the farmers had no barns or accommodations for storage, the wheat was carried to the nearest railroad station, where it lay for days, and sometimes weeks, exposed to rain and sun. Consequently much grain arrived at its destination in bad condition; gave rise to heavy claims for deficient quality; and caused some millers to abstain from using River Plate wheat.

But there were signs of improvement. Attempts were being made to establish a system of inspection, by which wheat would be graded by responsible and qualified persons, as in the United States. There were improvements, too, in threshing. Formerly threshing had been conducted by means of troops of horses, that were driven round and round on a piece of hard ground and made to trample out the grain, the chaff being up to their knees. This concluded, the straw, being very brittle, was thrown up against the wind and blown away, leaving a mixture of grain and dirt. By the late eighties and early nineties, however, steam threshing machines and winnowers were in fairly general use; and reaping, which formerly had been done by hand with a sickle, was effected by machines which reaped, bound, and left the wheat in sheaves ready for stacking.

In addition to these improvements, grain elevators were being built in the ports of shipment. There were three in Rosario in 1892, with an aggregate capacity of 26,000 tons, one at Villa Constitución, with a capacity of 10,000 tons, and one in the port of Buenos Aires, of 6,000 tons. Also, with the extension of the railroads new shipping-ports for grain were being created. Rosario, the chief city of Santa Fé, the richest grain province, had every facility for export. The extension of the railroads created Villa Constitución, San Lorenzo, and Colastine, all on the River Paraná, navigable for steamers drawing sixteen to eighteen feet of water. In the province of Buenos Aires, the opening of docks at La Plata was a great boon to exporters, for from all parts of the country the railroads converged on the quays alongside ocean-going steamers. With such a group of forces as these which have been reviewed,—the expansion of railroads, the great wave of immigration, the land boom, the mortgage-bank operations, the improvements in agricultural methods, and in the methods and facilities for storage, classification, and shipment,— it is not surprising that the wheat trade should have shown in the decade 1884–94 a greater expansion than in any other ten-year period in Argentine history. It is probable that that expansion would have occurred even without the artificial stimulus of a rise in the premium on gold.

The course of European prices, so injurious to wool, particularly between 1889 and 1893, when the value of wool exports declined 50 per cent, tended also to restrict the wheat trade, so far as the value figures are concerned. The chart indicates that in 1892 "quantity exported" increased 20 per cent; in 1893 and 1894 the increase in quantity exported was phenomenal. There was an increase from 396,000 tons in 1891 to 1,608,000 tons in 1894, an increase of over 400 per cent. The increase in value was much less. In 1892, despite the increase of 20 per cent in the quantity exported, the value figures fell 42 per cent. In 1893, the value was about equal to that of 1891 ($23,000,000 gold), though the quantity exported the latter year was almost three times that of the former. Comparing 1893 with 1894, we find an increase of 60 per cent (600,000 tons) in quantity, but of only 16 per cent in value.[1] The extraordinary increase in quantity of wheat exported in these years was due to the enormous increase in the acreage sown[2] during the late eighties and early nineties, under the stimulus of expanding railroads, heavy immigration, and a rising gold premium. The failure of the value

[1] Statistics of the value and the quantity of wheat exported, 1880–1900:

WHEAT EXPORTS, 1880–1900

Year	Value (gold pesos)	Quantity (tons)
1880	$46,747	1,166
1881	11,111	157
1882	66,864	1,705
1883	2,430,184	60,755
1884	4,339,970	108,499
1885	3,139,736	78,493
1886	1,510,378	37,864
1887	9,514,635	237,866
1888	8,248,614	178,929
1889	1,596,446	22,806
1890	9,836,824	327,894
1891	23,733,312	395,555
1892	14,696,089	470,110
1893	23,459,926	1,008,137
1894	27,118,142	1,608,249
1895	19,471,652	1,010,269
1896	12,830,027	532,002
1897	3,470,351	101,845
1898	22,368,900	645,161
1899	38,078,343	1,713,429
1900	48,627,653	1,929,676

Extracto Estadistico, 1915, pp. 72–73.

[2] INCREASE IN CULTIVATED AREA, 1883–92

(ooo's omitted)

Crop	Number of hectares cultivated in: 1883	1892	Increase Absolute	Per cent
Wheat	244	1,322	1,078	400
Corn	203	908	705	350
Alfalfa	143	662	509	360
Grapes	15	30	15	100
Sugar-cane	10	28	18	200
Others	316	952	636	200
Total	929	3,902	2,973	300

(See *Exposición sobre el Estado Económico y Financiero*, p. 86.)

figures to respond is an indication that the gold price of wheat was falling, and tending to neutralize the increase in quantity exported.

Information concerning European prices is given by the correspondent of the *Economist*. In February, 1893, he writes:

> The fall in the price of wheat in European markets will neutralize the much larger quantity exported.[1]

In July, 1893, he says:

> The past season has not been a favorable one in international commerce for the Argentine Republic, as the fall in the price of wheat and wool in the consuming markets has left much less to her credit than she expected.[2]

And in August, 1894, referring to the exports of the first half of the year, he says:

> The great fall in the price of wheat in Europe quite neutralized the heavy increase in production.[3]

These citations are sufficient to indicate that European wheat prices, like wool prices, were generally falling between 1890 and 1895, the period of the rapid rise and high general level of the premium on gold, and that they therefore tended to offset the stimulative influence of depreciating paper money on exports. With wool, as has been said, the falling European price effected a positive decline in the value figures, the quantity exported remaining about stationary. On wheat, the effect was not so great, owing to the enormously increased acreage and the consequent growth of the quantity figures. Some increase in value there was, and it is ascribable, among the other causes that we have mentioned, to the stimulating effect of a rising premium on gold.

---

[1] *Economist*, 1893, i, p. 355.   [2] *Ibid.*, ii, p. 1059.

[3] *Economist*, 1894, ii, p. 1195. Mr. J. H. Sams, one of the best authorities on the wheat industry in the River Plate, gave the paper-money price obtainable by the farmer at the nearest railroad station as $4.70 paper in 1893–94, as against $6.50 paper in 1892–93; and ascribed the fall to a decline in wheat prices in Europe. *Economist*, July 14, 1894, Trade Supplement, pp. 8–9. (Note that the gold premium was higher in the latter year than in the former, and would therefore tend to raise the paper price.)

B. *Corn*

Wool and wheat were the great staples. Since most of the major changes in the export trade during our period are traceable to fluctuations in the one or the other of these two items, they sufficiently serve the purpose of general illustration of the nature and effect of the forces operating upon Argentine exports. To illustrate again, however, the extraordinary fluctuations in the crops occasioned by irregularities of rainfall and the inroads of the locusts, the statistics of corn exports are given in the following chart.

The irregularities of the corn harvest were extreme; climatic conditions and the locusts influenced the export figures to such a degree as to over-ride almost completely all other factors. The year 1890 was an unusually good corn year; the increase in exports would appear to be due to that, rather than to the rising gold premium. In 1891 the premium rose much more sharply than in any other year, but corn exports sank to an insignificant figure, three-fourths of the crop having been destroyed by locusts. In 1892, the gold premium fell sharply, but corn exports were normal, in consequence of a fair crop. In 1893 the tendency of the premium was upwards, and in 1894 it rose sharply, but the corn crop was a failure in both years. In 1895 and 1896, the premium was falling, but corn was abundant, and exports reached their highest point. In 1897, the crop was again spoiled by locusts. In 1898 and 1899, with the premium falling violently amid the protests of producers and exporters, corn exports were rising because the crops were good. Any reasoning about the corn trade which does not begin and end in the purely natural, seasonal conditions of cultivation seems futile.

QUANTITY OF CORN EXPORTED, 1886–1900

INDEX NUMBERS

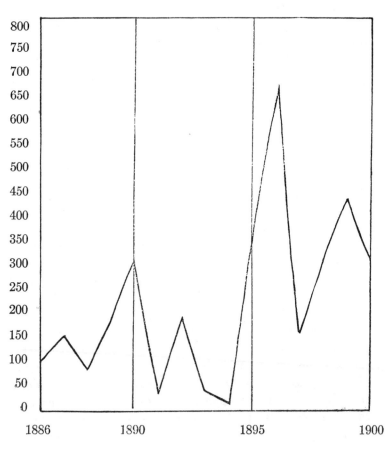

III. Conclusions

The study of the three major exports,— wool, wheat, and corn,— together with the discussion of the statistics of total exports in Chapter XIII, has shown the character and course of the export trade, and the forces at work upon it. The purpose of the investigation has been to determine how far the Argentine export trade in the period of depreciated paper money was in accordance with theoretical expectation. We may sum up the result.

According to theory, a rising gold premium stimulates exports. It does so by virtue of the fact that export prices rise more rapidly than costs, creating an extra profit or "bounty" for the producing and exporting classes. The index numbers of Argentine export prices and of wages move in accordance with theoretical expectation. The premium on gold appeared in 1885 and began to rise rapidly in 1888, reaching its climax in 1891. Export prices followed suit, showing extreme sensitiveness to movements of the gold premium. Wages, on the other hand, rose but sluggishly. The "bounty," or "gap," between export prices and wages does certainly appear.

Evidence that the gold premium did affect exports is shown, too, by the operations of producers and exporters, who, in so far as possible, regulated their activity with an eye to the premium on gold. When the premium fell, those who were able to do so, as the wool-growers, stored their produce in the hope of a higher premium later on.

A rising gold premium, then, was undoubtedly a stimulus to the export trade. When one turns to the statistics of exports, however, the expected expansion of exports does not appear. Some increase of quantity exported there was,— a really remarkable increase as regards wheat. But the "value of exports," which are the significant figures for our purpose, show an increase of a bare $3,000,000 between 1888 and 1891, although in the intervening years the premium on gold had ascended violently.

The failure of "value of exports" to expand in accordance with theoretical expectation, and in accordance with the evidence afforded by the index numbers of prices and wages, we have seen to be due to the presence of other factors working at cross-purposes to the gold premium. The most important factor was European prices. These were falling between 1890 and 1895: their fall neutralized the effect of the rising gold premium. Though quantity of exports increased, the greater quantity was sold for a lower gold price per unit; with the result that "value of exports" remained virtually stationary. The fall of European prices acted as a restraint upon the wheat trade, though it could not prevent a considerable increase even in "value of exports" because of the enormously increased wheat acreage. In the wool trade, where the quantity was about stationary, the fall of prices abroad produced a decided decline in "value of exports." The general result was that the decline in the wool trade offset the growth of the wheat trade, and kept "value of exports" about stationary during the period of the high premium on gold.

A second complicating factor is the character of the Argentine exports. They were purely agricultural and grazing products, and therefore extremely susceptible to vagaries of climate. Argentine rainfall is very irregular. Moreover, there was the locust, which in some years did but little damage and in others practically destroyed the cereal crops. In 1889 the wheat crop was spoiled by excessive rain. In 1891 the locusts ate three-fourths of the corn crop.

If one seeks to discount the seasonal mishaps by calculating a moving average of seasons, and asks whether, taking the period of the rising gold premium as a whole, there was not some considerable increase in exports, the case is but little improved. Total value of exports, as was just pointed out, show but little increase during the period. The one striking fact is the increase in wheat, especially in the quantity produced and exported. But even this is not ascribable solely to a rising gold premium. Other factors, at least equally powerful, coöperated to the same end: the growing railway net, the inrush of immigrants, the land boom, the mortgage-bank operations, the building of new shipping ports and the improvement of old ones, the improvement in threshing and reaping. Why, among so many, choose a single factor, the rising premium on gold, as chiefly responsible for the remarkable growth of wheat cultivation and exports? The truth, clearly, is that all were responsible. There was no *chief* cause, but many causes working in combination, and of these, one undoubtedly was the rising gold premium.

Aside from wheat, it is difficult to point out any striking instance in which the gold premium increased exports. The wool trade, most important of all, affords some favorable evidence, but appears in the main to have depended on the state of foreign demand as reflected by European prices. The corn trade was so irregular that virtually no conclusions can be drawn from it.

We must leave our examination of the export trade with the statement that, as regards verification of theory, the Argentine case, so far as the export trade is concerned, is inconclusive. The stimulus to exports supposed to be afforded by a rising gold premium was undoubtedly present. The index numbers of prices and wages show that clearly enough. "Other things being equal," an expansion of exports would have taken place: but owing to the presence of other factors working at cross-purposes to the gold premium, the actual increase in the export trade was only slight.

CHAPTER XV

PAPER MONEY AND PRICES IN RELATION TO THE IMPORT TRADE

In the discussion of principles in Chapter XI it was shown that, according to theory, depreciating paper money, or, in other words, a rising gold premium, has just the contrary effects on exports and imports. It stimulates exports and depresses imports. It is by this dual influence, says theory, that the overturn of the trade balance in a paper-money country is brought about. As regards the first half of the statement, the stimulation of exports, we have seen that the evidence afforded by the Argentine case is inconclusive. We have now to examine the second half of the theory,— that concerning the diminution of imports.

The examination of imports is a simpler matter than that of exports, and the results are more decisive. In the first place, the particular factor to be studied, the effect of depreciated paper money, is not overlaid by so many other factors as in the case of exports, though other factors were present, as we shall see. In the second place, the expected diminution of imports did occur, and to a striking degree. We have simply to determine to what extent the diminution is ascribable to a rising premium on gold. The following table shows the change that occurred in the import trade, as compared with that in the export trade during the four years 1889–92, in which the overturn of the Argentine trade balance took place.

BALANCE OF TRADE, 1889–92

(Thousand gold pesos)

Year	Exports	Imports	Excess of Exports	Excess of Imports
1889..........	$90,145	$164,570	..	$74,425
1890..........	100,819	142,241	..	41,422
1891..........	103,219	67,208	$36,011	
1892..........	113,370	91,481	21,889	

The table makes it clear that the overturn took place not by an increase of exports, but by a diminution of imports. The overturn occurred in 1891, the year when the gold premium mounted to 287 per cent (yearly average). An "unfavorable" balance of over forty-one millions in 1890 is converted into a "favorable" balance of over thirty-six millions in 1891. Yet the exports of 1891 are less than 3 per cent in excess of those of 1890. On the other hand, imports amounting to 142 millions in 1890, are followed in 1891 by imports of only sixty-seven millions, a decrease of about 53 per cent.

INDEX NUMBERS OF EXPORTS AND IMPORTS, 1886–1896

(BASE-AVERAGE OF THE ELEVEN YEARS)

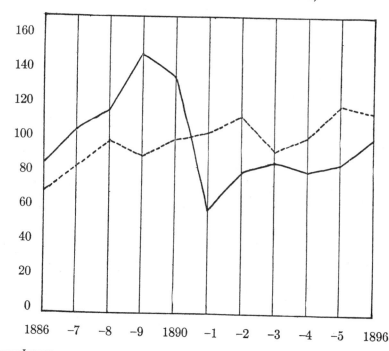

——— = IMPORTS
– – – – = EXPORTS

The chart on p. 237 shows the relative changes in the value of imports and of exports in the period 1886–96. The curves represent the index numbers of exports and imports, the average of the eleven years being taken as the base. The outstanding fact is the expansion of imports between 1886 and

INDEX NUMBERS OF VALUE OF IMPORTS AND THE GOLD PREMIUM, 1886–1896

(BASE-AVERAGE OF THE ELEVEN YEARS)

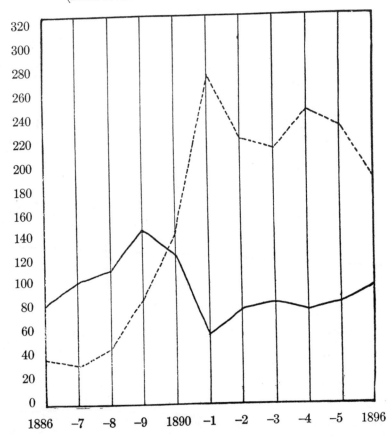

——=IMPORTS
- - -=GOLD PREMIUM

1890, and the sudden contraction of imports in 1891. Exports, meantime, show only a slight increase.

The period here presented is the period of chief interest as regards the depreciation of paper money. It includes the years when the premium on gold rose to its highest point, and also the year of the first marked decline of the premium, 1896. In the chart on page 238 the index number of the value of imports is compared with the premium on gold for this period, 1886–96. After 1889 the movements of the two curves are entirely in accordance with expectation. As the gold premium rises, imports decrease. The spectacular rise of the premium in 1891 is matched by the remarkable shrinkage of imports in that year. And in the following years also, without exception, the curves are in inverse relation to each other.[1]

---

[1] This period, 1889–96, is the one of primary significance for the purpose of our study. It is the "transition period," the period in which the overturn of the trade balance was effected. The excess of imports over exports, until 1891 the character-istic situation in Argentine foreign trade, reaches its maximum in 1889, in conse-quence of the extraordinary inflation of imports in this year. Thereafter imports decline rapidly; exports increase gradually. In 1891 exports exceed imports. In 1893 the situation is again, temporarily, reversed,— imports exceeding exports. But the following year exports again exceed imports; and since that time, despite marked fluctuations due principally to bad harvests, as in 1897, exports have exceeded imports in every year except one, 1911. The "favorable" balance in-creases even in spite of a falling gold premium in the closing years of the nineties, reaching over $68,000,000 gold in 1899, and about $118,000,000 gold in 1905. The transition period, from the condition of an unfavorable trade balance which had existed prior to 1891 to the favorable balance which has since then characterized Argentine foreign trade, clearly falls within the years 1889–96. In these years we have all the factors which have been mentioned as bringing about the overturn of the trade balance. After 1889 borrowings decrease and interest charge grows, the overturn in the balance of borrowings occurring in 1890. The years 1890 and 1891 are the panic years which mark the subsidence of the borrowing fever and the overturn of the trade balance. The years 1891–95 constitute the period of recovery from the panic. By 1896 borrowings, on a moderate scale, have again begun; trade is picking up. The worst effects of the panic are past. Regarding the gold premium, too (and this is the matter of chief significance in our study of the course of imports), the period 1889–96 is the period of paramount importance. The marked rise of the gold premium does not begin until 1889; in the next two years, there is an increase of one hundred and ninety-six points in the premium.* The general level thereafter is high until 1896, when the premium falls forty-eight points in a single year. It is in this transition period, therefore, that one looks for

* From 91 per cent in 1889 to 287 per cent in 1891.

The years prior to 1889 are of secondary interest. The transition stage in the foreign trade had not then commenced. The overturn in the balance of borrowings, which was the underlying cause of the overturn in the balance of merchandise trade, had not taken place. Borrowings were in full swing; and the excess of borrowings over interest charge was at its maximum in 1888–89. The gold premium, though rising slowly, had not yet assumed alarming proportions. The average premium for 1888 was only 48 per cent, which is but eleven points above the premium of 1885, the year in which specie payments were terminated. In 1886 and 1887, the premium, on an average, remained about stationary.

Our chart of imports and the gold premium (p. 238) shows that the inverse relation between imports and the gold premium does not appear prior to 1889. Despite the fact that the gold premium is rising, imports do not decrease, but on the contrary show an extraordinary degree of inflation, which reaches its maximum in 1889, with imports of about $165,000,000 gold, as compared with $95,000,000 in 1886. The apparent failure of theory to "work" in these years, 1886–89, requires explanation. As in the case of exports, we have to recognize the presence of "other factors." In the first place, it may be pointed out again that the rise of the premium in those years was only moderate; not sufficient to dominate the import trade in opposition to other forces. In the second place, these were the "boom" years; the years in which personal credit over-extended itself to a degree never witnessed in any other period of Argentine history. The expansion of credit applied to the import trade quite as much as to any other phase of commercial or financial activity, and tended to increase purchases from abroad. The spirit of "easy come, easy go" was in the air. It appears in the increased purchase of articles of luxury, of "consumption goods" generally, despite the fact that these articles, like imports in gen-

the effect of movements of the gold premium upon the value of imports; and the fact that the chart shows in every year an inverse relation between the movements of imports and of the gold premium, establishes a very strong presumption of the soundness of the theory that a rising gold premium discourages, and a falling premium encourages, imports.

eral, were rising in price, under the influence of a rising gold premium.

In the following table are shown the combined imports of manufactured foods, drinks, tobacco, and textiles; that is, the pure consumption goods. With them are compared the total imports for the period 1886–96.

TOTAL IMPORTS, AND IMPORTS OF FOOD, DRINKS, TOBACCO, AND TEXTILES, 1886–96

(Thousand gold pesos)

Year	Absolute Figures		Relative Figures [1]	
	Total Imports	Foods, Drinks, Tobacco, Textiles	Total Imports	Foods, Drinks, Tobacco, Textiles
1886	$95,409	$50,811	87%	92%
1887	117,352	62,756	107	114
1888	128,412	57,510	117	105
1889	164,570	67,778	151	123
1890	142,241	61,780	130	112
1891	67,208	29,556	61	54
1892	91,481	54,277	83	99
1893	96,224	52,057	88	95
1894	92,789	46,624	84	85
1895	95,096	58,869	87	107
1896	112,164	63,361	103	115

The chart on page 243 shows the relative changes in these two categories,— all imports, and imports of pure consumption goods,— and compares with them the movements of the gold premium. It is seen that the imports of consumption goods did rise between 1886 and 1889, in spite of a rising gold premium. Compared with that of all imports, however, the rise is less pronounced, more in conformity with theoretical expectation. In fact, in only one year, 1889, do imports of consumption goods move in the same direction as the gold premium. In 1887 the premium on gold falls, this class of imports increases; in 1888 the directions of the two curves are reversed. In the later period,

[1] The average of the eleven years equals base.

too, that after 1889, imports of consumption goods move in closer sympathy with the gold premium than do general imports, particularly in 1891–92 and in 1895–96.

Imports of "luxury" and other consumption goods, then, do not sufficiently explain the extraordinary inflation of total imports in the period 1886–89, in the face of a rising gold premium. In only one year, 1889, did this kind of imports fail to respond to the influence of the gold premium. The main cause of the inflation of imports was the character of the other imports in these years,— the imports of construction materials and other reproductive goods. The consideration of these necessitates fuller discussion than has heretofore been given of the relation between imports and foreign borrowings.

At various points in Part I of this study, as well as in Chapter XII of the present section, we have discussed the relation between the balance of borrowings and the balance of trade. And it has been shown that the overturn of the balance of borrowings in 1890 was responsible for the overturn in the trade balance in 1891. That is to say, prior to 1890 Argentina annually borrowed more from abroad than she was required to pay out in interest charge; new annual borrowings exceeded interest charge; but with the virtual cessation of borrowings after the outbreak of the panic in 1890 the situation was reversed; interest charge annually exceeded new borrowings. This overturn in the balance of borrowings communicated itself to the balance of trade in the following year, 1891. When prior to that date borrowings had exceeded interest charge, imports had exceeded exports; and when after 1890, interest charge exceeded new borrowings, exports exceeded imports, the change taking place, as has been shown in the present chapter, not by an increase of exports, but by a diminution of imports.

This relationship between borrowings and merchandise trade is a familiar fact of international trade, and beyond the calculation of the balance of payments, as presented in Part I, requires no special discussion. The real matter for examination, the central point of this study, has been to explain the *mechanism* whereby the overturn of the balance of borrowings com-

IMPORTS OF FOODS, DRINKS, TOBACCO AND TEXTILES, COMPARED WITH ALL IMPORTS AND WITH THE GOLD PREMIUM, 1886–1896

(INDEX NUMBERS: BASE = ELEVEN–YEAR AVERAGE)

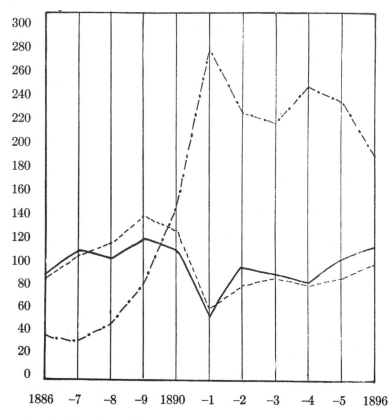

= IMPORTS OF FOODS, DRINKS, TOBACCO AND
TEXTILES

- - - = ALL IMPORTS

—.— = GOLD PREMIUM

municated itself to the trade balance. There is no need to recapitulate the situation: how in most discussions of international trade the mechanism is gold movements and gold exchange; how in Argentina this mechanism was lacking because paper money was depreciated and gold, being always at a premium, could not circulate. The nature of our problem has been already sufficiently explained. The only point requiring restatement for our present purpose is the relation between imports, borrowings, and exchange operations.

The balance of borrowings affects the trade balance through its effect upon the value of paper money; and it affects the value of paper money through its effect on the rate of exchange. This is the gist of the discussion of principles in Chapters II and XI. Thus, Argentina borrows from England; Argentine borrowers draw on the English lenders; the supply of exchange in Buenos Aires is increased; the rate of exchange rises. If the borrowing is heavy, exchange rises to gold import point; gold flows into Argentina. The gold cannot, however, flow into circulation, and this is the point at which the Argentine case, despite the fact that the Argentine exchange was a gold and not a paper exchange, differs from that of the gold-standard countries. Gold was at a premium. The inflow of gold would alter the ratio of exchange between gold and paper. The gold supply being increased, gold would fall in terms of paper; that is, paper money would appreciate. In contrary manner, when as in 1891 the interest charge on former borrowings grew larger than the new annual borrowings, the contrary process would begin, ending in an outflow of gold and a rise of the premium on gold.

It is in this manner, as has been shown in Part I, that the balance of borrowings affected the value of paper money. From that, in Part II, we turned to the second half of the process. The balance of borrowings governs the value of paper money; the value of paper money governs the relative movements of imports and exports. A rising premium through its effects on prices and costs encourages exports and discourages imports. Thus is established, through the mechanism of depreciated paper money, the relation between balance of borrowings and balance of trade.

This relationship, however, depends entirely upon the fact that borrowing operations give rise to foreign-exchange operations. This is the step that sets in motion the whole series of consequences. Some of the Argentine borrowings, however, and a very considerable part of them, did not give rise to exchange transactions at all. It is to make clear the significance of this fact that the argument underlying our study has been recapitulated.

Much of the capital borrowed in England was borrowed for the express purpose of buying materials in England. It did not leave England either in bills of exchange or in gold: it left England in the form of goods, in the form of imports into Argentina. It is these imports, which have no relation whatever to depreciated paper money, to fluctuations of the premium on gold, but which came as the *direct* result of borrowing operations, which are mainly responsible for the failure of the Argentine import trade to show an inverse relation to the movement of the gold premium in the years prior to 1889.

The imports referred to are railroad construction and operating materials. They were imported almost exclusively from England by the English-owned railroad companies of Argentina. They represent a considerable part of the heavy railroad borrowings in the last half of the eighties.

In the following chart the railroad borrowings and the imports of construction materials are compared, in millions of gold pesos. In addition is plotted the curve representing "construction materials"[1] plus "iron and manufactures thereof." It is seen that the great outburst of borrowings for the construction of new lines and the expansion of old ones in the late eighties is accompanied by large imports of construction materials and iron goods. In 1891, the panic year, railroad borrowings virtually ceased; construction materials continued to be imported

---

[1] These are the two main branches of the Argentine classification of imports which refer to "reproductive" goods, and which may therefore be expected to show the closest relation to borrowings for purposes of construction.

in considerable quantity as a result of the borrowings of former years. Railroad construction does not come to a halt until 1892. After 1891 railroad borrowings are insignificant, as also are imports of construction materials.

RAILROAD BORROWINGS AND IMPORTS OF CONSTRUCTION GOODS
1886-1896

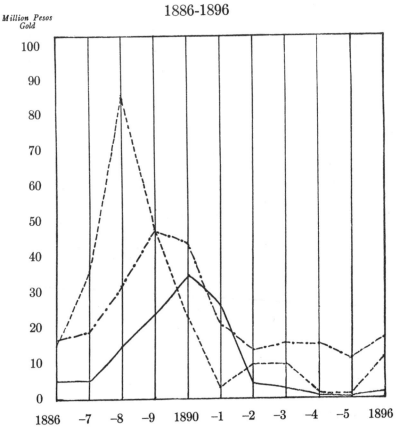

——— = RAILROAD CONSTRUCTION MATERIALS
ALONE
—•— = RAILROAD CONSTRUCTION MATERIALS
PLUS IRON AND MANUFACTURES
THEREOF
– – – = RAILROAD BORROWINGS

In the following table the general course of imports of construction materials is compared with that of all imports. Both the absolute and the relative figures are given. The percentage figures are based in each instance on the average of the eleven years 1886–96.

ALL IMPORTS, AND IMPORTS OF CONSTRUCTION MATERIALS, 1886–96

	Absolute Values (Thousand gold pesos)			Percentages (Based on average for the eleven years)		
Year	1 All Imports	2 Construction Materials plus Iron and Manufactures Thereof	3 Construction Materials Alone	1° All Imports	2° Construction Materials plus Iron and Manufactures Thereof	3° Construction Materials Alone
1886	$95,409	$17,396	$5,103	87	73	48
1887	117,352	19,398	5,039	107	81	47
1888	128,412	33,115	15,472	117	139	146
1889	164,570	48,901	24,174	151	205	228
1890	142,241	45,841	36,274	130	192	342
1891	67,208	22,398	17,881	61	94	169
1892	91,481	13,885	3,546	83	58	33
1893	96,223	16,319	3,280	88	68	31
1894	92,789	16,165	1,914	84	68	18
1895	95,096	11,723	1,922	87	49	18
1896	112,164	17,754	1,940	103	74	18

On page 249 are plotted the relative variations of these three categories, (1) all imports, (2) construction materials plus iron and manufactures thereof, (3) construction materials alone. The most striking curve is that of "construction materials alone." In the early years, when railroad borrowings were heavy, it ascends much more sharply than do imports in general. In the later years, railroad borrowings having virtually ceased, it falls to insignificance. Total imports, meanwhile, rise and fall in sympathy with the movements of the premium on gold.

The data just presented explain, then, the failure of total imports to move inversely to the gold premium in the early years, 1886–89. Imports and gold premium rose together in those years mainly for the reason that a large portion of the imports

were goods imported as the *direct* consequence of railroad borrowings. These borrowings did not result in exchange operations
and had therefore no effect on the value of paper money; and
the imports to which they gave rise were, in turn, unaffected by
the fluctuations of the premium on gold.

This *direct* connection between borrowings and imports,
however, extends only to a portion of total borrowings and of
total imports. Investments in railroads were only one item in
the balance of borrowings. There were besides the government
borrowings,— national, provincial, and municipal; the cédulas;
the investments in other forms of private enterprise. Moreover,
not all of the railroad borrowings could have been expended
directly on construction materials abroad. Some part of them
would be needed in Argentina to buy domestic materials, and
particularly, to pay wages and salaries for the building of the
roads. In the late eighties, with construction of new roads
proceeding at a pace never equalled in Argentine history, expenditures *within* the country were certainly very large. And
for these the railroads would need to receive a part of their
capital in the form of money. This portion of the new railroad investments would give rise to exchange operations, and
would therefore exert an influence on the value of paper money;
as would also the very large borrowings for purposes other than
railroad construction.

In like manner, only a part of the imports, even in the late
eighties, were construction materials. The major portion of the
imports had no *direct* connection with borrowing operations.
They, therefore, might be expected to rise or fall in accordance
with the fluctuations of the premium on gold, or, stated more
exactly, in accordance with import prices as these were affected
by the movement of the premium on gold. Such indeed we have
seen to be the case, once the interfering factor of railroad borrowings and imports of railroad materials was removed. The
depressing effect of a rising gold premium is so great that total
imports begin to decline from 1889, notwithstanding the fact that
imports of construction materials (as shown in the chart on
page 249) do not reach their maximum until 1890.

INDEX NUMBERS OF ALL IMPORTS AND OF IMPORTS OF CONSTRUCTION MATERIALS
1886–1896

BASE = AVERAGE OF ELEVEN YEARS

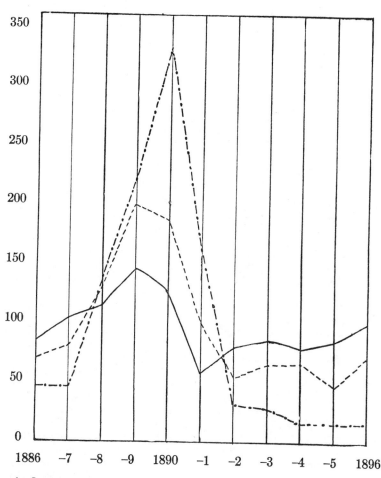

——— = ALL IMPORTS
- - - = RAILROAD CONSTRUCTION MATERIALS
PLUS IRON AND MANUFACTURES
THEREOF
—•— = RAILROAD CONSTRUCTION MATERIALS ALONE

As regards the import trade, then, the facts of the case are clear. Imports did diminish simultaneously with the rising premium on gold. Since throughout the important period, 1889–96, the curves of imports and of gold premium move inversely to each other, there would appear to be no doubt that an inverse relationship did exist between them. There remains to be considered the manner in which this relationship made itself felt. By what means does a depreciating paper currency exercise a discouraging effect upon imports?

This question brings us to the comparison of import prices with wages and the premium on gold.[1] Concerning Argentine import prices there are but few sources of information even today. There are no officially published import prices. One or two trade journals devoted to the import trade did exist in the period of this study; but most of their numbers have long since been lost. I have data for only eighteen imports, and these for only three years, 1886, 1890, and 1896. These years represent the beginning of the depreciation of paper money, the period of greatest depreciation, and the first year of marked appreciation.

---

[1] There is no need to restate the theory in detail. A rising gold premium discourages imports through the difference in the degree to which it affects import prices and wages. The former are more sensitive to movements of the premium than are the latter. The reason for the greater sensitiveness of import prices is that the importer buys abroad in gold and sells at home for paper. Were there no gold premium, a sterling bill for £1000 of imported goods would cost 5040 paper pesos (mint par). With gold at 100 per cent premium the same bill would cost 10,080 paper pesos: with gold at a premium of 200 per cent, 15,120 paper pesos.* As the premium rises, then, the paper cost of imported goods increases. The importer raises his selling price to recuperate himself. Meanwhile, the paper-money income of consumers, especially wage-earners and salaried clerks, rises more slowly. They are less able to purchase; and imports decline in consequence.

Imports decline, too, because of the instability of a paper-money situation, which by its very nature is abnormal. The premium on gold constantly fluctuates. The importer does not know what his goods may cost; the premium may change one hundred points between the date of drawing and that of settlement of a ninety-day bill. Though covering operations become habitual and to some degree remove the element of uncertainty, legitimate business is impaired. The importer becomes, perforce, a gold speculator. The more conservative reduce their purchases, or withdraw from business.

* The bill would be bought with Argentine gold, as previously explained: but the gold would have to be bought with Argentine paper. The above calculation, therefore, represents accurately the underlying transaction.

The articles are representative, but pertain wholly to two classes of imports, foods and textile goods.[1]

The following table compares, in the form of index numbers, import prices with wages and with the price of gold. On page 252 the same data are shown in a diagram.

INDEX NUMBERS OF IMPORT PRICES, WAGES, AND THE PRICE OF GOLD, 1886–96

Year	Wages		Import Prices		Price of Gold
	Mean	Median	Mean	Median	
1886	100	100	100	100	100
1887	..	..	..	..	97
1888	..	..	..	..	106
1889	..	..	..	..	138
1890	125	120	347	313	181
1891	..	..	..	..	278
1892	138	133	..	..	239
1893	..	..	..	..	233
1894	146	146	..	..	257
1895	..	..	..	..	248
1896	161	161	308	293	213

The data on import prices are, of course, too scanty to allow any but the most general conclusion to be drawn from them. Particularly are we ignorant of the course of import prices between 1886 and 1890, and again between the latter date and 1896. There appears little doubt, however, in view of the enormous gap between the curves of import prices and of wages, that import prices were affected to a greater degree and more quickly by the rise in the price of gold than were wages. The evidence from the eighteen representative articles included in the index numbers appears to indicate, indeed, that import prices rose even higher than the price of gold; that, in other words, depreciated paper had a greater effect on import prices than upon

[1] List of articles: cotton sheetings, flannel, muslins, calico, stockings; tea, coffee, chocolate, whiskey, olive oil, preserved ham, tinned salmon, preserved tongue, oatmeal, rice, sugar, bacon, raisins. Data taken chiefly from W. I. Buchanan, "La Moneda y la Vida" and from *La Comercial*.

INDÉX NUMBERS OF IMPORT PRICES, WAGES AND THE PRICE OF GOLD, 1886–1896

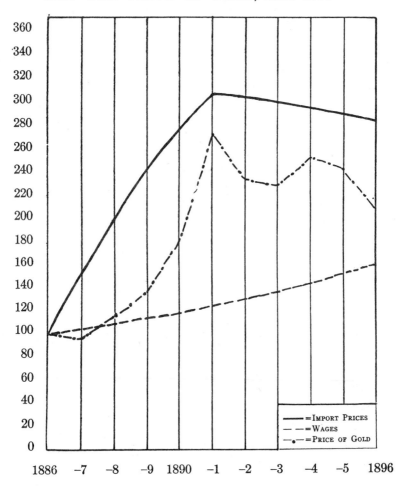

export prices (cf. chart in Chapter XIII, p. 193). That such was very probably the case one is led to believe by the other aspects of the situation already reviewed,— the particularly hazardous nature of the import trade under the unstable conditions of depreciated paper; and the fact that other forces, particularly falling prices of Argentine products abroad, tended to offset the influence of the rising gold premium on export prices. Whether import prices did in fact, however, rise higher than the price of gold is a matter of secondary importance. The important matter, and here a general conclusion appears amply warranted notwithstanding the scantiness of the evidence, is that import prices were much more sensitive to the rising price of gold than were wages. Import prices increased markedly and rapidly; wages rose but slowly, and even by 1896 had not caught up with import prices. The power to purchase imported goods was clearly reduced.

Summing up the examination of the import trade, then, we find first of all that the diminution of value of imports asserted by theory as the result of a rising gold premium did occur: that, in fact, the diminution was very marked, and was principally responsible for the overturn of the trade balance in 1891. On comparing the course of imports with the gold premium, we find that in the period of chief importance, 1889–96, there was in every year an inverse relation between imports and the premium on gold. Finally, by a comparison of import prices (though the data are scanty) with wages and the price of gold, we find the reason for the depressing effect of depreciating paper money on imports. As the price of gold rises, import prices rise more rapidly than wages, and power to purchase imports is thereby reduced. In other words, the Argentine import trade appears to offer complete verification of theory.

CHAPTER XVI

CONCLUSION

THE purpose of this inquiry has been to test the theory of international trade under conditions of inconvertible paper money. The question has been to see whether from a mass of complex facts and forces there would emerge, upon analysis, a framework of tendencies and principles substantially in accord with theoretical expectation. For such a purpose, it has been necessary at each stage of the investigation to relate fact to principle and principle to fact, to formulate such conclusions as appeared clearly to be warranted, and with the threads of the situation well in hand, to pass on to the examination in similar manner of the succeeding phases of the problem. Such, at any rate, has been the writer's conception of a proper method of analysis, and such is the method which he has sought to pursue in this inquiry, even at the cost here and there of some repetition of argument or example.

There is no occasion at this point, therefore, for a detailed restatement of conclusions. More profitable and necessary is the consideration of the worth of those conclusions, their limitations, and their significance for the theory of international trade.

The question of the reliability of the data — a point of major importance in any investigation of a statistical character — has been discussed in detail, and need not be reconsidered here. Despite some deficiencies, especially in the official statistics of merchandise trade and in wage data, the essential features of the situation stand forth unmistakably. The main movements and changes — in the balance of payments as a whole, in borrowings, in the import trade, in prices and wages, in the gold premium; and in the quantity of paper money in circulation — were so marked and spectacular, and were supported so amply by the general course of events, especially in the most significant period, that leading up to and including the Baring Panic, that one need have no hesitation in basing conclusions upon them. Moreover, it may be said again that in an inquiry of the character of the present one, which aims chiefly to trace broad underlying tendencies, small errors are of small consequence. What is required in the data is substantial accuracy, sufficient for purposes of general comparison and interpretation. In passing upon the data, also, the fact should not be overlooked that, though some of the evidence is defective, other portions of it possess unusual merit, owing to the fact that the government played so large a part in the situation and that in consequence much of the data may be drawn from official records. This is especially true of the balance of borrowings, and renders the computation of that balance much less liable to serious error than would be the case for most other countries.

Accepting the data as on the whole adequate for our purpose, what they indicate is a pretty general correspondence with theoretical reasoning. The investigation provides substantially the same explanation of the overturn of the Argentine trade balance as is offered by theory. Especially clear-cut is the interrelation between the balance of international payments and the value of inconvertible paper money. It is upon the clear proof of this relationship that the entire theory fundamentally depends. The further assertion of theory, that changes in the value of paper money bring about changes in exports and imports through the varying intensity with which movements of the gold premium affect prices and costs, is also sustained, though, as we have seen, the theoretically expected result upon the foreign trade is apparent in the Argentine case only in the import trade. So far as the export trade is concerned, the results of the inquiry are inconclusive, since, notwithstanding the fact that the particular set of forces that we have analyzed was undoubtedly at work, exports failed to expand, because of the presence of more powerful conflicting forces.) Viewing the investigation as a whole,— when one recalls the multiplicity and complexity of forces which are at work in any industrial or

commercial situation, and especially in a period of expansion
and panic such as has been reviewed, the degree of verification
of theory which the facts of the Argentine case provide is rather
striking.

Two points brought out in the inquiry deserve special emphasis, as indicating possible modifications, or at least the need of
a more careful restatement, of theory. The first is suggested by
what has just been said regarding the foreign merchandise trade.
In most discussions of the problem that we have been considering the emphasis has been placed too exclusively upon the
"bounty" that is afforded to exports by a rising gold premium.
Too little attention has been given to the depressing effects of
the rising premium upon imports. Yet, as we have seen, in the
Argentine case it is the imports that afford the most clear-cut
example of how the premium actually makes itself felt. In the
writer's opinion this greater sensitiveness of imports to the
movements of the premium on gold is not a mere vagary of Argentine foreign trade, and therefore incapable of a more general
application. It would seem to be a characteristic condition in
any agricultural country on a depreciated paper money basis,—
and to be so by virtue of the marked difference in the character
of the products (as well as in the general conditions) which make
up the export trade and the import trade of any predominantly
agricultural country. The exports of such a country are, of
course, mainly agricultural products, whereas the imports are
mainly manufactured goods. The exports are usually few in
number; or at least a comparatively small number of staple
products usually comprise the major part of the exports. The
imports, on the contrary, are numerous and are drawn from
many sources. Finally, the exports ordinarily constitute but
a minor portion of the total supply available for the world's
markets. Cases of the contrary sort, of agricultural products
drawn so largely from a single country as to dominate the world
market — such cases as Brazilian coffee or our own cotton —
are exceptional.

These differences between the general characteristics of export
and import trade in agricultural countries are significant as

regards the comparative effects of inconvertible paper money on exports and imports, or to state the matter more carefully, as regards the likelihood of those effects being allowed to work themselves out unimpeded. Since the exports are of an agricultural character, they are subject, as we have seen, to the uncontrollable vagaries of nature. Natural irregularities occur which are in no wise connected with domestic monetary and price conditions, but which interfere profoundly with any set of forces which are dependent on conditions of money and prices. On the other hand, the imports, being manufactured goods and drawn from a variety of foreign sources, are relatively unaffected by fluctuating natural conditions. Again, since the exports form only a minor part of the world's supply, and therefore do not fix, but merely reflect, the world price, fluctuations in the world price (which is a *gold* price) affect the total value of exports far more deeply than does the effect of a fluctuating gold premium upon domestic paper prices. And when, as is likely to be the case, the export trade is composed chiefly of a few major exports, the effect of changes in the world price of any one of these major exports is likely to have a greater effect upon the total value of the export trade than is the influence of a shifting premium on gold. The import trade, on the contrary, being made up of a great number and variety of smaller items, is less apt to undergo marked alteration by reason of fluctuations in individual prices abroad.

In other words, it would seem probable that as regards agricultural countries "other things" are more apt to remain "equal" in the case of imports than in the case of exports. In any event, there seems to be no reason why the depressing effect of depreciating paper upon the import trade should not receive as much consideration from theorists as the "bounty" upon exports, which has more commonly engaged their attention.

The second point brought out by the investigation which may be regarded as indicating in some degree a modification of theory, or at least the need of a more careful statement of it, is that which has to do with the mechanism of foreign exchange in depreciated paper-money countries. At various points in the

inquiry attention has been called to the fact that in most statements of the theory a depreciated paper exchange is presupposed
or, as more commonly stated, a condition of "dislocated exchange." It has been shown in this study, however, that the
presence of depreciated paper money by no means renders
necessary any dislocation of exchange, and that so far as exchange
mechanism is concerned the Argentine situation differed in no
wise from that of gold countries. Gold exchange did in fact
exist throughout the period. Except for a few brief months in
1884 there was no "dislocation" whatever. It was shown too
that the question of exchange mechanism does not touch upon
the essential problem, which is one arising entirely out of the
presence of depreciated paper money within the country, and
the necessity in international dealings of constant comparison
between the domestic paper and the international gold standard.
The term "dislocated exchange," therefore, though genuinely
applicable to those cases where a depreciated paper exchange
does in fact exist (as in Chile, for example) would appear to be
a misnomer in so far as it is used to designate the theory of international trade under conditions of depreciated paper; for in the
first place, it does not apply to such cases as that of Argentina
at all, and in the second place, it puts the emphasis upon a
matter which is of purely incidental importance.

In conclusion, it need scarcely be repeated that this inquiry
has been concerned mainly with events and consequences growing immediately and directly out of a disturbance in the balance
of international payments,— the disturbance occasioned by the
heavy borrowings of the eighties and the consequent increase
of the interest charge in the early nineties. It has been concerned
with following through the train of sequences whereby this
disturbance eventually brought about an overturn in the trade
balance. In other words, the purpose has been to find out what
really happened in what is called the "transition period" between "states of equilibrium" in the balance of payments, and to
compare the findings with the conclusions of theory. No attempt
has been made to inquire into ultimate consequences, the event-
ual terms of commodity exchange, the possible benefits or losses

accruing to the people of Argentina from the series of changes reviewed. It is generally conceded that these larger implications of the theory of international trade — working out their consequences over long periods, and overlaid, as they are bound to be, by other factors — are extremely difficult (probably impossible) to verify even in the relatively simple situation of gold-using countries. To endeavor to test their validity under the infinitely more complex conditions of depreciated paper money would be futile.

BIBLIOGRAPHY

BIBLIOGRAPHY

Agote, Pedro:
  Informe del Presidente del Crédito Público sobre la Deuda Pública, Bancos y Emisiónes de Papel Moneda y Acuñación de Monedas de la República Argentina. Referred to in text as *Finances of the Argentine Government.* Buenos Aires, 1881–88, 5 editions.
Albarracin, Santiago J.:
  Bosquejo Historico, Politico y Económico de la Provincia de Córdoba. (Official edition.) Buenos Aires, 1889.
Alberdi, J. B.:
  Organisación Politica y Económica de la Confederación Argentina. Besanzon, 1856.
Alcorta, Amancio:
  Estudio sobre el Curso Forzoso. Buenos Aires, 1880.
Allard, A.:
  Proyecto para la Acuñación de las Monedas de Oro de la República Argentina. Buenos Aires, 1864.
Alsina, Juan A.:
  Memoria del Departamento General de Inmigración, Correspondiente al Año 1895. Buenos Aires, 1896.
  La Inmigración Europea en la República Argentina. Buenos Aires, 1898.
  El Obrero en la República Argentina. Buenos Aires, 1905.
Alvarez, F. A.:
  Estado de las Sementeras de Trigo y Lino en la Provincia de Entre Rios, en Diciembre, 1900. Buenos Aires, 1900.
Anales de la Sociedad Rural Argentina.
Annual Bulletins of the Caja de Conversión.
Anuario de Estadística del Comercio y de la Navegación. (Annual reports of the Dirección General de Estadistica de la Nación.) Buenos Aires, 1880–1900.
Anuario Estadístico de la Provincia de Buenos Aires. (Emilio R. Coni, Director.) Buenos Aires, 1884 on.
Anuario Estadístico de la Ciudad de Buenos Aires. (Annual statistical publication of the city of Buenos Aires.)
Anuario de la Prensa Argentina. Buenos Aires.
Anuario Oficial de la República Argentina. Buenos Aires, 1912.
Argentine International Trade; a Few Figures on its Development. (Published by the Dirección General de Comercio é Industria.) Buenos Aires, 1907 on.
Argentine Year Book. R. Grant & Co. Buenos Aires, 1902.
Arias, D. M.:
  Historia del Papel Moneda de Argentina. Buenos Aires, 1912.

Baker, E. L.:
  The Argentine Republic. Washington, 1896.
Balance Sheet of the Caja de Conversión, 1890. Buenos Aires, 1890.
Ballestran, Samuel:
  Estado de las Sementeras de Trigo y Lino en las Provincias de Santa Fé y Córdoba, en Diciembre de 1900. Buenos Aires, 1900.
Balloé, Antonio:
  Falsificación de Moneda. Buenos Aires, 1901.
Banco de la Nación Argentina. (Published by the bank on its twenty-fifth anniversary.) Buenos Aires, 1916.
Banco Hipotecario Nacional, 1886–1916. (Official publication.) Buenos Aires, 1916.
Banco Hipotecario Nacional:
  Leyes y Disposiciones. Buenos Aires, 1916.
Bankers' Magazine. London.
Belin Sarmiento, Augusto:
  Una República Muerta. Buenos Aires, 1892.
Bodaró, D.:
  Capitales Extranjeros. Buenos Aires, 1892.
Boletínes de la Bolsa de Comercio.
Boletínes del Departamento Nacional de Inmigración.
Boletínes del Departamento Nacional del Trabajo.
Borain, Jules:
  La République Argentine et ses Créanciers Européens. Brussels, 1891.
Bruyssel (van), Ernest:
  La République Argentine: ses Ressources Naturelles; ses Colonies Agricoles; son Importance comme Centre d'Immigration. Brussels, 1888.
Buchanan, W. I. (Ex-United States Minister to Argentina):
  "La Moneda y la Vida en la República Argentina." In *La Revista de Derecho, Historia y Letras,* 1898, vol. ii. Buenos Aires. (The same investigation appears in United States Special Consular Reports, vol. xiii, "Money and Prices in Foreign Countries.")
Buenos Aires Handels Zeitung. (Trade journal.)
Buenos Aires *Standard,* The.
Bulletins of the Dirección General de Comercio é Industria. Buenos Aires.
Bulletins of the International Bureau of the American Republics.
Bunge, A. E. (Director General of Statistics):
  El Intercambio Económico de la República Argentina en 1916. Buenos Aires, 1917.
Burton, T. E.:
  Financial Crises and Periods of Industrial Depression.
Callender, H. B.:
  "The Argentine Crisis." *Fortnightly Review,* vol. liv.
Calvet, L.:
  L'Immigration Européenne, le Commerce, et l'Agriculture à la Plata (1886–88). Paris, 1889.

Canderlier, G.:
La Verité sur l'Immigration des Travailleurs et des Capitaux Belges dans la République Argentine. Brussels, 1889.

Carcano, Ramón J.:
Historia de los Medios de Comunicación y Transporte en la República Argentina. Buenos Aires, 1893.

Carmona, Enrique:
Descripción y Movimiento Comercial del Puerto de Buenos Aires en el Año 1897. Buenos Aires, 1898.

Carranza, A. B.:
Anuario Financiero y Administrativo de la República Argentina. Buenos Aires, 1904.

Carrasco, Gabriel:
La Colonisación Agricola de la Provincia de Santa Fé. Buenos Aires, 1893.
Intereses Nacionales de la República Argentina. Buenos Aires, 1895.

Castro, J. J.:
South American Railways. (Official publication.) Montevideo, 1893.

Censo Agropecuario de la Nación. (See especially the section entitled "Stock Breeding and Agriculture.") Buenos Aires, 1908.

Censo de la Cidad de Buenos Aires, 1904.

Censo General de Población, Edificación, Comercio y Industrias de la Ciudad de Buenos Aires. (Compiled by F. Latzina, M. Chueco, Alberto B. Martinez, and N. Perez.) Buenos Aires, 1887.

Censo de la Provincia de Buenos Aires, 1887.

Censo de la República Argentina, Buenos Aires, 1895.

Chueco, C. Manuel:
Finanzas de la Municipalidad de Buenos Aires, 1880–91. Buenos Aires, 1892.

Clarke, F. S.:
Finances of the Argentine Republic for the Years 1898, 1899, 1900. (Diplomatic and consular reports of the Foreign Office.) London, 1900.
Agricultural and Commercial Condition of Argentine Republic for the year 1899. Ibid., 1900.

Clémenceau, Georges:
South America Today: A Study of Conditions Social, Political and Commercial in Argentina, Uruguay and Brazil. Paris, 1911.

Comisión Nacional del Centenario:
La Historia de Argentina, 1810–1910. Buenos Aires, 1910.

Conant, Charles A.:
A History of Modern Banks of Issue. 1909.

Cornador, J. B.:
Ganadería. Buenos Aires, 1894.

Daireaux, Émile:
La République Argentine: le Commerce et les Finances; le Papier Monnaie; les Banques Particulières, la Bourse, le Crédit Publique, etc. Paris, 1889.

Del Busto, Rodriguez:
  El Proteccionismo en la República Argentina.   Buenos Aires, 1899.
*Deuda Pública.   Informe Presentado por el Poder Executivo al Congreso
  Nacional sobre la Deuda Pública, Reconocida hasta el 31 de Mayo de 1890.*
  Buenos Aires, 1890.
De Vedia, A.:
  El Banco Nacional.   Buenos Aires, 1854.
Diarios de Sesiones de la Camera de Senadores y de la Camera de Diputados.
  Buenos Aires, 1900.
Drago, J. M.:
  La Ganadería en la República Argentina.   Buenos Aires, 1900.
Duclot, J.:
  *Deuda Pública Exterior y Capitales Europeos Empleados por Sociedades
  Anonimas.*   Buenos Aires, 1890.
Economist, The.   London.
El Economista.   Buenos Aires.
*Estadística de los Ferrocarriles en Explotación.   (Annual Report of the Bureau
  of Railroads.)*   Buenos Aires.
Exposición sobre el Estado Económico y Financiero de la República Argentina.
  (Official publication.)   Buenos Aires, 1893.
Extracto Estadístico de la República Argentina Correspondiente al Año 1915.
  (Published by the Dirección General de Estadística de la Nación.)
  Buenos Aires, 1916.
Financial News, The.   London.
Fliess, A. E.:
  El Presente y el Porvenir de la Agricultura.   Buenos Aires, 1890.
  La Producción Agricola de la Provincia de Santa Fé.   Ibid., 1891.
Floro Costa, Angel:
  El Banco Nacional.   Buenos Aires, 1874.
Fragueiro, Antonio:
  Consideraciones sobre Nuestra Actualidad Económica.   Buenos Aires,
  1897.
Fraser, John Foster:
  The Amazing Argentine.   New York and London, 1914.
Galanti, A. N.:
  La Industria Viti-Vinicola Argentina.   Buenos Aires, 1900.
Gandolfo, Carlos:
  Apuntes sobre la Ganadería en la República Argentina.   Buenos Aires,
  1901.
Gesell, Silvio:
  El Sistema Monetario Argentino, sus Ventajas y su Perfeccionamiento.
  Buenos Aires, 1893.
Gibson, H.:
  "The History and Present State of the Sheep-Breeding Industry in
  the Argentine Republic."   (In the Bulletin of the National Associa-
  tion of Wool Manufacturers, 1904.)
Gonzales, M. P.:
  Recopilación de Leyes Nacionales.   Buenos Aires, 1899.   5 vols.

Grinfeld, I.:
"Monetary Experiences of Argentina." *Political Science Quarterly* (Columbia University), vol. xxv, No. 1.

Guasalaga, S. A.:
Estudio de los Tratados de Comercio de la República Argentina. Buenos Aires, 1898.

Guerrico, A. A.:
Finanzas Argentinas. (Estudios é Ideas sobre Nuestros Emprestitos Externos.) Buenos Aires, 1887.

Guilaine, Louis:
La République Argentine, Physique et Économique. Paris, 1889.

Guzman, V.:
Oro. Buenos Aires, 1890.

Hammerton, J. A.:
The Real Argentine. New York, 1915.

Hansen, Emilio:
La Moneda Argentina. Buenos Aires, 1916.

Hirst, W. A.:
Argentina. London, 1912.

Hurley, E. H.:
Banking and Credit in Argentina, Brazil, Chile, and Peru. United States Department of Commerce.

Informe sobre los Bancos Locales en las Provincias Nacionales. (Published by El Ministerio de Hacienda.) Buenos Aires, 1894.

Journals of the Royal Statistical Society. London.

Justo, J. B.:
El Papel Moneda. Buenos Aires, 1903.

Koebel, W. H.:
Argentina, Past and Present. London, 1910.

La Comercial. (Trade journal, 1886–90.) Buenos Aires.

Lahitte, Emilio:
La Ganaderia Argentina. Buenos Aires, 1899.
Cosecha del Año 1898–99. (Datos estadísticos de la División de Estadística y Economia Rural.) *Ibid.*, 1899.
Cosecha del Año 1899–1900. Ibid., 1900.

Lamas, Andres:
Estudio Historico y Cientifico del Banco de la Provincia de Buenos Aires. Buenos Aires, 1886.

Lamas, Domingo:
Revista Económica, 1892.

Lamas, Pedro S.:
Exposé Sommaire de la Situation Économique et Financière de la République Argentine. Paris, 1888.

La Nación. (Newspaper.) Buenos Aires.

La Prensa. (Newspaper.) Buenos Aires.

Latzina, Francisco:
The Argentine Republic as a Field for European Immigration. Buenos Aires, 1883.

Las Vicisitudes de Nuestra Moneda Fiduciaria en los Últimos Sesenta y Cinco Años. Buenos Aires, 1891.
La Argentina Considerada en sus Aspectos Fisico, Social, y Económico. Buenos Aires, 1902.
Comparaciones Estadísticas Internacionales. Buenos Aires, 1895.

Lawson, W. R.:
"The Argentine Crisis." *Fortnightly Review,* vol. liv.

Lemee, C.:
Agricultura y Ganadería en la República Argentina. Buenos Aires, 1894.
Datos para la Estadística Agricola para la Provincia de Buenos Aires. Buenos Aires, 1896.

Leroy Beaulieu, P.:
"La Depréciation du Change dans les Pays à Finances Avariées." (Argentina, Brazil, and Spain, etc.) (In *Économiste Française, August 24, 1901.*)

Lix Klett, Carlos:
La República Argentina, sus Recursos y su Comercio Internacional. Buenos Aires, 1897.
Estudios sobre Producción, Comercio, Finanzas & Intereses Generales de la República Argentina. (Preface by Enrique M. Nelson.) Buenos Aires, 1900. 2 vols.

Lobos, E.:
Apuntes sobre la Legislación de Tierras. Buenos Aires, 1900.

Lorini, Eteocle:
La República Argentina e i Suoi Maggiori Problemi di Economia e di Finanza. Rome, 1902, 1904, 1910. 3 vols.

Lough, W. H.:
Banking Opportunities in South America. United States Bureau of Foreign and Domestic Commerce, 1915.

Lyon, Jacques:
"La Politique Monétaire de l'Argentine." (In *Questions Monétaires Contemporaines.*) Paris, 1905.

Mabragaña, H. (Editor):
Los Mensajes. (Messages of the Presidents of Argentina.) Buenos Aires. 6 vols.

Martinez, A. B.:
El Presupuesto Nacional. Buenos Aires, 1890.
La Estadística en la República Argentina. (Su pasado, su presente y mejorías de que es susceptible en el porvenir.) Buenos Aires, 1891.
Finanzas Comunales de Buenos Aires. (Collection of articles published in *La Nación.*) Buenos Aires, 1892.
Les Finances de la République Argentine. (Budget, dépenses, revenus, et dette publique.) Buenos Aires, 1898.
Baedeker de la República Argentina. Buenos Aires, 1900.
Les Valeurs Mobilières de la République Argentine. Paris, 1908.
"Los Valores Mobiliarios de la República Argentina." (In *Censo de la Ciudad de Buenos Aires.*) Buenos Aires, 1905.

Martinez, A. B., and Lewandowski, M.:
La República Argentina en el Siglo XX. Madrid, 1912, 4th Edition.
(Published originally in French. English translation of 3d Edition,
1911.)
Massé, J. B.:
Informe sobre el Estado de las Clases Obreras en el Interior de la República. Buenos Aires, 1904.
Masson-Forestier, L.:
Réforme Monétaire en Argentine et au Brazil. University of Paris, 1913.
Memorias del Banco Hipotecario de la Provincia de Buenos Aires: 1886–91.
(Annual reports of the bank.) Buenos Aires.
Memorias del Banco Hipotecario Nacional: 1887 on. (Annual reports of the
bank.) Buenos Aires.
Memorias de Hacienda. (Annual reports of the Ministry of Finance.)
Buenos Aires.
Mills, G. J.:
Argentina. London, 1914.
Mulhall, M. G.:
Handbook of the River Plate Republics. Buenos Aires, 1863; *Ibid.*,
1875; *Ibid.*, 1885; *Ibid.*, 1892.
The British in South America. Buenos Aires, 1878.
Between the Amazon and the Andes. London, 1881.
Parliamentary Papers, LXXXI, No. 1000.
Patroni, Adrian:
Los Trabajadores en Argentina. (Datos acerca de salarios, horarios,
habitaciones, costo de vida, etc.) Buenos Aires, 1898.
Peña, J. B.:
La Deuda Argentina. (Complete collection of laws, contracts, etc.,
pertaining to the foreign debt of the nation.) Buenos Aires.
Deuda de la Municipalidad de la Capital. (Laws, decrees, and con-
tracts pertaining to the municipal debt.) Buenos Aires, 1907.
Perez, T. S.:
Desde Lejos. Buenos Aires, 1907.
Perugia, F.:
Unificación y Consolidación de las Deudas Argentinas. Buenos Aires,
1901.
Pillado, Ricardo (formerly Director of the Bureau of Commerce and Indus-
tries):
*Anuario Pillado de la Deuda y Sociedades Anónimas Establecidas en las
Repúblicas Argentina y Uruguay.* Buenos Aires, 1899, 1900.
La Crisis Económica. Buenos Aires, 1893.
Revista Económica y Financiera. Buenos Aires, 1890–95. (An annual
resumé of events, appearing in the anniversary number — January 1st
— of *La Prensa*.)
Apuntes y Datos. Buenos Aires, 1903.
Argentine Loans. Buenos Aires, 1908.
Estudio sobre el Comercio Argentino con las Naciones Limítrofes. Buenos

Aires, 2d Edition, 1910.
  Tratados de Comercio Argentinos. Buenos Aires, 1915.
Pinero, O. M.:
  La Conversión del Billete. Buenos Aires, 1899.
Quesada, Ernesto:
  La Deuda Argentina. Buenos Aires, 1898.
  Las Finanzas Municipales. Buenos Aires, 1889.
  Las Finanzas de la República Argentina. Ibid., 1892.
Quesada, S. J.:
  El Banco Hipotecario de la Provincia de Buenos Aires. Ibid., 1894.
Ramón, Doman:
  Manual de la Bolsa de Buenos Aires. Buenos Aires, 1914.
Ramón, S. C.:
  Bolsas y Mercados de Comercio. Buenos Aires, 1896.
Rebora, Juan Carlos:
  Las Finanzas de Buenos Aires. Buenos Aires, 1911.
Review of the River Plate.
Revista de Derecho, Historia y Letras.
Revista de Economía y Finanzas.
Revista Económica del Rio de la Plata.
Revista Económica. (Domingo Lamas, Director.)
Revista Mensual de la Camera Mercantil. (C. Lix Klett, Director.)
Roca, J. A.:
  La Conquista del Desierto. Buenos Aires, 1881. 2 vols.
Rosa, J. M.:
  La Reforma Monetaria en la República Argentina. Buenos Aires, 1909.
Schmitz, O.:
  Die Finanzen Argentiniens. 1895.
Seeber, Francisco:
  Estudios Económicos. Buenos Aires, 1878.
  Nacionalización del Banco de la Provincia de Buenos Aires. Ibid., 1882.
  Situación Económica y Financiera de la República Argentina. Ibid., 1884.
  Apuntes sobre la Importancia Económica y Financiera de la República Argentina. Ibid., 1888.
  Finanzas y Administración. Ibid., 1888.
  Great Argentina. Ibid., 1904.
Segui, Francisco D.:
  Provincia de Buenos Aires. (Investigación parlamentaria sobre agricultura, ganadería, industrias derivadas y colonisación.) Buenos Aires, 1898.
South American Journal, The. London.
Statesman's Year Book, The.
Statist, The. London.
Subercaseaux, G.:
  El Papel Moneda. Valparaiso, Chile, 1916.
Taussig, F. W.:
  "International Trade under Depreciated Paper," *Quarterly Journal of Economics,* vol. xxxi, May, 1917.

Terry, A. José:
   Le Crisis (1885–92). Buenos Aires, 1893.
   Sistema Bancario. *Ibid.*, 1893.
   Finanzas. (Apuntes taquigráficos de las Conferencias en la Facultad de Derecho.) *Ibid.*, 1898.
   Questiones Monetarias. (Conferencias en la Facultad de Derecho.) *Ibid.*, 1899.
Thery, R.:
   Rapports des Changes Avariés et des Règlements Extérieurs. Paris. 1912.
Thiriot, L. F.:
   Estudios sobre los Presupuestos de la República, las Provincias y los Municipios Argentinos. Buenos Aires, 1901.
Torino Damian, M.:
   Estudios Económicos. Buenos Aires, 1914.
Tornquist, Carlos Alfredo:
   El Balance de Pagos de la República Argentina, 1914–15. Buenos Aires, 1916.
   Ibid., 1915–16, Buenos Aires, 1917.
   Ibid., 1916–17, Buenos Aires, 1918.
   Ibid., 1917–18, Buenos Aires, 1919.
   The Argentine Republic of Today. Buenos Aires, 1916.
Tornquist, Ernesto y Ca., Lda.:
   Manual of Argentine National, Provincial and Municipal Loans. Buenos Aires, 1913.
Tornquist's " Clippings."
Walle, Paul:
   L'Argentine Telle Qu'elle Est. Paris.
Williams, John H.:
   "Latin American Foreign Exchange and International Balances during the War," *Quarterly Journal of Economics*, vol. xxxiii, May, 1919.
   "Foreign Exchange, Prices, and the Course of International Trade," *The Annals of the American Academy*, May, 1920.
Wolff, Julius:
   Die Argentinische Währungsreform von 1899. Leipzig, 1905.
Year Book of the London Stock Exchange.
Zeballos, E. S.:
   La Concurrencia Universal y la Agricultura en Ambas Americas. Washington, 1894.
   Discurso sobre el Banco Hipotecario Nacional. Buenos Aires, 1886.
   "Capital Extranjero en Argentina," *La Revista de Derecho, Historia y Letras*, January, 1899. Buenos Aires, 1899.
   "La Crisis Económica," *La Revista de Derecho, Historia y Letras*, vol. iv. Buenos Aires, 1899.
   "Legislación Agraria," *La Revista de Derecho, Historia y Letras*, vol. xii. Buenos Aires, 1902.
   Le Crédit et le Régime Hypothécaire. Brussels, 1910.

INDEX

INDEX